PURSUING THE DIVINE IMAGE

TOWARD AN EXEGETICALLY BASED THEOLOGY OF HOLINESS[1]

BY

H. RAY DUNNING, PH.D.

PROFESSOR EMERITUS OF THEOLOGY
TREVECCA NAZARENE UNIVERSITY

---

[1] This subtitle is intended to suggest a disclaimer that I think I have spoken a last word, or perhaps even a penultimate word on the subject. It is rather an exploratory probe proposed with the intention of stimulating discussion to the end of maintaining a theologically and exegetically viable understanding of sanctification in the 21st century.

DEDICATION
TO THE MEMORY OF

DR. W.M. GREATHOUSE

WHOSE COURAGE, OPENNESS AND COMMITMENT TO
BIBLICAL TRUTH OVER TRADITION TO HIS OWN
DISADVANTAGE AT TIMES INSPIRED MANY OF HIS
STUDENTS TO FOLLOW THAT TRUTH WHEREVER IT LEADS.

Dr. Dunning has a fierce devotion to Scripture and an uncompromising commitment to the holiness heritage as understood by the likes of Wesley, Wynkoop, and Greathouse. *Pursuing the Divine Image* offers a humble but honest look back at the inadequacies of sanctification understood as removal, and a compelling way forward emphasizing sanctification as renewal in the image of God. Exegetically sound. Existentially livable. Absolutely essential for anyone serious about living or proclaiming the holy life to which scripture constantly calls, and for which God's grace continuously provides.

> --Dr. Steve Estep, Pastor Grace Church of the Nazarene, Clarksville, TN; Adjust professor of preaching Nazarene Theological Seminary

For me this book resolves the issues that almost led to my rejecting the holiness message I was taught. . . . What I was initially taught and what I experienced in my life and observed in the lives of others just did not conform to the message I was hearing. I struggled with this for decades. *Pursuing the Divine Image* will save countless serious disciples from that pain. Mildred Bangs Wynkoop in *A Theology of Love* identified the "credibility gap" between the theology of the 19th and early 20th centuries and life. In this book, H. Ray Dunning has bridged that gap.
> ---Rev. Rodney Shanner, Pastor, Little Rock, Arkansas

Dr. Dunning reveals that sanctification is not a noun but a verb--a pursuit--and makes it relevant for all who desire to follow Christ.
> --Dr. Peggy Cooning, Vice President for External Relations, Trevecca Nazarene University

As a builder, I have appreciated a tool simply called a level. By use of a liquid-filled tube and a little bubble, you can tell whether something is plumb or not. From this, we have gotten the image that something is "half a bubble off level". I have sensed this about our doctrine of holiness for years. Too many Biblical texts had to be bent a bit to fit human experience. Dr. Dunning has helped us significantly in his newest work. As I listened to an oral presentation of these thoughts, my heart and experience echoed a loud amen. I suspect many of you will do the same. I think this brings the bubble closer to the center of Biblical theology and human experience.

--Dr. Dan Boone, President, Trevecca Nazarene University

In *Pursuing the Divine Image*, Dr. H. Ray Dunning offers a fresh understanding of the doctrine of sanctification that is faithful to God's unfolding redemption story throughout the whole of scriptures, consistent with Wesleyan theology, and true to human experience. It reflects honesty in relation to experience. Theologically, it is creation-rooted and eschatologically oriented and thus faithful to the whole scope of salvation history. In a word, it closes the credibility gap identified by Dr. Mildred Wykoop regarding the holiness message.

--Rev. Daron Brown, pastor Waverly, TN.

TABLE OF CONTENTS

> Thesis: The relevance of the holiness movement in the 21st century is dependent on the formulation of a paradigm that avoids the pitfalls of the 19th century holiness theology that has resulted in an identity crisis, but that also maintains the Biblical essence of the message.

> Thesis: The modern holiness movement has largely been preoccupied with the "when" and the "how" of sanctification whereas the "why" is the basis for a sound theological and biblical rationale for the importance of the holy life.

> Thesis: The holiness of God is the logical ground of the call to holiness in human experience rather than the model to be reproduced.

> Thesis: Exegetically, purity is the prerequisite of holiness as a status, which is the possibility of sanctification as total consecration thus providing a biblical basis for the "secondness" of "entire sanctification."

> Thesis: The goal of salvation broadly understood is the renewal of humanity in the image of God with a view to the new creation.

> Thesis: While not a biblical term, entire sanctification may be an exegetically sound designation of Christian experience when referred to the whole person rather than to the act/process of renewing humanity in the image of God.

Thesis: The relation of the Holy Spirit to sanctification in the New Testament is a fulfillment of the Old Testament hope for inner transformation and is the enabling Agent in the pursuit of the image of God as embodied in Jesus Christ

Thesis: Certain atonement metaphors from the New Testament have significant implications for the experience of sanctification.

Thesis: The varieties of human personality, understanding and situations require great latitude in prescribing patterns of experience, allowing the Holy Spirit freedom in leading seekers of spiritual development in a diverse pattern of experiences.

Thesis: Consistent with the thoroughgoing eschatological orientation of New Testament theology, the dynamic of sanctification is not an experiential event in the past but the goal of the new creation anticipated in the death and resurrection of Jesus Christ.

Thesis: The proper and valid role of rules (or laws) in the holy life is to function as guideposts pointing in the direction of the actualization of the *telos* of the image of God rather than evidences of the validity of a past experience.

Thesis: The actualization of the virtues that constitute the ideal of the image of God is the result of deliberation and decision to manifest them in the various contexts in which they are appropriate with the consequence that their expression moves their practice toward "second nature," or habituated virtue similar to Aristotle's (or Thomas Aquinas) ethics, which provided the structural paradigm for John Wesley's ethics.

Thesis: Traditionally the holiness movement has interpreted the Pauline dichotomies (flesh/spirit, etc.) as "psychological" elements (virtual entities) within the regenerated person whereas as seen in Paul's perspective they are references to "spheres or modes of existence" corresponding to the "eschatological dualism" that is the sub-structure of New Testament theology.

Author's Foreword

My earliest "preaching" should probably never have taken place. I did not grow up in the church and became a Christian shortly after my 15th birthday. Some two years later I felt a "call to preach," which I announced to my pastor after the Sunday evening service on July 4, 1943. Our church was conducting a tent revival at the time as an outreach program so he immediately announced that I would preach my first sermon on Thursday evening. Thus four days later I delivered my first masterpiece. I now know that it probably never should have occurred—I was not prepared in any sense of the word. Nonetheless before I had completed high school I had been assigned to two churches as the "pastor." Actually they were alternating Sunday afternoon preaching points. Again, from my present perspective, that should probably never have occurred either but it did give me a lot of experience attempting to preach—such as it was.

Quite obviously, in my immaturity (although I was pursuing an educational program of ministerial preparation through a home study course, little of which I understood) I inevitably reflected the folk theology that I had heard from pastors and evangelists, including the proclamation of sanctification as a "second work of grace," although I had almost no idea what that meant. Through college and seminary studies I was never really challenged to explore the implications of that folk theology. I was able to articulate it more clearly and more decisively but early on after becoming pastor of a "real" church, I made a disturbing discovery. In proclaiming the message of holiness as it had been delivered to me, I found it sounding rather hollow both to myself and my congregation, It felt as if it was bouncing back in my face. It didn't help that I quite often observed glaring ethical discrepancies in the lives of some of the most vociferous (and legalistic) professors of the "second blessing." A friend who was a European pastor described his similar experience:

As a pastor in Rotterdam, I found myself more involved with laying a solid foundation of grace in the lives of the people, than with challenging them to go on unto perfection. The times I did preach holiness or explain it in membership classes I was strengthened in my impression that the traditional way of presenting entire sanctification was not relevant to the modern congregation. In my preaching I always tried to search for different terminology and a non-traditional approach.[2]

During those years I was quite slow in coming to think for myself in the sense of critically analyzing theological and biblical interpretations and being willing to speak about it. In no sense did I ever have doubts that there was a deeper life than nominal Christianity and an experience with the Lord that transcended formal religion. A number of parishioners experienced such a deeper relationship with God under my ministry. But as I continued further education and began to teach, the nature of this task involved critical evaluation of the *theology* that informed the deeper life. The major turning point in my understanding occurred with my "discovery" of John Wesley's teaching while researching my doctoral dissertation. My formal education had not exposed me to Wesley in any holistic way. In fact I do not remember any teacher in the holiness institutions I attended talking about Wesley's theology at all, but it's been a long time.[3]

The discovery of Wesley effected a major transition in my teaching and preaching as a result of which numerous students, as well as lay persons, found a sense of relief that there was another way of talking about "scriptural holiness" than the folk teaching they had heard while growing up. A number of ministerial students have confided that they now felt that they could continue as a part of and minister in the holiness denomination they had joined. The truth is that a transition had occurred so naturally and subtly that I never fully realized I was departing from the "party line," until someone characterized my work as "a subversive theology."[4]

[2]Antonie Holleman, "Entire Sanctification in Our Modern Times," paper presented at the European Theology Conference, 1998.

[3]This is one evidence for Wesley Tracy's indictment that "If you question ministers, as I have, who received their training in so-called Wesleyan colleges and seminaries within the holiness movement during the '40s, '50s, and '60s you will find that it was not at all unusual for a theological student to go through four years of college and three years of seminary without being required to read one page of Wesley's writings." Foreword to H. Ray Dunning, *A Layman's Guide to Sanctification* (K.C.: Beacon Hill Press of Kansas City, 1991), 11.

[4]Mark Quanstrom, *A Century of Holiness Theology* (K.C.: Beacon Hill Press of Kansas City, 2004), 157-166.

Perhaps most significant is the fact that as I was invited to preach in "revivals," often by my former students, the lay people responded very positively and enthusiastically to an understanding of sanctification that both made sense out of scripture and did not call for a level of perfection they knew they could not and did not approximate. After retirement, with greater freedom to study and write, I have attempted to put together some of the insights that have come to me over the years. I had the privilege of being a colleague of Mildred Bangs Wynkoop while she was developing her proposal for dealing with what she correctly called a "credibility gap" between the folk theology of the 19th and early 20th centuries and life.[5] We had numerous discussions during that time and I feel privileged to attempt to continue and perhaps further develop the vocation which she felt God had given her.

My commitment in this project is to the belief that the message of heart holiness is both a soundly biblical message and the answer to the need of the contemporary church. I am, with most of my contemporaries—lay, clergy and academic--convinced that the perpetuation of that message in the 21st century is dependent on the development of a different theological paradigm from the one that dominated the 19th and early 20th century holiness revivals. It is not merely that this way of understanding has been institutionalized and thus atrophied; it is that it no longer sounds the note of authenticity. My necessary critique of aspects of this paradigm is not simply the expression of a revolt against the past but a recognition that its inadequacies must be exposed in order to move forward. It is in no sense an indictment of the sincerity, spirituality or integrity of those who propagated that paradigm. But as John Wesley said in a letter to Joseph Benson, "sometimes we must write and speak controversially,"[6] My sentiments are well expressed in the words of Christopher Stead in his Preface: "In the pages that follow, I have sometimes had to deal

---

[5]Mildred Bangs Wynkoop, *A Theology of Love* (K.C.: Beacon Hill Press of Kansas City, 1972).

[6]John Telford, ed., *The Letters of the Rev. John Wesley*, 8 vols. (London: Epworth Press, 1931), 6:35

roughly with friends, and with beliefs, that I hold in loyalty and affection. But I can trust in the generosity of those friends; and of

> My Friend indeed
> Who at my need
> His life did spend.[7]

I am not a "lone ranger" in this task since many of the biblical and theological scholars of the church whom I know are engaged in this work as well. A few of them have confided that my work in writing a systematic theology for the church, which broke from the traditional way of doing theology in the holiness movement, opened the door for them to pursue their work in freedom and honesty. Not all of them, of course, will fully agree with my interpretations but that is the nature of the theological enterprise.

There is a significant distinction between tradition and heritage. The former involves the theological formulation of a teaching, the latter the commitment to a vision. While the tradition can undergo changes, the heritage to which we are committed remains intact. Melvin Dieter (historian of the holiness movement)[8] says that every generation in the holiness movement will look at its heritage as if it were an estate sale. At such an event all the belongings of a house or a family are placed on display in unoccupied rooms, the veranda, and the lawn. Among the items up for bid are priceless family heirlooms, valuable works of art, useful tools – and lots of junk. The task of each generation is to tell the difference between parts of the heritage that have timeless value and the parts of the heritage that are just "stuff."

One of the classic passages from the 19th century tradition comes from the pen of Richard S. Foster. His rhetorical lines were quoted by almost everyone who wrote on the subject of sanctification subsequent to the publication of his book, *Christian Purity*. They still sparkle with significance:

---

[7]Christopher Stead, *Divine Substance* (Oxford: Clarendon Press, 1977), ix.

[8]*History of the 19th Century Holiness Movement* (K.C.: Beacon Hill Press of Kansas City, 1998).

It [holiness] breathes in the prophecy, thunders in the law, murmurs in the narrative, whispers in the promises, supplicates in the prayers, sparkles in the poetry, resounds in the songs, speaks in the types, glows in the imagery, voices in the language, and burns in the spirit of the whole scheme, from alpha to omega, from its beginning to its end. . . . It is the truth glowing all over, webbing all through revelation; the glorious truth which sparkles and whispers, and sings and shouts in all its history, and biography, and poetry, and prophecy, and precept, and promise, and prayer; the great central truth of the system. The wonder is that all do not see, that any rise up to question, a truth so conspicuous, so glorious, so full of comfort.[9]

Unfortunately however, most of the popular literature of that period (including Foster's) failed to pick up on the great vision embodied in these words. Instead of mining from the deep vein of gold to which Foster's words point, they seemed to settle for picking up a few nuggets off the surface and unfortunately along with the genuine nuggets, a lot of pyrites. This suggests the nature of the challenge to preserve the heritage.

How shall we proceed with this task? As has been the case throughout Christian history, the way forward has been back to the source, in this case, the scripture. But the real issue here is the interpretation of scripture. It is at that point that I fear the early holiness movement has suffered in its departure from John Wesley's principle of appealing to "the whole tenor of scripture."[10] Hence the critical question in proposing a "new paradigm" is exegetical.

The development of more adequate methods of biblical interpretation by holiness scholars has outdated the proof-texting approach generally used by the early holiness apologists and set the Bible free to be heard in its own idiom. The result has been that some facets of the holiness apologetic has fallen on hard times and the increasing number of biblical scholars produced from the holiness movement has intensified the strain on the fabric woven out of certain

---

[9]R.S. Foster, *Christian Purity*, abridged by John Paul (K.C.: Beacon Hill Press, 1944), 80.

[10]It is true that Wesley did not always conform to this principle as noted in the following pages.

proof-texts. It has threatened, in some quarters, to be torn asunder. In-depth biblical studies, including the significance of the original languages and the historical and linguistic contexts of many of what were considered passages that had been traditionally used to defend the unique teaching of the holiness movement, revealed them to have been based on faulty exegesis, or more accurately, on eisegesis. Interesting in this regard is the affirmation of James B. Chapman in his lectures on *The Terminology of Holiness*: "We have nothing to fear from genuine biblical scholarship."[11]

The good news is that the emergence of scientific biblical scholarship among the younger scholars within the holiness movement has not led to an abandonment of the "faith of our fathers." To the contrary, it has led to a deeper grounding of the message on even more solid biblical footing, not in terms of more "texts," but in terms of finding the truth of sanctification firmly anchored in the major currents of biblical theology. And it is the emergence of biblical theology as a discipline that has provided the strongest support for the paradigm to be explored in the succeeding pages. Furthermore, scholarship of the wider church has become more and more interested in the biblical teaching of sanctification. N.T. Wright makes the illuminating parenthetical comment: "why one should assume that scholars are not interested in holiness I do not know, but it sometimes appears to be the case, just as pietists are not always interested in what the text actually says."[12]

Historical scholarship has made its own contribution to what might be called the "recovery of the holiness message." Like my personal experience, under the influence of leaders like W.M. Greathouse, the holiness movement in the latter 20th century has "rediscovered" John Wesley, the theological father of the modern holiness movement. And in doing so they have discovered that Mr. Wesley had unearthed the "mother lode" of holiness teaching in the Bible and explained it in terms of the broad teachings of scripture in a way that makes Bishop Foster's words take on flesh and blood. It is our task to continue mining ore from this "strike" and also to continue

---

[11]J.B. Chapman, *The Terminology of Holiness*, 20.

[12]"Romans," in *The New Interpreter's Bible* (Nashville: Abingdon Press, 2002), 552.

the process of refining the ore. A process that, as we shall see, is greatly needed.

This is, of course, not to make John Wesley an authority within himself, and certainly not a "cult hero." Rather we must think of Wesley as a guide to the authority to which he, himself, submitted. He tested everything he said by the word of God and then verified it by experience.

I did not realize until I had completed this study and read the entire manuscript the extent to which I had drawn on the work of New Testament scholar, N.T. Wright. In recent years since my retirement I have immersed myself in his writings and have clearly had my views impacted to the point that I believe the so-called "new perspective" on Paul, of which Wright is one proponent, is the soundest interpretation of scripture to this point. Not being a biblical scholar, I am of course subject to correction. But I have been taken by the work of Wright for four reasons: 1) his deference to biblical authority over tradition; 2) his exegesis makes excellent sense of the text, 3) he reinforces many interpretations I had taught for years but expressed them with greater authority, and 4) without using traditional theological language he has articulated from scripture an understanding of sanctification that is, in essence, consistently Wesleyan.

Chapters 2, 3 and 6 are probably the most difficult parts of this book for the average reader. However, these two chapters contain the heart of the exegesis that underlies the paradigm I am exploring. I have attempted to explain the argument as clearly as possible and believe it will be worth the effort to follow it.

The overall plan of this book moves through three phases: a statement of the problem to a proposed solution to suggested practical applications. It is easy to stop with the analyses so that the result is what has been called "the paralysis of analysis." Thus we are offering a proposed theological solution based on the exegesis of scripture. The "proof of the pudding" is in the livability of a theory so I seek to develop some practical guidelines in the final chapters. In this way I believe I have implicitly utilized what Albert Outler called the Wesleyan "quadrilateral." This was not Wesley's term but he did, on more than one occasion, refer to his use of scripture, tradition, reason and experience as resources for his conclusions about the Christian life.

There is some repetition among the chapters in this book since each subject was developed in some independence from the others, but taken as a whole, I believe they represent a theology of holiness that is biblically, theologically and practically sound. An effort has been made to cross reference the central themes. And further, to repeat myself, it is my belief that some such understanding is essential to the perpetuation of the message of Wesleyan holiness in the 21st century.

Introduction
Resolving the Contemporary Dilemma

There is little disagreement, if any, among analysts of the holiness movement that it is in the midst of an identity crisis and has been for some time. This truth was brought home with a shock in 2004 when Keith Drury announced in his presidential address to the Christian Holiness Partnership that "the holiness movement is dead." After several years, this "bombshell" still reverberates throughout the holiness community. Timothy Smith anticipated this development in his official history of the first 25 years of the Church of the Nazarene by musing that his story should provide the information for persons to thoughtfully ponder "the relevance of Wesleyan perfectionism to a generation awed by its rediscovery of the deep sinfulness of man."[13] Mark R. Quanstrom demonstates the way this "rediscovery" matured in his history of the theology of sanctification in the Church of the Nazarene. His research validated the identity crisis beyond question as well as demonstrated conclusively the necessity of a new paradigm. His introductory description summarizes the situation as it developed during the 20th century:

As the [20th] century wore on, the very optimistic expectations of entire sanctification became less and less credible in the light of the apparently intractable nature of sin. By mid-century, the extravagant promises of the grace of entire sanctification began to be tempered. Theologians in the denomination began to define the sin that could be eradicated more narrowly and the infirmities that were an inescapable consequence of fallen humanity more expansively. This led to an increasing dissatisfaction with traditional formulations of the doctrine.[14]

---

[13]*Called Unto Holiness* (K.C.: Beacon Hill Press of Kansas City, 1962), 352.

[14]Mark R. Quanstrom, *A Century of Holiness Theology* (K.C.: Beacon Hill Press of Kansas City, 2004), 11. This book is an adaptation of Quanstrom's Ph.D. dissertation that was significantly titled: "The Doctrine of Entire Sanctification in the Church of the Nazarene: From the Conquest of Sin to a New Theological Realism, 1905-1997," St. Louis University, 2000. In my opinion this is one of the most

He concluded his research by observing, "the question in the last decades of the 20th century was whether or not the Church of the Nazarene had a coherent and cogent doctrine of holiness at all." In 1958, General Superintendent Hardy C. Powers declared at the 50th anniversary of the formation of the denomination:

> To properly understand the Church of the Nazarene in 1908 or today it is necessary to think of it as more than an organization. In the minds of the founders it was spiritual in nature. Actually, the organization that we have today is the child of a message and was called into being to preserve, propagate and perpetuate that message. The message which brought the Church into existence included all the generally accepted doctrines of evangelical Christianity with special emphasis on the doctrine of entire sanctification as a second work of grace, the heritage of all believers.

However, in a denominational magazine published in 2014 exploring the Church's identity, holiness scarcely appeared as a central element and that was to emphasize the lack of a uniform understanding and included virtually no reference to the "doctrine of entire sanctification as a second work of grace."

While evidence for an "identity crisis" can be multiplied from both academic and popular sources, the bottom line is that the paradigm to which the Church early committed itself has resulted in numerous anomalies and that paradigm is no longer sufficient to deal with these anomalies. Yet the Church continues to insist that one of its core values is "holiness."

What Went Wrong?

Two factors may be identified that contributed to what Mildred Bangs Wynkoop referred to as a "credibility gap." This terminology has a two-fold implication. It describes the "gap" between what Quanstrom repeatedly referred to as the "extravagant claims" for entire sanctification and the actual experience of many people. It also refers to a gap between the arguments for "entire sanctification" and good biblical interpretation.

---

important books for the holiness movement published in recent years for it makes clear the unavoidable necessity of a new theological paradigm.

The source of the first "gap" was the rediscovery of the "intractable nature of sin." The historical period during which the holiness revivals flourished was, for good reason, known as the "age of progress," characterized as highly optimistic, believing in the perfectibility of human nature. Many factors contributed to the loss of this optimism in the general ethos of the world, including the emergence of a more profound sense of the hidden, often unsuspected, depths of human personality. This awareness is the basis for the shocking declaration of Henry H. Knight, III that "our present appreciation of the role of unconscious motives in our lives makes Wesley's talk of Christian perfection seem hopelessly naïve, if not dangerously presumptive."[15]

The second "gap" was highlighted by W.M. Greathouse in a paper presented at the 1969 Nazarene Theology Conference. He argued that a source of much negativism toward the "holiness movement" by outside scholars was "its lack of broad and deep biblical grounding," whereby "it has reduced the many-splendored scriptural truth of sanctification to simply 'the second blessing' understood as a sort of watertight 'experience' which will keep us secure until Christ returns to gather up the little flock of holiness professors." He further noted that "A thoughtful reading of Wesley's *The Plain Account* [*of Christian* Perfection] will quickly reveal how seriously this 'folk theology' has departed from the more scriptural Wesleyan view of sanctification."

In analyzing what went wrong with the "holiness movement," Gordon J. Thomas identified one reason as "biblically, the exegesis of Holiness proof-texts has generally failed to convince others," resulting in its being marginalized in the wider church.[16] In his Ph.D. dissertation exploring the biblical interpretation of the 19th century holiness movement, Steven Lennox found that one reason for this was that the movement was built on one doctrinal distinctive, the experience of entire sanctification and this was used as a lens through which to read the entire scripture, thus finding "two works of grace" in

[15]Henry H. Knight, III, *The Presence of God in the Christian Life* (Metuchen, NJ: Scarecrow Press, Inc., 1992), 1.

[16]Introduction to a series of papers on "Reminting Christian holiness."

all sorts of unlikely places. Lennox's research identified many examples of this:

> When the movement read the Bible through experience, it discovered entire sanctification [by which they meant two works of grace] in places where a natural reading of the text does not suggest it. They found holiness proof-texts in the prohibition against wearing a garment mixed with wool and linen, the process of cleansing the leper, and many other places. Old Testament texts were interpreted to show how the second blessing came to Abraham, Jacob, Isaiah, and many others. Wherever Scripture spoke of two of anything or when something occurred twice, this was seen to teach a second definite work of grace. Passages like the second cleansing of the temple by Jesus, the two sisters of Lazarus, the two elements which flowed from Christ's side and the double touch on the eyes of the blind man were all treated as holiness texts."[17]

At best this reflects Martin Luther's criticism of the papists who, he said, turned scripture into "a wax nose" to be twisted into any shape they desired. This was clearly, as Lennox demonstrated, the result of drawing their understanding from "experience" and imposing it on scripture. This is substituting "eisegesis" (reading a meaning into the text from outside the text) for "exegesis" (identifying the meaning from within the text). With even those texts that were less imaginative in the interpretation, my sense is that they inherited the proof-texting method of doing Biblical theology from 17th century Protestant orthodoxy. Those systems of doctrine derived texts from throughout the scriptures indiscriminately, ignoring to a great extent the historical setting and larger context from which they came. This approach often kept the scripture from speaking for itself.

How did they justify this procedure? The first reason was objective. Believing that entire sanctification (as they understood it) was the central truth of scripture, they permitted this doctrine to shape and guide their interpretation of the Bible. The second reason was subjective. It had a two-pronged aspect. Along with Christian faith in general they believed that the Holy Spirit not only inspired the writing of scripture but he also enabled the interpreter to properly grasp its

---

[17] "Biblical Interpretation, American Holiness Movement, 1875-1925," *Wesleyan Theological Journal*, vol. 33, no. 1, Spring 1998, 28.

truths. By identifying entire sanctification with the baptism with the Holy Spirit, they inferred that only the entirely sanctified believer could understand the truth of the text. Stephen Lennox describes this assumption: "It professed to be completely purified of the sinful nature, indwelt by the Spirit of God, and thus perfectly prepared to interpret God's Word. 'Now for the first time,' remarked Beverly Carradine concerning the results of entire sanctification, the real depth of certain Bible expressions are understood and the heart fairly revels in them'[18] On this basis many of the interpreters found "second blessing holiness" in places and passages that would not be recognized by the average Bible reader, and certainly not by the trained biblical exegete.

Wesley Tracy points to a further factor that contributed to what today we would recognize as irresponsible biblical interpretation. The holiness movement emerged during a period that saw the rise of biblical criticism, Darwinian evolution, Freudian psychology and other new ideas that were radically changing the world they had inherited from their fathers. Tracy made the point that out of a resistance to these ideas and an instinct for survival, the holiness people "cut themselves off from the biblical scholarship, the theological reflection, and the philosophical hypothesizing then taking place. Avoiding such things, it is not surprising that the good people of this movement came early to rely heavily on testimony and religious experience. They developed a way of being that was long on personal experience and short on in-depth understanding of the scriptures and open-minded theological reflection." The result of this was that they became largely self-sufficient with no need for outside counsel. By talking only with themselves, they "became more and more self validating." The consequence of this was that the movement lacked the capacity to check its own interpretation.[19]

---

[18] "Biblical Interpretation, American Holiness Movement," *Wesleyan Theological Journal* vol. 33, no. 1, Spring 1998, 21.

[19] Wesley D. Tracy, "Foreword" to H. Ray Dunning, *A Layman's Guide to Sanctificaion* (K.C.: Beacon Hill Press of Kansas City, 1991).

Possible Responses to the Crisis

There are six possible responses to the problem, each with its own consequences: (1) the ideal of Christian perfection can be abandoned with the consequence that holiness churches will simply become generic evangelical churches. This was, to some extent, what occurred with the old-line churches that originally had a holiness emphasis. (2) The traditional paradigm can be vigorously defended[20] in which case there will be continued irrelevance. The major spokesmen among the theologians of the Church for this approach have now graduated to the more excellent glory thus largely resulting in the first response. John L. Peters points out the "Scylla and Charybdis of these first two options. If the claim is established that perfection can be actually and consciously attained in this life, Pharisaism immediately threatens. If, on the other hand, one gives up on the possibility, moral complacency tends to take over. . In other words, what can save the teaching from spiritual pride on the one hand or from acquiescence in spiritual mediocrity on the other?[21] (3) It can be ignored with the consequence that the problem will merely be perpetuated. This seems to be the widespread response at the grassroots level, both lay and clergy, and to a great extent by many Wesleyan scholars who focus their work on other issues.

(4) Minor *ad hoc* adjustments can be proposed to the traditional interpretation in an attempt to preserve its major claims, which will only perpetuate the problem. This has generally taken the form of an increasing emphasis on the role of "infirmity" in the sanctified life accompanied by a minimizing of the sin "eradicated" in entire sanctification.[22] Alternately, many have suggested simply using

---

[20]See J. Kenneth Grider, *Entire Sanctification* (K.C.: Beacon Hill Press of Kansas City, 1980); Richard S. Taylor, "Why the Holiness Movement Died," *God's Revivalist*, vol. 111, No. 2, March, 1999, 7-27; Richard S. Taylor, *The Theological Formulation*, vol. 3 of *Exploring Christian Holiness* (K.C.: Beacon Hill Press of Kansas City, 1985); Donald Metz, *Studies in Biblical Holiness* (K.C.: Beacon Hill Press of Kansas City, 1971).

[21]John L. Peters, *Christian Perfection and American Methodism* (Nashville: Abingdon Press, 1956), 186.

[22]Cf. Quanstrom, *Holiness Theology*, 11. For a detailed and painstaking attempt to distinguish between "carnality" and "infirmity," see Richard S. Taylor, *A*

different terminology, which is more understandable by the current generation. However, without coming to terms with the underlying theology, the crucial issues are not really addressed.

(5) One widespread response is to return to John Wesley's teaching. This has resulted in the widely recognized result that there are now two major understandings of sanctification in the holiness movement, the Wesleyan and the American holiness teaching. While this move is helpful and represents a sounder approach, the problem is that Wesley left a number of unresolved issues to his successors. Wesleyan scholar, Rob L. Staples stated that one of the purposes of his doctoral dissertation was to "resolve the inconsistencies in his [Wesley's] thought—inconsistencies which are recognized by most Wesley scholars." Hence, to take this approach uncritically will likely result in continuing ambiguity.

Samuel Chadwick, in *The Call to Christian Perfection*, one of the more perceptive "holiness classics," made some very interesting comments relevant to this issue. He declared that "Wesley's statement of [the doctrine of Christian Perfection] was obviously incomplete, but had it been complete it would have needed a new birth for a new age." Chadwick further said of the literature of his own day,

> The literature upon the subject is singularly disappointing. I have for years urged the young biblical scholars of the ministry to explore and restate the teaching of the Scriptures on the subject of Holiness. I hope some of them are doing it. I am sure it must be done, for while the witness may be sincere, the teaching is confused, unrelated and incomplete."[23]

Right Conception of Sin (K.C.: Nazarene Publishing House, 1939), 96ff; J. Kenneth Grider, "Carnality and Humanity," *Wesleyan Theological Journal*, Vol. 11, Spring, 1976, 81-91; Ortho Jennings, "Areas of Growth After Sanctification," *Further Insights into Holiness* (K.C.: Beacon Hill Press, 1963), 141-162; Leo G. Cox, "The Imperfections of the Perfect," *Further Insights into Holiness*, 179-196; Cornelius P. Haggard, "Temptation and the Sanctified Life," *Further Insights into Holiness*, 197-212.

[23]Samuel Chadwick, *The Call to Christian Perfection* (K.C.: Beacon Hill Press, 1943), 24.

Albert Outler, dean of Wesley studies until his death, observed that Wesley "did not guard himself as carefully as he might have" against the idea of "sinless perfection," which he explicitly rejected, holding rather to a "perfectible perfection." The result was a shift among some of Wesley's successors to the claim for a "perfected perfection" expressed, said Outler, in the dubious distinction between "a perfect heart and a perfect character," or between "purity and maturity," a distinction still widely defended in the holiness movement.[24]

One significant ambiguity in Wesley concerns the nature of sin and its relation to sanctification. He occasionally referred to the instantaneous aspect of sanctification as the destruction of the "evil root," a divine action in which "inbred sin subsists no more." This implies the idea that sin is a "substance" that can be removed.[25] But he is equally emphatic on the moment by moment relational nature of the sanctified life.[26]

Unfortunately, Wesley's followers in the 19th and early 20th centuries followed the substantialist implications of this ambiguity with confusing results, at least at the popular level. Wynkoop comments that "It has always been the most profound conviction of Wesleyanism that the Bible speaks to the moral relationships of men and not about sub-rational, nonpersonal areas of the self," and bemoans the results of interpreting scripture in this "nonpersonal" way as "both alarming and dangerous . . . a spiritual tragedy."[27]

---

[24]Albert C. Outler, *Theology in the Wesleyan Spirit* (Nashville: Tidings, 1975), 79-80. See Chapter 3 on "Sanctification and Purity" of this work.

[25]E.H. Sugden, ed., *Wesley's Standard Sermons*, 2 vols. (London: Epworth Press, 1964) said: "Both he [Wesley] and many of his followers have been brought into some confusion of view by the idea that the carnal mind is something in man which can be removed, like an aching tooth or a cancerous growth; or a sort of stain or defilement which can be washed away, like an ink-blot, or patch of filth on the body. Now the carnal mind is not a *thing* at all," 2:148-149.

[26]Hoo-Jung Lee provides an extensive discussion of this ambiguity in "The Doctrine of New Creation in the Theology of John Wesley," Ph.D. dissertation, Emory University, 1991, pp. 56-7.

[27]*Theology of Love*, 51.

Harald Lindström calls attention to a further ambiguity in Wesley relating to the use of sanctification terminology. He says:

Sanctification itself is rarely presented in its full range. The conception is normally restricted. Sometimes it connotes Christian perfection only, no regard being had to the gradual development of sanctification, from its commencement in the New Birth. Sometimes, it is true, the latter is included, but then entire sanctification is minimized. In neither alternative, moreover, has the significance, for Wesley's total view of salvation, of the principle of entire sanctification, been clearly expounded.[28]

Mildred Bangs Wynkoop, in giving her presidential address to the 10th Anniversary meeting of the Wesleyan Theological Society challenged the membership to make Wesley their mentor rather than a guru. A mentor, she defined, "is a guide and critic. His task is to introduce his charge to sources of information; to prevent the student from drifting into unfruitful, erroneous byways; and to encourage him to exploit his own potential as he learns to master his field. A mentor is satisfied when his student outpaces him." On the other hand "The guru is a master. . . . Innovation is not the prerogative of the follower. He sets aside personal initiative. The guru is a little god." She concluded her challenge with the observation "We have no excuse for thrashing [sic] old straw."[29]

It is certainly the case that there are elements in Wesley's descriptions (at least at various stages of his career) that need re-examination and perhaps reformulation.[30] Or it may be that there are

---

[28] Harald Lindström, *Wesley and Sanctification* (Wilmore, KY: Francis Asbury Pub. Co., reprint, 1980),15.

[29]Mildred Bangs Wynkoop, "John Wesley—Mentor or Guru?" *Wesleyan Theological Journal*, vol. 10, Spring, 1975, 5-15.

[30] Richard S. Taylor makes an interesting observation that addresses this issue while discussing "Holiness and the Meaning of Maturity:" "Problems arise when we are reminded that John Wesley often ascribed maturity to entirely sanctified people; in fact, he wrote as if the second blessing brought one at once into spiritual maturity." *The Preacher's Magazine*, September/October/November, 1994, 4-6.

implications of Wesley's teaching that we have yet to properly recognize and appropriate.[31] We will be highlighting some of these emphases throughout this study. The authentic way to be faithful to the Wesleyan heritage is not to use Wesley's teaching in lieu of a careful study of the scripture and acknowledging its authority based on the best exegetical methods available. We can certainly say of him as N.T. Wright said of the Protestant Reformers: "Luther, Melanchthon, Calvin, and the rest would certainly have advised us to read the New Testament even better than they did, not to set up their own work as a new authoritative tradition, a fixed lens through which the Bible would have to be viewed for ever afterwards."[32]

A New Paradigm

Finally, one can propose a new paradigm altogether, and this is usually met with considerable resistance.[33] The concepts of "paradigm" and "paradigm shift" have become popular ways of talking about how we experience the world. A "paradigm" may be simply defined as something like a pair of lenses through which one views the world. There is a sense in which complete objectivity in our experience is impossible since we all come to our experiences with a set of presuppositions or perspectives in the light of which we interpret what we see. For most people, their paradigm is subconscious as it is normally derived from the culture of the context in which they exist. It is sometimes the case that when one comes to the realization that their paradigm is unable to make sense of all their experience that they self-

---

[31]For a full-scale analysis of the elements in Wesley's works that *avoids* the pitfalls that have created major theological and practical problems for his followers, and formulates them into a consistent vision of Christian perfection see Rob L. Staples (unfortunately unpublished) Ph.D. dissertation: "John Wesley's Doctrine of Christian Perfection; A Re-Interpretation."

[32]N.T. Wright, "Redemption from a New Perspective," in *RedemptionI,* ed. S.T. David, et. al. (Oxford: Oxford University Press, 2006), 76.

[33] Cf. the descriptions of the furor surrounding the publication of Mildred Bangs Wynkoop's book in Quanstrom, *Holiness Theology*, 150ff. as well as the criticisms of H. Ray Dunning, *Grace Faith and Holiness* described by Quanstrom, pp. 157ff.

consciously develop another "set of lenses." This transformation is what is termed a "paradigm shift."

The classic example of these concepts is the Copernican Revolution in which the geocentric view of the universe was challenged by the heliocentric one. There was much opposition by the traditionalists and much pain suffered by those who proposed the paradigm shift. But science was stymied by the old paradigm and progress could only be made on the basis of a new hypothesis. It appears that we are in the same situation in the holiness movement. Of course, it is not without significance that the structure and function of the universe did not change with the shift in humanity's model for understanding it.

The fact that the "Copernican revolution" in science did not actually change the structure of the heavens should remind us that in order not to lose the value of the tradition by proposing a paradigm that alters that essence, we must attempt to identify that which is the genius of the tradition, without which it becomes something else (i. e. we must keep the stars in their orbits). I would propose that the heart of the holiness message may be reflected in a little referenced quotation from John Wesley in his sermon, "The More Excellent Way:"[34]

> From long experience and observation, I am inclined to think that whoever finds redemption in the blood of Jesus—whoever is justified—has the choice of walking in the higher or the lower path. I believe the Holy Spirit at that time sets before him the 'more excellent way,' and incites him to walk therein—to choose the narrowest path in the narrow way—to aspire after the heights and depths of holiness—after the image of God. But if he does not accept this offer, he insensibly declines into the lower order of Christians; he still goes on in what may be called a good way, serving God in his degree, and finds mercy in the close of life through the blood of the covenant."

This statement provides the rationale for Wesley's guidance to his preachers that they should preach perfection in a drawing rather

---

[34]*The Works of John Wesley*, 14 vols. (K.C.: Nazarene Publishing House, reproduction of 1872 edition), 7:28.

than a driving manner. It also implies how entire sanctification must be understood in thoroughly ethical terms since the response to the "high road" is a commitment to the pursuit of the image of God as embodied in Jesus Christ.

The implication is that an authentic "holiness church" is one composed of those who have chosen to respond to this calling but who are not therefore bigoted in relation to those Christians who do not respond to that call. *An adequate paradigm must consistently develop the nature of this "high road" including how it plays out in experience.*

Paradigm Shifts not Unusual

The truth is that during the history of holiness teaching from the 18th century to the present, there have been a number of significant paradigm shifts. One can even identify changes in John Wesley's understanding that took place over his lifetime as a result of experience.[35] Mark Olsen demonstrates that Wesley's interpretation of sin was quite fluid, evolving over time in relation to his understanding of holiness and concludes that "Wesley bequeathed to his posterity . . . . a theology of holiness bound with unresolved tensions."[36]

In the transition of Methodism to America, some major paradigm shifts took place in Wesley's theology of holiness resulting in this context having a somewhat different character from Wesley. Generally, these changes are the ones that have been the major source of the malaise of the movement in the present time.[37] One of the most obvious shifts occurred with Wesley's consistent emphasis on both gradual and instantaneous sanctification.

---

[35]Cf. Don Marselle Moore, "Development in Wesley's Thought on Sanctification and Perfection," *Wesleyan Theological Journal*. Vol. 4 (1969), 3-15.

[36]Mark Olsen, "John Wesley's Doctrine of Sin Revisited," *Wesleyan Theological Journal*, Vol. 47, No. 2, Fall 2012, 51-71.

[37]Cf. Victor Reasoner, "The American Holiness Movement's Paradigm Shift Concerning Holiness," *Wesleyan Theological Journal*, vol. 31, No. 2, Fall, (1996), 132-146; Kevin T. Lowrey, "A Fork in the Wesleyan Road: Phoebe Palmer and the Appropriation of Christian Perfection," *Wesleyan Theological Journal*, vol. 36, no. 2 (2001), 187-222.

Although not universal[38] a widespread tendency in the holiness movement resulted in reducing complete sanctification to a single moment of experience whereas the Methodist tendency was in the opposite direction. John L. Peters describes this dual movement among Wesley's followers in an incisive summary:

This consideration—instantaneous and gradual—was to become the watershed in the development of Wesley's doctrine. Down one slope would move the absolutist interpreters until Christian perfection would come to mean an almost exclusive emphasis upon a single climactic experience. Down the other slope would move the accommodative interpreters until Christian perfection would come to mean little more than a dimly remembered tradition.[39]

The grounds for this development may be partly the consequence of the fact that Wesley was never able to provide a satisfactory explanation of how these were to be integrated. After carefully analyzing Wesley's struggles to synthesize these two aspects of sanctification Rob L. Staples concludes that "it is our thesis that Wesley's synthesis is intrinsically problematic and therefore open to serious criticism," and suggests that the fallout between the two emphases in the 19th century is the result of the inherently inadequate and structurally inconsistent nature of Wesley's attempted synthesis.[40]

---

[38]In his General Superintendent's address to the 1928 General Assembly of the Church of the Nazarene, Roy T. Williams declared "The church must place emphasis both upon the *crisis and the process* in religion. . . For many years the holiness people felt that the work to which they were called ended at the altar, when the crowds who came forward received the blessing of regeneration and sanctification, but it became evident that our work has only begun at this point. . . The Church of the Nazarene is combining these two great principles, namely the crisis and the process. Leading men to God and the edification of the body of Christ in initial salvation and the development of Christian character." *General Assembly Journal*, 1928.

[39]*Christian Perfection and American Methodism*, 47-48.

[40]Staples, "John Wesley's Doctrine of Christian Perfection," 77-122. Matthew R. Schlimm, "The Puzzle of Perfection: Growth in John Wesley's Doctrine of Perfection," *Wesleyan Theological Journal*, vo. 38, no. 2 (Fall, 2003) also

This does not mean that there was a uniform understanding in the 19th century American context. There was actually a variety of paradigms present during this period. One researcher identified at least 6 different varieties of the holiness message.[41] Paul M. Bassett has demonstrated that the holiness movement had a constantly shifting understanding of the concept of original sin, a major component of the doctrine of sanctification, during the period from the mid-nineteenth century to 1920.[42] While these were not all major paradigm shifts they do reflect that the message of holiness in the Wesleyan tradition has been in near constant flux throughout the history of the American Holiness movement that spawned the Church of the Nazarene and other contemporary "holiness denominations." The result is aptly described in E. Dale Dunlap's conclusion about the 19th century holiness movement in the Methodist Church: "'Scriptural holiness' is what Methodism is all about, even if there is not universal agreement as to what 'Scriptural holiness' is all about."[43]

Proposed Paradigm Shifts

The first *published* comprehensive attempt to formulate a more adequate paradigm for "holiness theology" was the *magnum opus* of Mildred Bangs Wynkoop, *A Theology of Love*.[44] Wynkoop identified

---

explores Wesley's difficulty in affirming the possibility of both perfection and growth.

[41]Myung Soo Pak, "Concepts of Holiness in American Evangelicalism: 1835-1915," Ph.D. dissertation, Boston University, 1992.

[42]Paul M. Bassett, "Culture and Concupiscence: the Changing Definition of Sanctity in the Wesleyan Holiness Movement, 1870-1920." *Wesleyan Theological Journal* 28 (1993): 59-127.

[43]"Tuesday Meetings, Camp Meetings, and Cabinet Meetings: A Perspective on the Holiness Movement in the Methodist Church in the United States in the Nineteenth Century," *Methodist History/A.M.E. Zion*, 13, no. 3, Apr. 1975, 85.

[44]Rob L. Staples, in his unpublished Ph.D. dissertation, developed a significant paradigm shift in Wesley's teaching about sanctification by identifying two major strands in Wesley's teaching concerning the instantaneous and gradual element—which he himself never really correlated—and interpreting the instantaneous element, which Staples said was the core commitment of Wesley's thought, in relation to the dialogic theology of Jewish philosopher/theologian Martin

what she conceived to be the major tensions in the prevailing paradigm and offered an alternative perspective based on her reading of John Wesley. The three major issues she identified as needing attention involved contrary worldviews: "(1) the Greek versus Hebrew anthropology [see our chapter 6]; (2) the substantial versus relational concept of sin, and (3) the magical versus moral concept of salvation."[45] In her proposals she began breaking new ground but like most pioneering attempts her work needs more clarification and sharpening up but the direction she pointed out is toward what I believe to be the way out of the "credibility gap" she was attempting to bridge.

There are several issues that need to be addressed in attempting to formulate a more adequate paradigm, including the ones Wynkoop identified. I have herewith offered a tentative proposal regarding some of these issues that includes a positive affirmation of Wynkoop's basic proposals. My proposals have been hammered out over the years of study and teaching, usually in a seriatim fashion. New ideas are often like a jigsaw puzzle when you do not have a picture of the finished product. You have all the pieces, and sometimes they are beautiful in themselves but ideally there comes the time when they all fit together and you see them in an integrated whole.

One major caveat needs to be made regarding the experience of that great host of persons who experienced and testified to a deeper relationship with God during the first half of the 20th century. Finding a way forward inevitably involves calling attention to the inadequacies of the prevailing theology and biblical interpretation. It is very important to recognize that in no way does this impugn the reality of their relation to God, the depth of their spirituality, or the purity of their integrity. It is true, however, as some analysts have pointed out, that their theological inadequacies resulted in some cases in faulty experience and ethics. In offering his answers to "Why the Holiness Movement Died," Richard S. Taylor identified one contributing factor as the "shabby demonstration of holiness on the part of so many of its professors."[46] But this does not invalidate the fact that many

---

Buber, thus offering a viable paradigm for contemporary theology and experience.

[45]*Theology of Love*, 50.

24

demonstrated a depth of commitment and quality of character that expressed a relationship to God, others and themselves that transcended nominal Christianity. Even though recognizing the theological problems involved, Wesley Tracy's positive evaluation should be taken seriously:

> They believed in traditional Christianity, the Bible, social justice, and holiness of heart and life. They were passionate and compassionate, conservative and tough, innovative and courageous, energetic and shrewd. They believed that what persons and nations needed was the doctrine and experience of entire sanctification. Like John Wesley they believed that sanctifying grace was God's cure for the private and corporate ills of the race.
> This group spread revival, organized churches, established orphanages, and planted holiness colleges all over the landscape. They proclaimed timeless truths. They did a lot of things gloriously right."[47]

---

[46]Richard S. Taylor, "Why the Holiness Movement Died," *God's Revivalist*, vol. 111, No. 2, March, 1999, 7-27. Taylor ultimately placed the blame on the people who "refused to pay the price to be entirely sanctified" rather than the unrealistic claims of at least the popular preaching and the understanding of human nature that has become prevalent in the late 20th and 21st centuries.

[47]Wesley Tracy, "Foreword," to H. Ray Dunning, *Becoming Christlike Disciples* (Bloomington, IN: Westbow Press, 2010), 4.

Chapter 1
Sanctification in Perspective

Thesis: The 19th century/early 20th century holiness movement was largely preoccupied with the "when" and the "how" of sanctification[48] whereas the "why" is the basis for a sound theological and biblical rationale for the importance of the holy life.

In order to properly address the question of why sanctification is an important aspect of the Christian life, one must first make a preliminary effort at defining what is meant by the concept. One may approach this task in one of two ways. The first is to do a survey of the biblical material seeking to identify the characteristics essential to "holiness" in human experience. Unfortunately, traditional attempts to do this have tended to focus on what might be termed a "canon within the canon." This approach tends to highlight the "texts" that have been used to reinforce the structure of the traditional understanding.[49] Jack

---

[48]A case can be made that the formative voice in the theology of the American Holiness Movement was Phoebe Palmer, who has been called "the mother" of the movement. Timothy Smith, in an analysis of her theology, concluded that her "theology of Christian holiness" was largely a theology of means or method. "Clarity with respect to method is her main goal—describing the nature or essence of entire sanctification or holiness is very clearly a minor concern. In fact, it is not at all easy to 'pin her down' at the point of definition or description because she so seldom addresses herself to that concern!" Handwritten lecture shared privately with the author. In "A White Paper on Article X," Paul Bassett, et. al. make the same analysis of the American Holiness emphasis. www.didache.nts.edu; (summer, 2010) For an interesting critique of a series of volumes of primary sources from the entire sweep of Christian history where the terminology and structure of 19th century holiness theology relative to these issues was imposed on the material, see Victor Reasoner, Wesley Center Online, Northwest Nazarene University. Reasoner rightly critiques the imposition of a 19th century grid upon this material, specifically reviewing the first volume edited by Paul M. Bassett. What he did not know is that Bassett resisted doing this, it was forced upon him, and furthermore this author as a member of the advisory committee objected to this approach but to no avail. This approach reflects the implicit fact that tradition took priority over objective scholarship.

[49]This is the greatest weakness of W. T. Purkiser, Exploring *Christian Holiness, The Biblical Foundations* (K.C.: Beacon Hill Press of Kansas City, 1983).

Ford, in exploring the teaching of the holiness movement at the mid-point of the 20th century commented: "Even friends of Wesley have to admit that he was inclined to use the Bible as an arsenal of proof texts rather than to deal with a text in its context and historical setting.[50] This method is still largely followed in the holiness groups. . . It is much more satisfactory to take a passage when seeking to make a point, and to relate a text to its context."[51] A much wider ranging

---

Cf. the negative review of this volume by Wayne McCown, *Wesleyan Theological Journal*, Vol. 19, No. 2 (Fall 1984), 90-92; Ralph Earle, *Sanctification in the New Testament* (K.C.: Beacon Hill Press of Kansas City, 1988); H. Orton Wiley, in his discussion of the biblical basis of entire sanctification, explicitly chose to base his argument on the traditional "proof texts." (*Christian Theology*, 2:442). It is of considerable interest that Wiley, in a lecture given in 1951 said that "I have come to see that while holiness may be substantiated by texts the main thing about our doctrine of holiness is the 'whole tenor of scripture.' Texts may be differently interpreted but not the whole tenor of scripture," and added that we must "give more attention to the cultivation of a holy life." Recorded for PalCon, 1976. W. T. Purkiser, in tension with his later work cited above, likewise emphasized the shift from "texts" to the "wholeness" of scripture": "The doctrine of Christian holiness is based upon the total thrust of the Scriptures. . . . a network of teaching which is an essential part of the fabric of the whole." *Interpreting Christian Holiness* (K.C.: Beacon Hill Press of Kansas City, 1971), 9.

[50]W.E. Sangster, *The Path to Perfection* (N.Y.: Abingdon Press, 1943) claimed that Wesley based his teaching of Christian Perfection on 30 texts, which he then identified and critiqued. But he ultimately concluded that "we have noticed the shadows of dubiety cast by scholarship on a translation, or interpretation, here and there, but, for the most part, the stones stand.", 52.

[51]Jack Ford in *What the Holiness People Believe, A Mid-Century Review of Holiness Teaching*, (Palm Grove, Birkenhead, Cheshire: Emmanuel Bible College and Missions, n.d.), 18. Leroy Lindsey devotes an entire chapter of his dissertation ("Radical Remedy") to arguing that the majority of Wesleyan-holiness thinkers were not "proof-texters" but basically used scripture similarly to John Wesley. The examples he uses and the concessions he makes, such as the use of circular reasoning and presuppositions derived from experience that "discarded" any conflicting evidence and widespread use of allegory for apologetics, make his argument unconvincing. One can agree that the holiness exegetes had "genuine respect" for divine revelation (212) but that is quite different from informed exegesis. Actually what he inadvertently demonstrates is clearly eisegesis. As N.T. Wright commented, "prayer and humility before the text do not guarantee exegetical success." "New Perspectives on Paul," found at www.ntwrightpage.com (2003). His further words are incisive: ". . . Christian theology needs biblical studies. To be truly Christian, it must show that it includes the story which the Bible tells, and the sub-stories within in. Without this it lapses into a mere *ad hoc* use of the Bible, finding bits and pieces

approach has been admirably undertaken by the faculty of Nazarene Theological College in England in a series titled "reminting Christian holiness."[52] Such an inductive approach has one significant difficulty in the light of the amazing diversity of the biblical material. Other than word studies, one must of necessity approach the material with an implicit concept of what constitutes "holiness" or "sanctification." Further, as with all inductive reasoning, to complete the task one must create a generalization from the material surveyed. This was the prevailing method of science up until the 17th century. Real progress only began to be made in science with the emergence of the use of a hypothesis, which was then tested by experimentation. As Samuel M. Stumpf wrote: ". . . a modern scientist knows it is necessary to have an hypothesis in order to inspect facts in order to have some guide in the selection of facts relevant to the experiment."[53] It is this latter approach that I propose to take in this investigation.

This method creates an interesting logical situation since the definition must, at least to some extent, be a conclusion resulting from adequate research into the relevant material. To propose that we begin the discussion with a thesis is clearly to run the risk of "begging the question." But as N. T. Wright argues, all hypotheses are ultimately circular.[54] *Hence, what we propose here is to set forth a hypothesis or a series of hypotheses and proceed to test their adequacy in the context of the biblical story viewed holistically.* What this approach proposes is that a hypothesis is validated by its consistency and inclusiveness in

---

to fit into a scheme derived from elsewhere. If finding a proof-text, or even a proof-theme, from the Bible, is what counts then theology is simply reproducing the worst phenomenon of an earlier proof-texting Biblicism. *New Testament and the People of God*, 138.

[52]Gordon Thomas, "Re-Minting Christian Holiness: Our Global Opportunity" (Search "European Explorations in Christian Holiness" online for 51 essays).

[53]Samuel E. Stumpf, *Philosophy: History and Problems* (N.Y.: McGraw-Hill Publishing Co., 1989), 224.

[54]*Jesus and the Victory of God* (Minneapolis: Fortress Press, 1996), 50.

relation to what may be referred to as the biblical world view.[55] No clearer statement of such a perspective can be found than the brief summary of N. T. Wright who suggests that the Christian (biblical) world view can best be viewed as a "story:"

> The story is about a creator and his creation, about humans made in this creator's image and given tasks to perform, about the rebellion of humans and the dissonance of creation at every level, and particularly about the creator's acting, through Israel and climactically through Jesus, to rescue his creation from its ensuing plight. The story continues with the creator acting by his own spirit within the world to bring it towards the restoration which is his intended goal for it.[56]

The adequacy of a paradigm of holiness theology is the degree to which it integrates with this world view.[57] We have a good model of

---

[55]The concept of "worldview" has been influential in my thinking for a long time, influenced by, among others, Arthur F. Holmes, *Contours of a World View*, (Grand Rapids, Mich.: Eerdmans, 1983). More recently, N.T. Wright has written brilliantly on the importance of "worldview" as essential to exegetical integrity. This is simply another way of saying that the larger context of biblical theology must inform microscopic exegesis of texts. In discussing the question of "Pauline theology," Wright says, "In the last analysis, theology is all about the great wholes, the world-views which determine and dominate the day-to-day handling of varied issues. When all is said and done, most, perhaps all, great thinkers and writers can and should be studied at this level." *Climax of the Covenant* (Continuum International Publishing), 3. In one of his latest writings, he describes "worldview" as a level "one does not normally talk about, but which informs everything else one thinks, says and does." *Paul and the Faithfulness of God*, 2 vols. (Minneapolis: Fortress Press, 2013), 1:375.

[56]*The New Testament and the People of God* (Minneapolis: Fortress Press, 1992), 132. Hoo-Jung Lee argues that the mature Wesley came to emphasize "the *grand scheme* of redemption that embraced the whole drama of God's creation, the Fall of humanity, and the far superior New Creation," thus substantially expressing the same world view. "The Doctrine of New Creation in the Theology of John Wesley," Ph.D. dissertation, Emory University, 1991, 53.

[57]Mildred Bangs Wynkoop describes the failure to conform to this principle as a "provincialism," which she defines as "Lifting one aspect of doctrine into a central dominating position, away from its proper place in the whole doctrine." *Foundations of Wesleyan-Arminian Theology* (K.C.: Beacon Hill Press of Kansas City, 1967), 22. The post-Civil War holiness movement, with rare exceptions, tended to become a one-issue theology as described by Rob L. Staples: "in many of the

this in the Apostle Paul who "grounds his theology again and again not in isolated proof-texts but in a reading of scripture which, like many second Temple Jewish readings, picked up its fundamental quality as the story of the creator and covenant God with the world and with Israel. It is central to Paul's world-view that this long story has now come to its climax in Jesus, the Jewish Messiah."[58] But much more needs to be said to sharpen the world view perspective. We must examine the structure of New Testament theology since particular passages of scripture bring to expression some aspect of the overarching theology that informs the biblical material. This is such a wide ranging task that we can only, in this place, offer a summary statement of what contemporary New Testament scholars have generally agreed is the underlying structure of New Testament theology. This theological structure involves the reformulation of the rabbinic teaching of the "two ages," an eschatological concept. According to this understanding, history is divided into two ages, "the present age," and "the age to come."[59] As a result of the continued failure of the promises of a glorious future depicted by the prophets to become reality, there emerged the belief that God had removed himself from active involvement in the world and this "present age" was under the control of demonic powers, with Satan as the "prince of the powers of the air." The hope for the coming of the kingdom of God was the expectation of a cataclysmic event when God will break into history with a traumatic upheaval of the social order, probably marked by cosmic signs,[60] thus defeating the enemy and thus ushering in the

---

smaller Wesleyan sects the doctrine [of entire sanctification] is held as the basic tenet, often to the exclusion of other vital emphases in the Christian faith," "John Wesley's Doctrine of Christian Perfection," 2. A member of a ministerial credentials committee once said to me, "if the candidate is O.K. on the doctrine of sanctification, the others do not matter.'

[58]N.T. Wright, "Redemption from the New Perspective," 76-77.

[59]This language is explicitly found in the following passages: ("this age:" Romans 12:2; 1 Corinthians 1:20; 2:6, 8; 2 Corinthians 4:4), ("the present evil age:" Galatians 1:4), ("the present age:" 1 Timothy 6:17; 2 Timothy 4:10; Titus 2:12).

[60]This aspect of eschatology has been referred to as "apocalyptic." Many biblical scholars have argued that the texts that reflect apocalyptic imagery dealing

"age to come," which was the kingdom age. This was a horizontal view of history, not a vertical one in which the redeemed would escape this world. It rather involved a "new heavens and new earth," a renewal of creation.

With the advent of Jesus, particularly with his death/resurrection, the early Christians saw that the age to come had broken into history even though the present age had not come to an end. They were living in the overlap of the ages, in the time between the times. In Ephesians 1:21, Paul speaks of the power of God that has been given to Christ through his resurrection from the dead "not only in this age but also in the age to come."[61]

Herman Ridderbos points out how this structure has become generally accepted in Pauline scholarship:

> [Biblical theology] has no longer sought the basic motif of this preaching in one particular soteriological aspect, whether in justification by faith or in victory over the flesh through the Spirit,[62] but, transcending all these partial viewpoints and antecedent to them, in the eschatological or redemptive-historical starting point of Paul's proclamation. The whole content of this preaching can be summarized as the proclamation and explication of the eschatological time of salvation inaugurated with Christ's advent, death, and resurrection. It is from this principle point of view and under this denominator that all the separate themes of Paul's preaching can be understood and penetrated in their unity and relation to each other.[63]

---

with cosmic upheaval are actually referring to historical events and investing them with theological or cosmic significance by the use of this imagery. E.g. the so-called apocalyptic passages in the Synoptic Gospels (Mark 13, par.) do not refer to the end of the world but to the fall of Jerusalem that took place in 70 A.D. Adam Clarke actually recognized this interpretation.

[61]Unless otherwise indicated, all scripture quotations are from the New Revised Standard Version.

[62]These were the two major proposals for the "center" of Pauline theology.

[63]Herman Ridderbos, *Paul: An Outline of His Theology*, trans. John Richard de Witt (Grand Rapids: Eerdmans Pub. Co., 1966), 44. George Eldon Ladd, *A Theology of the New Testament*, Revised Ed. (Grand Rapids, Eerdmans Pub. Co., 1974) demonstrates how this structure informs every segment of NT literature, not just Paul's.

In the light of this theological perspective, we will first analyze the prevailing paradigm of the 19th and early 20th centuries that can be adequately summarized by the following definition: "Entire Sanctification is essentially defined as an instantaneous cleansing from Adamic sin, and an empowerment, which Christian believers may receive by faith, through the baptism with the Holy Spirit."[64] A fuller spelling out of the paradigm states: "We believe that entire sanctification is that act of God, subsequent to regeneration, by which believers are made free from original sin, or depravity, and brought into a state of entire devotement to God, and the holy obedience of love made perfect. It is wrought by the baptism with the Holy Spirit, and comprehends in one experience the cleansing of the heart from sin and the abiding, indwelling presence of the Holy Spirit, empowering the believer for life and service."[65] Our task here is to analyze and determine how this understanding would answer the "why" question.[66]

To begin with, the major concern of this formulation is to deal with "sin" individualistically understood. While consistent with a dominant cultural understanding since the Enlightenment of the 18th century, and intensified in America by the frontier experience, such

---

[64]Grider, *Entire Sanctification*, 11.

[65]Wiley, *Christian Theology*, 2:466-7. The reference to entire sanctification being a *state* suggests a static idea. W. M. Greathouse points out the fallacy of this perception: "Even after the issue of sovereignty has been settled, victory over Sin is not inevitable. For this reason, it is a mistake to speak of a 'state' of holiness; it is always a maintained 'condition.' Since it exists only by virtue of a sustained relationship of loving obedience to the holy God, it can never be conceived of as a human possession." *Romans 1-8, New Beacon Bible Commentary* (K.C.: Beacon Hill Press of Kansas City, 2008), 187.

[66]Most discussions of sanctification during this period focused almost exclusive on the idea of *entire* sanctification with little recognition of an important distinction between "sanctification" as the more general term and "entire" sanctification as sub-set of it. As a matter of fact, for all practical purposes, the terms were synonymous. In fact, the entire holiness word group was generally used interchangeably with entire sanctification.

individualism is in tension with Biblical faith, which is thoroughly corporate in nature. Ben Meyers observed that ". . . it would be difficult to adduce a single text to exemplify a religious self-understanding which positively abstracted from 'membership' in God's people."[67] Not only are we as individuals involved in an organic relation with the remainder of humanity resulting in what has been termed "systemic evil,"[68] but the redeeming work of Christ has its intention to bring into being a "community of faith," a "holy nation" as a corporate reality. This is not to deny the personal nature of salvation but to recognize, at least in part, what it means to be a human person, and this entails being in relation.[69]

Two other features of this definition raise exegetical questions. The use of the term "cleansing" implies a number of other terms that are widely used in holiness literature, terms such as "purity," "corruption," and "defilement." In fact, this complex of idioms became a dominant conceptuality used by the American holiness movement to embody its central claim concerning the nature of entire sanctification.[70]

---

[67]Ben M. Meyers, *The Aims of Jesus* (San Jose, CA: Pickwick Pub., 2002), 135.

[68]Albert Truesdale, "Christian Holiness and the Problem of Systemic Evil," *Wesleyan Theological Journal*, Vol. 19, no. 1, Spring 1984.

[69]Cf. Ray S. Anderson, *On Being Human* (Grand Rapids: Eerdmans, 1982); John MacMurray, *Persons in Relation* (Atlantic Highlands, NJ: Humanities Press, 1979).

[70]See for example, J. A. Wood, *Purity and Maturity,* abridged by John Paul (K.C.: Beacon Hill Press, 1944); R. S. Foster, *Christian Purity* (Holiness Data Ministry, NNU website, 1997); Jesse T. Peck, *The Central Idea of Christianity,* (K.C.: Beacon Hill Press, 1951); G. A. McLaughlin; *Clean Heart* (Holiness Data Ministry, NNU website, 1995); H. Orton Wiley used the concept of "cleansing" almost exclusively in his discussion of entire sanctification. *Christian Theology,* 2:487-517. Cf. representative phrases found throughout his treatment of sanctification: ". . . the first essential element in entire sanctification is the purifying of the believer's heart from inbred sin or inherited depravity," (488); "Sanctification is an act of cleansing, and unless inbred sin be removed, there can be no fullness of life, no perfection in love," (476). For a history of the emergence of the emphasis on cleansing in the holiness movement see Leroy Lindsey, Jr.,"Radical Remedy: The Eradication of Sin and Related Terminology in Wesleyan-Holiness Thought, 1875-1925," Ph.D. diss, Drew University, 1996, 127-130.

The New Testament use of these concepts have their roots in the Old Testament and present a complex picture. Since these terms arise from the cultic context and are primarily ceremonial in nature, and sanctification as developed in the New Testament is a thoroughly ethical concept (though its idioms are derived from the cult and informed by it), the question arises as to how it is used and what is the relation between holiness, sanctification and purity. Much work has been done on these concepts in recent scholarship and we shall explore some of the implications of this research in chapter three. This is an important exercise since, as Gordon Wenham says:

> . . . Christians should be especially anxious that the significance of sacrifice and other biblical rituals should be clarified, for, because they are so fundamental to Old Testament, they are also fundamental to New Testament theology. The New Testament writers thought in largely Old Testament categories. In particular, Christ's death is interpreted in term of Old Testament sacrifice, not just in the epistle to the Hebrews but in many other places.[71]

However, in general, 19th century holiness literature demonstrates little awareness of the significance of the Old Testament background. One result is that its use in this literature manifests little if any evidence of other than an individualistic, very private, understanding of sanctification as noted above whereas "moral impurity" in the Old Testament extends beyond the individual to defile the sanctuary, the land and others and therefore this defilement must be addressed by means of purification. Furthermore, as understood by both the Qumran Community and St. Paul, "purity" is a corporate concept ideally characteristic of the community of faith based on the assumption that the community [the church for Paul] is the New Temple.[72] A further problem arises from the way the concept of

---

[71]Gordon Wenham, "The Perplexing Pentateuch," *Vox Evangelica* 17 (1987), 18.

[72]Michael Newton, *The Concept of Purity at Qumran and in the Letters of Paul* (Cambridge: Cambridge University Press, 1985; R. J. McKelvey, *The New Temple* (London: Oxford University Press, 1969); B. Gäutner, *The Temple and Community in Qumran and the New Testament* (Cambridge: Cambridge University

"cleansing" is interpreted, suggesting a materialistic concept or a substantive understanding of "sin." Wynkoop clearly identifies this implication: "The difficulties relative to expressing the concept of sin and its 'removal' in terms of substance are involved here. Does God 'do something' to the soul to make it pure? Do men make themselves clean? What is it that is not clean? How is it unclean? What is purity"[73] This substantive mode of thinking is unsound philosophically, theologically, psychologically and from the Biblical point of view, anthropologically (see chapter 3).

The other element in the paradigm we are exploring is the claim that in entire sanctification one is "cleansed" from "Adamic sin," or in more theological language, "original sin."[74] This claim is accompanied by a repeated denial of "sinless" or "Adamic" perfection with extensive qualifications resulting in the tendency of the claim to "die the death of a thousand qualifications." Another standard element in this paradigm is the identification of entire sanctification with "the baptism with/of the Holy Spirit." While no one would question that the Holy Spirit is the dynamic of the holy life, the use of this terminology as the equivalent of entire sanctification has been seriously questioned on the basis of exegetical grounds by the majority of biblical scholars of the modern holiness movement.[75] Further, as has been often pointed

---

Press, 1965); R. Kempthorne, "Incest and the Body of Christ," *New Testament Studies* 14 (1967-68), 568-74; L Cerfaux, *The Church in the Theology of Paul* (N. Y.: Herder & Herder, 1959).

[73]Wynkoop, *Theology of Love*, 250.

[74]In the words of J. A. Wood: "When the 'blood of Jesus Christ' 'cleanseth from all sin,' all that corruption which the Church of England calls 'original, or birth sin, which is the fault or corruption of the nature of every man, whereby he is very far gone from original righteousness,' is totally destroyed, the soul is pure. Then, where there is pure love, there is no anger or malice; where there is pure humility, pride is extinct; where there is pure patience, impatience and fretfulness are not found; and where there is pure meekness all wrath and bitterness are excluded. *Purity and Maturity,* 5. Here is a classic example of the "extravagant claims" for entire sanctification repeatedly described in Quanstrom's history of holiness in the 20th century.

[75]Cf. essays in the *Wesleyan Theological Journal.* E.g., Herbert McGonigle, "Pneumatological Nomenclature in Early Methodism," *Wesleyan Theological Journal,* 8, 1973, 61–72; Donald W. Dayton, "Asa Mahan and the Development of American Holiness Theology," Ibid. 9, 1974, 60–69; John A.

out, this pneumatological terminology opens the door to a diversity of interpretations, many of which are not essentially ethical in nature, which is the basic New Testament understanding of sanctification. Ultimately, the answer to the "why" question is relatively simple for this paradigm, at least in its expression in popular theology. One must be "entirely" sanctified, cleansed from all sin, in order to qualify for final acceptance, in a word, to get to heaven.[76] This conclusion is reinforced by identifying the "holiness" referred to in

Knight, "John Fletcher's Influence on the Development of Wesleyan Theology in America," Ibid. 13. 1978, 13–33; Robert W. Lyon, "Baptism and Spirit-Baptism in the New Testament," Ibid. vol. 14, No. 1 (Spring 1979) Alex R. G. Deasley, "Entire Sanctification and the Baptism with the Holy Spirit: Perspectives on the Biblical View of the Relationship," Ibid. Paul M. Bassett, et. al., "White Paper," say "Little or no support can now be found among Nazarene biblical scholars or theologians for the 'Oberlin' view of Charles Finney and Asa Mahan (adopted into the Wesleyan holiness tradition by Phoebe Palmer and later Daniel Steele) that the Pentecostal 'baptism of the Spirit' in Acts 2 can be regarded as the *exact* equivalent of the entire sanctification *of the individual.*"

[76]Jesse T. Peck, *The Central Idea of Christianity*, 12; J. A. Wood, *Purity and Maturity*, 17; J. A. Wood, *Christian Purity*, has a detailed expression of this perspective: "Justification and regeneration do not supersede entire sanctification, which is a full preparation and the only preparation for heaven. A state of continued justification, in the gracious order of God, includes the assurance of entire sanctification. All justified souls are God's children, are heirs of eternal life, and have a title to heaven, and cannot fail of their inheritance if they do not forfeit their justification by apostasy. All men will be saved who die in a justified state before God, as all such are children of God by adoption, are absolved from the guilt of actual sin by pardon, and are free from any voluntary antagonism to holiness. Sudden death to such finds them covered with the covenant of grace, similar to the dying infant, which entitles them to the merits of Christ and heaven. Justified believers, in the event of their sudden death, stand in the same relation to God that infants do, and He (not death) perfects that which is lacking in them. Infants are justified, but they are not entirely sanctified. Dying infants go to heaven, but not without first being entirely sanctified, not by death, but by the blood of Christ." 107 In his "Introduction" to the American Edition of Henry E. Brockett, *Scriptural Freedom from Sin* (K.C.: Beacon Hill Press, 1941), C.W. Ruth stated: "Since no one can hope to pass through the pearly gates into the City of God while any sin remains within his heart (Heb. 12:14), it should be self-evident to thoughtful men that no subject should more sincerely engage the attention of sinful men than to know the way to scriptural freedom from sin." 11.

Heb. 12:14 with the "second blessing."[77] Here we have individual redemption viewed almost exclusively in a negative mode and furthermore without any necessary connection with the wider scriptural vision of the redemption of the total creation.

An Alternate Paradigm

The alternate understanding of sanctification I want to explore in the light of the biblical world view is pervasive in scripture, thoroughly informs both John and Charles Wesley's understanding[78] and is generally accepted by classical Christian faith. It may be summarily stated as the renewal of human persons in the image of God.

The Wesleys were influenced by Henry Scoval's *Life of God in the Soul of Man* who defined true religion as

a union of the soul with God, a real participation of the divine nature, the very image of God drawn upon the soul, or, in the apostle's phrase, 'It is Christ formed within us.'—Briefly, I know not how the nature of religion can be more fully expressed, than by calling it a *Divine Life*: and under these terms I shall discourse of it, showing first, how it is called a life; and then, how it is termed divine.[79]

---

[77]In rejecting the position that culpability attaches to original sin in the context of arguing that entire sanctification "eradicates" original sin, J. Kenneth Grider correctly notes that "A spin-off of this way of seeing the matter is that it is incorrect to preach 'holiness or hell.' Justification is what changes eternal destiny, not entire sanctification. The exhortation to 'pursue after holiness, without which no man shall see the Lord' (Heb.12:14), refers to holiness in the broadest sense, begun in regeneration." "Carnality and Humanity," *Wesleyan Theological Journal*, vol. 11, Spring, 1975, 82.

[78]Patrick Alan Eby, "The One Thing Needful: The Development of Charles Wesley's Theology of the Restoration of the Image of God," Ph.D. diss. Drew University, 2010. Theodore Runyon affirms that "the renewal of the creation and the creatures through the renewal in humanity of the *Image of God* is what Wesley identifies as the very heart of Christianity," *The New Creation* (Nashville: Abingdon Press, 1998), 8.

[79]www.grace-ebooks.com, 11.

This understanding is succinctly expressed in the more modern and formal words of E.C. Blackman: Sanctification is "the realization or progressive attainment of likeness to God or to God's intention for men. It may be regarded both as a status conferred by divine grace and as a goal to be aimed at."[80] This is not to suggest that the concept of the image of God is totally absent from the American holiness movement but a fair representative use of the concept, found in Peck's *Central Idea of Christian Perfection*, defines it as *purity* with the attendant problems mentioned above and others as well (see chapter 3). Unfortunately, even when the concept of the image of God is recognized the tendency is to interpret it as being completely and perfectly restored in entire sanctification. Instead of affirming, as does the New Testament, that sanctification is a lifelong process of restoring the image of God, Wiley states rather bluntly that "sanctification restores the image of God."[81] His emphasis on the "completeness" of this restoration is reinforced by his affirmation that "holiness . . . is . . . perfected by the cleansing at a single stroke from inbred sin, and brings the soul to a constantly existing state of perfected holiness."[82] One of the most influential voices in the post-Wesley development of holiness theology was Adam Clarke who correctly notes that "The whole design of God was to restore man to his image, and raise him from the ruins of his fall," but tends to interpret this restoration in a perfectionist mode.[83]

[80]"Sanctification," *Interpreters Dictionary of the Bible*, ed. George Buttrick, 4 vols. (N. Y.: Abingdon Press, 1964).

[81]*Christian Theology*, 2:470.

[82]Ibid. 446.

[83]Cf. John L. Peters, *Christian Perfection and American Methodism* (Nashville: Abingdon Press, 1956), 106; Paul M. Bassett and William M. Greathouse, *Exploring Christian Holiness, The Historical Development* (K.C.: Beacon Hill Press of Kansas City, 1985), 244-246; H. Ray Dunning, "Nazarene Ethics as seen in Historical, Theological and Sociological Context," Ph.D. Dissertation, Vanderbilt University, 1969. An extended critique of Clark on these points is made by George E. Failing, "Developments in Holiness Theology after Wesley," *Insights into Holiness,* comp. by Kenneth Geiger (K.C.: Beacon Hill Press, 1963), 14-17.

On the surface, renewal of mankind in the image of God may sound like an individualistic goal but when one grasps the wide sweep of the concept, it actually takes in the full vision of the biblical worldview as summarized in the quotation above from N. T. Wright. As Ray S. Anderson says: "In taking up the question of what the *imago Dei* means for human personhood, we address an issue that touches virtually every other tenet of Christian belief."[84]

The key to understanding the full implication of sanctification as the renewal of the *imago Dei* is the meaning of the concept of "image." Numerous ways of explaining this concept have been proposed.[85] What I am here suggesting is that the now wide-spread interpretation of it as a relational category is the door that opens up the idea of sanctification to the full scope of the biblical worldview.[86] In a survey of various theories about the meaning of the *imago* David J. A. Clines highlights the emergence of this perspective:

A fresh and provocative interpretation has been advanced by Karl Barth, following hints from W[ilhelm] Vischer and D[ietrich] Bonhoeffer. . . . The relation and distinction in mankind between male and female, man and wife, corresponds to the relation and distinction of the 'I and Thou' in God himself. There is thus between God and man an *analogic relationis*; God's image in man is the reciprocal relationship of human being with human being. . . . Thus the image describes the "I-Thou" relationship between man and man *and* between man and God.[87]

---

[84]*On Being Human*, 70. Hoo-Jung Lee argued that John Wesley's emphasis on the recreation of the image of God provided the hermeneutical clue with which to read his work. He argued that by reading Wesley through this lens, one could avoid an overly individualistic approach to salvation, "The Doctrine of New Creation in the Theology of John Wesley," Ph.D. diss. Emery University, 1991.

[85]A good survey is found in David Cairns, *The Image of God in Man* (N. Y.: Philosophical Library, 1953).

[86]In his magisterial work on Paul, N.T. Wright demonstrates exegetically how the "renewal of humanity in the image of God" is at the heart of the Apostle's world view. He says, in summary, "Bearing the image of God, through the agency of the Messiah, thus emerges as one of the foundation themes of Paul's vision for what we may call 'new humanity'. . . . It is part of the world view." *Paul and the Faithfulness of God*, 2 vols. (Minneapolis: Fortress Press, 2012), 1:441-2.

Bonhoeffer adds a third relation to the *imago* derived from an exegesis of Genesis 1-3: a relation to the earth.[88] This relation is developed theologically and practically by Douglas John Hall.[89] Arguing for the relational understanding of the *imago* as interpersonal, Hall affirms "that already implicit within this biblical logic of being is yet a third dimension: the inarticulate but 'unsilent' creation, the physical universe that is our home, the creatures whose 'otherness' is more conspicuous still than the otherness of those of our own kind—in short, what we call nature."[90] The implication of this relation is found in what Hall refers to as "Christian culpability in a groaning creation," clearly reminiscent of Paul's words in Romans 8:19-22.[91]

There is finally what might be termed an "anthropological" rationale why sanctification is important. This reason is based on the Creator's intention for the human race. From the Wesleyan perspective, the Lord intended the happiness of his creation and provided every condition for this to be realized, including, in particular, creating the structure of humanhood in his own image. John Wesley stated it succinctly: "[God] made all things to be happy. He

---

[87]"The Image of God in Man," Tyndale *Bulletin* 19 (1968), 60-1. Cf. also F. Horst, "Face to Face. The Biblical Doctrine of the Image of God," *Interpretation* 4 (1950), 259-170. Rob Staples' reinterpretation of Wesley's doctrine of Christian perfection is proposed in terms of the "I-Thou" theology of Martin Buber.

[88]D. Bonhoeffer, *Creation and Fall* (London: SCM, 1959), 37ff.

[89]*Imaging God* (Grand Rapids: Wm. B. Eerdmans Pub. Co., 1985.

[90]Ibid. 124.

[91]Some, including myself, feel that a fourth dimension should be added to the *imago*, a relation to the self. It is here that the concept of sin enters the picture as a distorted relation resulting from original sin, which may be simply interpreted as egocentricity. Hence all the other relations can only be restored to God's original intention when "sin," the self's distorted relation to God, is adequately addressed. Douglas John Hall's pungent words capture this point: "sin as such is something at the heart of us, so deeply ingrained in our persons that it is impossible to isolate, or even to describe, very satisfactorily. It belongs to the mystery of the self and refers in a particular sense to the distortion of the self's relationships." Ibid. 10.

made man to be happy in Himself. He is the proper center of spirits; for whom every created spirit was made," and "He made "*you;*" and he made you to be happy in him; and nothing else can make you happy."[92] In support of this claim he quotes St. Augustine's classic statement, "Thou hast formed us for Thyself, and our hearts are restless till they find rest in Thee."[93] When this arrangement was violated through human rebellion, God's intention did not change. Rather than abandoning his intention he initiated a means whereby that original intention could be actualized. This arrangement implies that sanctification as the renewal of human beings in the image of God as the means to their happiness is the ultimate goal of God's redemptive provision for the human race.

To see the significance of this rationale, we must have a proper understanding of the meaning of "happiness." Happiness is one of the more ambiguous words in the English language. The average dictionary defines it in more or less emotional terms and suggests the implication that it depends on "happenings" or "circumstances." This clearly is the popular concept of it. If we have money, or health, or other means to a carefree life, we can expect to be happy. But experience demonstrates in numerous cases that this is a faulty expectation. These material and physical benefits do not guarantee happiness.

By contrast happiness was a major component in the vision of the classical Greek philosophers, Plato and Aristotle, both of whom related happiness to the proper functioning of one's rational nature. The Greek word translated as happiness is *eudaimonia,* which can best be rendered as "well-being." More recent ethical philosophers have chosen to use the term "flourishing" to avoid the popular implications of the term "happiness." Both Greek philosophers grounded their understanding of happiness in their construal of human nature. Aristotle's definition of man as a "rational animal" expresses their general philosophical perspective. The "happy" person is one whose passions or desires are controlled by reason, thus functioning according to ones essential nature. This rationale informs Wesley's correlation of holiness and happiness.

---

[92]Wesley, *Works,* 7:266-7

[93]"The Confessions," *Basic Writings of St. Augustine,* 2 vols. (N.Y.: Random House, 1948), I, i.

The theme of happiness runs like a golden thread throughout the works of John Wesley. It played a central role in his first recorded sermon entitled "Death and Deliverance" from Job 3:17 (1725). He affirmed that "the desire of happiness is inseparably [bound] to our nature, and is the spring which sets all our faculties a-moving."[94] A reference to happiness appears in his discussion of virtually every central Christian doctrine and several sermons that do not speak directly about it have relevance to the subject. His fundamental premise about happiness was that it was the essence of God's creative intention for the human race. Since the essential nature of human personhood is embodied in the image of God, the restoration of the image is the goal of sanctification, this is the basis for his identification of happiness with holiness, an identification he makes throughout his sermons.[95]

In his sermon on "The End of Christ's Coming," based on 1 John 3:8, which defines the purpose of the manifestation of the Son of God to be to "destroy the works of the devil," he says:

> Here then we see in the clearest, strongest light, what is real religion: A restoration of man by Him that bruises the serpent's head, to all that the old serpent deprived him of; a restoration, not only to the favour but likewise to the image of God, implying not barely deliverance from sin, but the being filled with the fulness of God.[96]

In order to understand Wesley's point, it must be emphasized that the "holiness" to which he refers is more than outward conformity to certain behavioral disciplines. It includes both "inward and outward holiness." He repeatedly asserts that "without inward as well as

---

[94]Albert Outler, ed. *The Works of John Wesley*, Vols. 1-4 (Nashville: Abingdon Press, 1987), 209. Subsequently referred to as Outler, *Works*. This sermon is prior to his Aldersgate experience and reflects a rather morbid outlook about the possibility of happiness in this life.

[95]Outler notes that the relation of holiness and happiness appears in at least 30 of Wesley's sermons. Ibid. 35, n. 28.

[96]*Works*, 6:276.

outward holiness, you cannot be happy, even in this world, much less in the world to come."[97]

We have already suggested that it has become almost universally accepted that the *imago Dei* involves a four-fold relation. Randy L. Maddox argues that John Wesley himself understood it in this way. He says, "Wesley's anthropology recognized four basic human relationships: with God, with other humans, with lower animals, and with ourselves. A holy (and whole!) person is one in whom all these relationships is properly expressed."[98]

It now should be clear that the "why" of sanctification, understood as the restoration of the image of God as implied here, captures the entire worldview of the biblical story and touches on every aspect of God's redemptive project eschatologically embodied in the Christ event. Thus the title of Jesse T. Peck's "holiness classic," if properly understood, is totally appropriate: sanctification in its total scope is indeed "The Central Idea of Christianity."[99]

---

[97]"The New Birth," *Works*, 6:76. See 6:261 where he expresses sympathy to both Montanus and Tertullian who were considered heretics because they emphasized this belief. Of Montanus he says: "I believe his grand heresy was, the maintaining that 'without' inward and outward 'holiness no man shall see the Lord."

[98]*Responsible Grace*, 68.

[99]See chapters 4 and 5 for a fuller discussion of the meaning of the image of God.

Chapter 2
The Holiness of God

Thesis: The holiness of God is the logical basis of the call to holiness in human experience rather than the model to be reproduced.

Virtually every theological discussion of holiness in human experience begins with an analysis of the holiness of God.[100] This is both theologically and biblically appropriate since the most fundamental statement in scripture of the basis for the importance of the holy life is the repeated word of the Lord, "you shall be holy, for I am holy" (Lev. 11:44-45[101]; 19:2; 20:26; 1 Peter 1:16). The context of this declaration in the Old Testament and its use by Peter in the New is the covenant relation between Yahweh and Israel from which extensive theological themes emerge as normative for the divine-human relation. A proper understanding of this command must take into account the larger narrative concerning the establishing the covenant.

The significance of the holiness of God first appears explicitly in Exodus with Moses' experience at the burning bush and it is this encounter that initiates the narrative that consummates with the establishing of the covenant at Sinai. From this event we begin to learn essential characteristics about the holiness of God. It is also the beginning point for a proper concept of the holiness to which God's people are called. Jo Bailey Wells says that "This story is the foundation for all that ensues. The rest of the book of Exodus (and,

---

[100]Cf. Samuel M. Powell, *Holiness, Why it Matters Today* (San Diego, CA: Point Loma Press, 2010), "The place to begin is the Bible's portrayal of God's holiness," 9.

[101]There is huge theological significance in the fact that the NIV, the NEB, the Smith-Goodspeed version. The New American Standard and Moffatt's translation all render this passage as "consecrate yourselves and be holy for I am holy." In chapter 6 we will see how this is consistent with the understanding of the interpretation of entire sanctification" proposed in that chapter and elsewhere in this work.

indeed the whole story of Israel) flows out of this theophany. Not only the revelation of the divine name (YHWH) and the divine nature (holiness) but also aspects of the style of the narrative suggest that an important new beginning is depicted here."[102]

In this event, it is the *place* that is designated as holy, which has implications for future development in Israel's covenant life.[103] This place is not holy in itself but because of the presence of God. It was not holy before this encounter, but apparently remained a holy place to which Moses led Israel for the covenant encounter (Mt. Horeb/Sinai). Two other major implications emerge in this event that have further theological significance. One is the fact that "holiness" is associated with the personal name of God as Yahweh. The other is the connection with the Patriarchs (Abraham, Isaac and Jacob), which, as becomes clear later, connects the holiness of the people of Yahweh with election and its implications. "In the retelling of the story of the events of Sinai in the book of Deuteronomy, the language of election (כחר) comes into its own and, . . this is firmly associated with the matter of holiness."[104] The same relationship between election and holiness is present in 1 Peter 1:1-3 as applied to the "new Israel."[105]

A further significance of the burning bush theophany concerns the relation between holiness and purity. Because the ground is holy by virtue of the presence of Yahweh, Moses is instructed to remove his sandals before approaching the theophany. Although no purity laws have been promulgated as yet, the implication is clear. Sandals that have trod secular (profane) soil must be removed as an expression of purification, the qualification for coming into the presence of the holy, not to be equated with it (see chapter 3). The same order occurs when

---

[102]Jo Bailey Wells, *God's Holy People: A Theme in Biblical Theology* (EBSCO Publishing: e-book collection), 29.

[103]Jerome H. Neyrey, "The Idea of Purity in Mark's Gospel," *Semeia*, 35 (1986):91-128 following Mary Douglas' analysis points out that the "map" of purity in Judaism includes things, places, persons and times," to which some scholars refer as the "Holiness Spectrum."

[104]Wells, *God's Holy People*, 70. See Deut. 7:6; 14:2, 21; 26:19:28:9.

[105]H. Ray Dunning, *Partakers of the Divine Nature*, (Salem, Ohio: Schmul Pub. Co., 2006), 12-20.

the community returns to Sinai prior to Yahweh's appearance. The people are instructed to "consecrate" themselves by both rituals of purification (washing) and avoiding possibilities of contamination (19:15).[106]

The theology that informs these narratives enables us to understand the meaning of the holiness of God. The holiness of God is that characteristic that distinguishes him from all that is not God. He is unique, one of a kind, alone God. "Holiness," as Christopher J. H. Wright puts it, is "the biblical 'shorthand' for the very essence of God."[107] Langdon Gilkey gives an excellent summary of the proper understanding of the holiness of God: "Holiness is not primarily a moral attribute, as if it meant merely the perfect goodness of some super being with a white beard. Rather it refers to that absolute 'otherness' which distinguishes the divine from all that is creaturely, and so characterizes every aspect of God."[108]

The correlation between holiness and the personal name of Yahweh (see above) further implies that he alone is the holy one. This identification has far reaching implications for understanding the remainder of the Old Testament and for Israel's situation among the nations who worshiped many gods. It becomes the basis for the first three of the Ten Commandments as well as the summary of the commandments in Deuteronomy 6:3 (the Shema).

Since by definition, holiness belongs to God alone, it cannot be attributed to anything else (persons, things, places or times) except in a derivative sense by being in a proper relation to God. As Norman Snaith says, "God is separate and distinct because He is God. A person or thing may be separate, or may come to be separated, because he or it has come to belong to God. When we use the word 'separated' as a rendering of any form of the root *qodesh*, we should think of 'separated to' rather than of 'separated from'."[109] Right off, this tells

---

[106]In the Levitical law, sexual intercourse results in temporary impurity. Both these preparations as recorded here are anachronistic since the purity laws had not been spelled out.

[107]*An Eye for an Eye* (Downers Grove, ILL: Intervarsity Press, 1983), 27

[108]*Maker of Heaven and Earth* (N.Y.: Doubleday, 1959), 89.

us that holiness in human experience is foundationally a relational concept rather than a moral concept.[110]

Interpreting this understanding from the divine side, John Webster emphasizes that "it is difficult to overstress the importance of this relational character for grasping the nature of God's holiness. . . . The holiness of God is not to be identified simply as that which distances God from us; rather, God is holy precisely as the one who in majesty and freedom and sovereign power bends down to us in mercy."[111]

James D. G. Dunn makes the same point in his study of Pauline theology: "Paul's theology is relational. That is to say, he was not concerned with God in himself or humankind in itself. The classical Greek philosophical debates about existence and subsistence and the latter church debates about the natures of Christ are remote from Paul. As the opening of his exposition of the gospel in Romans 1:16ff. clearly shows, his concern was rather with humankind in relation to God."[112]

It is of utmost importance to recognize at the outset that the command does not enjoin God's people to be holy *as* God is holy but to be holy *for* or *because* God is holy.[113] *This means that God's holiness is the logical basis for the holiness to which his people are called.* Even some good scholars apparently fail to recognize this distinction and, for example, conclude that "this is a statement that

---

[109]Norman Snaith, *Distinctive Ideas of the Old Testament* (London: The Epworth Press, 1955), 30.

[110]Samuel M. Powell argues that the term "consecration" should be used to "designate the act of devoting something or someone to the service of God. Consecration thus signifies . . . a special relation to God." *Holiness*, 11. Dennis Kinlaw, "Old Testament Roots of the Wesleyan Message," *Further Insights Into Holiness* (K.C.: Beacon Hill Press, 1963), says "The OT may differentiate between things that are clean and unclean, but it knows nothing that is holy apart from its relation to God." 44.

[111]John Webster, *Holiness* (Grand Rapids: Wm. B. Eerdmans, 2003), 45.

[112]James D. G. Dunn, *The Theology of Paul the Apostle* (Grand Rapids: Wm. B. Eerdmans, 1998), 53.

[113]I am indebted to both Dr. Dan Spross and Dr. Tim Green for validating this from their knowledge of the Hebrew and Greek.

people can in some way, become like God."[114] Walter Houston's insistence that "purity became the guardian of monotheism" implicitly validates the proper interpretation.[115]

Unfortunately popular (as well as some academic) holiness literature has tended to interpret the holiness of God in moral terms.[116] This is clearly reflected in the comment of James F. Gregory, "When considering the holiness of God, we think more often of his moral quality."[117] A typical example from an early holiness manual reads like this: "God is a holy God, perfect in all His moral characteristics, absolutely sinless and separate from sin, opposed in His nature to sin, ever seeking its destruction."[118] Theologically and biblically, this statement has significant problems. To speak of God's holiness as meaning that he is "without sin," is extremely odd since rightly understood sin is a religious term that makes sense only as a distorted relation to God whereas there is no more ultimate reality to which God would have a distorted relation. This kind of interpretation implies that we must posit the existence of a standard of holiness to which God must conform, a higher reality. Furthermore, to define his holiness in moral terms is to inevitably and logically turn the call to human holiness into a moralism.[119] A careful examination of the descriptions

---

[114]Wells, *God's Holy People,* 31. There is a sense in which this emphasis is sound but is one drawn from other passages as described by Christopher J. H. Wright: "It is not simply that 'this is what God is like: follow his example.' Rather, 'this is what God has done *for you.* Therefore, out of gratitude you should do the same for others." *An Eye for an Eye,* 29. But this command we are exploring has a different emphasis.

[115]Walter Houston, *Purity and Monotheism* (Sheffield: Sheffield Academic Press, 1993), 123.

[116]For a full scale interpretation of God's holiness in moral terms resulting in holiness in human experience being interpreted in moralistic terms, see Richard S. Taylor, *Exploring Christian Holiness,* 3:13-28.

[117]James F. Gregory, *"*The Holiness of God," *Further Insights into Holiness* (K.C.: Beacon Hill Press, 1963), 33.

[118]D. Shelby Corlett, *The Meaning of Holiness* (K.C.: Beacon Hill Press, 1944), 20.

of holiness in the popular literature demonstrates that this occurred. The result was that holiness was popularly equated with moral behavior, quite often in terms of conformity to specific ethical rules. To speak of the holiness of God in moral terms makes it possible to posit a correlation between his holiness and that of his people. This conclusion is drawn by the source cited above when the author says: "In a sense holiness in man is the same as holiness in God for there are not two kinds of holiness."[120] Furthermore, some authors add the claim that the holiness of God is communicable.[121] Classical dogmatics has often distinguished between the communicable and noncommunicable attributes of God but holiness is not properly understood as in the former category, or even as one attribute among others. Gustav Aulën correctly notes that "If holiness were understood as a divine attribute among others, as has often been done, this definition would be both too ample and too limited . . . for holiness is not confined to any one phase or feature, but belongs to the idea of God as a whole. . . .Holiness is the background and the atmosphere of the conception of God."[122] It is unequivocal that an ethical life is the ultimate outcome of the call to holiness, and rules are important when they are rightly understood (see chapter 11) but such morality is the outworking of a more fundamental rationale that is the result of a biblical understanding of God's holiness.

A continued analysis of the establishing of the covenant leads to the conclusion that fundamentally, the holiness of Israel is a *status*.[123]

---

[119]For an extensive development of the idea of sin as moral rather than religious based on the assumption that God's holiness is moral see Donald S. Metz, *Studies in Biblical Holiness* (K.C.: Beacon Hill Press of Kansas City, 1971), 34ff.

[120]Corlett, *Meaning of Holiness*, 22.

[121]Baines Atkinson, *The Beauty of Holiness*, 24; J.H.J. Barker, *This is the Will of God*, 17-18; George Allen Turner, *The More Excellent Way*, 26.

[122]Gustav Aulën, *The Faith of the Christian Church* (Philadelphia: The Muhlenberg Press, 1948), 121.

[123]This is misunderstood if it is conceived in terms of an unconditional relation since, as Wells rightly observes, "The presence of the holy God in their midst means that any departure from the people's consecrated state will endanger their continued existence, because the holiness of God cannot coexist with what is

In Ex. 19:3-6, Yahweh—through Moses—recites his deliverance of Israel in the Exodus as the basis on which he offers them a covenant relationship that has the character of exclusiveness. He will be their God and they will be his "treasured possession," a relationship in which Yahweh will be their only God because he alone is holy and they will be his exclusive people. It is this special relationship that constitutes them as "a holy nation."[124] But this aspect of the relation is easily perverted unless it is recognized that they are also, in relation to the "nations," to be a "kingdom of priests."[125] It is this aspect of their national life that expresses their vocation. Thus the covenant entails both privilege and responsibility, both character and vocation.

It is in this context that we can see the ethical dimension of the call to be holy. It is on the basis of their status as "holy" that Israel is repeatedly enjoined to be holy because Yahweh is holy. In a sense it is an injunction to "be what they already are," namely a holy nation in both status *and* character. The relationship between their holiness as status and their holiness of character is the same as the repeated emphasis in the New Testament between the indicative and the imperative moods. On this basis, Paul repeatedly enjoins his converts to become what they are, i.e. live out ethically the status of having a relation to God that constitutes them as holy. The entire cultic provisions and rituals in the Pentateuch are designed to implement this principle. It is also the basis for Paul's efforts to call his converts to consistent ethical living. His ethical sections are essentially an appeal to bring their status and character into a consistent relation.

The relation between the "indicative" and the "imperative" is clearly expressed in Deuteronomy 14:2—". . . you are a people holy to

---

unholy, what is impure or 'unclean." *God's Holy People*, 79.

[124]Samuel M. Powell, *Holiness, Why It Matters Today*, says "As the Old Testament shows, Israel's corporate holiness depends primarily on election and only secondarily on the holiness of individual Israelites. It is the same with the church: in the New Testament, holiness pertains not only to our relationship to God as individuals but also to the church's relationship to God and our relationship to the church." 30.

[125]The phrase in Ex. 19:5, "indeed, the whole earth is mine," demonstrates that Israel alone is not the sole object of Yahweh's concern and sovereignty.

the Lord your God; it is you the Lord has chosen out of all the peoples on earth to be his people, his treasured possession" (NRSV). This indicative statement is immediately followed by the imperative of avoiding "unclean" food. This relation both emphasizes the ethical implications of the purity laws and, along with analysis of other passages, validates Jo Bailey Wells' statement that "This connection undermines the over-simple contrast which is sometimes set up between holiness in priestly and prophetic traditions, between cultic and moral/ethical demands, whereby the priestly notion of holiness focuses on God's transcendence while only the prophetic is relational."[126]

There are two types of purity/impurity: "ritual" and "moral." (see chapter 3). The primary distinction between them is the matter of intentionality. Because God is holy, and cannot be approached by the unclean, even ritual purity which is the result of unwitting acts or contact with a contaminating source (such as a corpse) needs purification. This is provided for by offerings as described in Leviticus 1-7. Intentional actions that bring "moral" impurity have no remedy in a sacrifice.[127] However, they may be dealt with by repentance.[128] These provisions are for maintaining the covenant relation.

We are now in a position to look more closely at the context of the call to "be holy *because* God is holy." It appears centrally in that section of Leviticus known as the "Holiness Code," which spells out the ethical "rules" given to both maintain Israel's relation to a holy God and live out their priestly vocation in relation to the nations. The spelling out of the implications of the call in Leviticus 19 is

---

[126]*God's Holy People*, 81.

[127]This background explains the passage in Hebrews 10:26—"For if we willfully persist in sin after having received the knowledge of the truth, there no longer remains a sacrifice for sin." This "is a clear warning that although the blood of Christ provides constant cleansing for inadvertent sin (or "mistakes"), if one deliberately goes against the known will of God, that person chooses to remove his or her life from the protective covering of the Blood and stands once more again under the condemnation of the judgment of God." H. Ray Dunning, *Superlative Christ* (K.C.: Beacon Hill Press of Kansas City, 2001), 91.

[128]Jacob Milgrom, "Sacrifices and Offerings, OT," *Interpreter's Dictionary of the Bible*, supplementary volume, Keith R. Crim, et. al. eds. (Nashville: Abingdon Press, 1976).

fundamentally a rehearsing of the Ten Commandments, including the injunction to "love your neighbor as yourself" (v. 18).

What may seem odd is that most of the elaborations of the call to ethical holiness in response to the divine holiness have to do with diet, with the distinction between clean and unclean foods. Various theories have been advanced to explain the food laws but the most adequate are those that reflect a theological rationale. Theologically, the implication is that the food laws, ethically understood, emphasize the unique relation between Israel and God, making them a separate people "for his own possession." Anthropologist Mary Douglas has made a significant contribution to our understanding in this area. She has demonstrated that the "division into clean (edible) foods and unclean (inedible) foods corresponded to the division between holy Israel and the Gentile world." "Through this system of symbolic laws Israelites were reminded at every meal of their redemption to be God's people. Their diet was limited to certain meats in imitation of their God, who had restricted his choice among the nations to Israel. It served, too to bring to mind Israel's responsibilities to be a holy nation."[129] Of great interest is the fact that with the inclusion of the Gentiles within the New Israel, these ethnic distinctions lost their significance with the result that from the New Testament perspective, all foods are clean (cf. the struggles over this issue in the Book of Acts).

Douglas has also identified further features of the holiness to which Israel was called. She insists that the concept of wholeness underlies the uncleanness law and is identified in the following fashion. In the Hebrew mind the natural world is divided into three spheres: land, air and water. Each sphere has its own natural inhabitants as simple observation recognizes. Creatures that seem to have characteristics of more than one realm are considered unclean. For example, the catfish lives in the water but does not have scales like a fish and therefore is unclean. This analysis reinforces the concept of integrity as of the essence of ethical holiness. This quality is further

---

[129]Mary Douglas, *Purity and Danger* (London: Routledge and Kegan Paul, 1966); this quotation summarizing her interpretation is from Gordon J. Wenham, "The Theology of Unclean Food," *Evangelical Quarterly* 53.1 (January/March 1981).

illustrated by the prohibitions to avoid mixtures of seeds, materials in clothes and marriages. This suggests wholeness as do the prohibitions against priests cutting themselves and the restriction of priests who are lame, blind or otherwise deformed from ministering in the tabernacle. Wholeness and integrity are thus suggested as the essence of holiness in those who "shall be holy to their God" (Lev. 21:5-6).[130]

The cultic provisions of the "Holiness Code" deal fundamentally with the relation to the presence of God, which is the locus of essential holiness. His locus in the holy of holies in the tabernacle requires the most rigid purity preparations for entrance. From that center the holiness of Yahweh spreads outward in a fashion that has been compared to a magnetic field. Hence there are degrees of holiness determined by proximity to the inner sanctum. While all degrees must be preceded by rituals of purification, those who come nearer the immediate presence or glory of God require the most stringent preparation. However, as Jo Bailey Wells notes, rituals of purity are "broadened to include issues of social organization and agricultural life. Thus laws concerning the temple and sacrifice are combined with social rules and agricultural practices, such that the essence of holiness comes to be seen as the perfection attained through the fulfillment of God's commandments in all walks of life."[131] This is consistent with the full-orbed understanding of the image of God as we briefly introduced it in the previous chapter, once again demonstrating that the understanding of sanctification as the renewal of the *imago* encompasses the entirety of God's restoration project and Israel is to embody and demonstrate this goal in their national life. By this lifestyle they are to carry out their function as a "priestly kingdom."

We have taken note of the contribution of Mary Douglas to an understanding of the theology of the purity laws, especially those relating to clean and unclean foods. Her studies in anthropology enabled her to move the discussion beyond earlier ways of attempting to provide a rationale for the distinction.[132] Her conclusions have

---

[130]Douglas, *Purity and Danger*, 41-57.

[131]*God's Holy People*, 81.

[132]These range from denying that there was a rationale but that the distinctions were arbitrary (Maimonides) to medical reasons. Cf. Gordon J. Wenham, "The Theology of Unclean Food."

influenced most subsequent treatments of the subject.[133] The basic premise that informs her work is that every society has a worldview that involves a classification system with distinguishing lines and boundaries, referred to as a "map." The process of ordering this system was called "purity" in contrast to "pollution," which stands for the violation of the classification system.[134] Walter Houston, while disagreeing with her exegesis at certain points, firmly supports this interpretation. He says "The worldview of the priestly writing not only revolves around the ritual of the sanctuary, but is dominated by a conception of *order* that extends through the cosmos, the sanctuary and human society."[135]

The operative word in this understanding is "order." "Holiness," Douglas avers, "means keeping distinct the categories of creation."[136] Jerome Neyrey, building on this interpretation, speaks of creation as "the ultimate act of ordering and classifying the world" which provides the original map. This map is reproduced by the purity requirements of the cult.[137] One can then conclude that the purity regulations are designed to direct attention to as well as order behavior in accord with God's original intention for his creation. This, as we have argued in the previous chapter, is what sanctification understood as the renewal of human persons in all aspects of the image of God is really about. This paradigm, solidly grounded in the Hebrew cult,

---

[133]E. g, Jacob Neusner, *The Idea of Purity in Ancient Judaism* (London: E.J. Brill, 1973); Philip Peter Jenson, *Graded Holiness: A Key to the Priestly Conception of the World* (Sheffield: JSOT Press, 1992).

[134]Mary Douglas, *Purity and Danger*. She insists that "the only way in which pollution ideas make sense is in reference to a total structure of thought whose key-stone, boundaries, margins and internal lines are held in relation by rituals of separation.", 41. The key-stone to which she refers is "holiness," both God's and human.

[135]Walter Houston, *Purity and Monotheism* (Sheffield: JSOT Press, 1993), 221.

[136]*Purity and Danger*, 53.

[137]"The Idea of Purity in Mark's Gospel."

embodies the essence of the biblical story of God's restoration program.

This discussion takes us one step further toward understanding the importance of holiness in human life. The expression of the love that epitomizes the relation of the human to the holy God, because of who God is, is the essence of worship. If the essence of ethical holiness is to "love God with all our heart, mind, soul, and strength" and that relationship is simply another way of describing worship, the purpose of God's call to holiness is so that he might have the respect and glory due to his name as "the holy one of Israel."

One of the significant aspects of this point is that there is a reciprocal relation between worship and holiness that may be expressed in terms of what N.T. Wright calls "two golden rules at the heart of spirituality:" The first one is *you become like what you worship*: "when you gaze in awe, admiration, and wonder at something or someone, you begin to take on something of the character of the object of your worship. Those who worship money become eventually, human calculating machines. Those who worship sex become obsessed with their own attractiveness or prowess. Those who worship power become more and more ruthless." This perception informs Paul's description of the holy life in 2 Corinthians 3:18 with Jesus as the "icon" of the holy God.

The second rule is based on the truth that we are created in God's image: *worship makes you more truly human.* "When you gaze in love and gratitude at the God in whose image you were made, you do indeed grow. You discover more of what it means to be fully alive."

> Conversely, when you give that same total worship to anything or anyone else, you shrink as a human being. It doesn't, of course, feel like that at the time. When you worship part of the creation as though it were the Creator himself—in other words, when you worship an idol—you may well feel a brief "high." But like a hallucinatory drug, that worship achieves its effect at a cost: when the effect is over you are less of a human being than you were to begin with. That is the price of idolatry."[138]

---

[138]N. T. Wright, *Simply Christian* (N.Y.: HarperCollins, 2006), 148.

If the purpose of the election of Israel was to be God's paradigm for the Creator's intention for the human race, and that purpose was to be manifested by their holiness, and that holiness was defined by the law, then the purpose of sanctification is illuminated by the function of the law. This brings us logically to a consideration of the role of rules in the holy life. We shall explore this in chapter 11.

Chapter 3
SANCTIFICATION AND PURITY

Thesis: Exegetically, purity is the prerequisite for holiness as a status, which is the possibility of sanctification as total consecration thus providing a biblical basis for the "secondness" of "entire sanctification."

While it must be recognized, as John Wesley observed,[139] that a right relation to God may co-exist with faulty theology, it is nevertheless the case that there is a mutual interaction between the two. When theological claims are invalidated by corporate experience, the proper response is a review of those claims. If those claims are supported by appeal to scripture, this review should take the form of a reappraisal of exegetical issues. Gordon J. Thomas points in this direction in analyzing why the holiness message "has been marginalized within the wider church:" "biblically, the exegesis of Holiness proof-texts has generally failed to convince others" and "doctrinally, it has been perceived (mostly unfairly) as claiming sinless perfection in this life." It seems clear that these two factors are intimately related. Thomas' suggestion as to how the situation should be addressed is a "rigorous scrutiny" of scripture, especially those traditional proof-texts.[140]

The presupposition of this chapter is that one crucial point contributing to the perfectionist tendency is the result of a significant shift in emphasis that took place in the transition of Wesley's theology to the 19th century holiness movement. A group of holiness scholars, in analyzing the developments in the American Holiness Movement, noted that "The whole focus and emphasis of Wesley's doctrine had . . . shifted from holiness understood as love to sanctification understood as cleansing. . ."[141] The concept of cleansing, along with its

---

[139]Sermon on the "Catholic Spirit," *Works*, 5:493.

[140]"The Need," in *Re-minting Holiness*, a project of the faculty of Nazarene Theological College, Manchester, England.

[141] In "A White Paper on Article X," Paul Bassett, et. al. www.didache.nts.edu; (summer, 2010). This shift was concomitant with the gradual shift from a positive focus (growth in the *imago Dei* in terms of love) to a negative emphasis (elimination of sin).

concomitant terms (especially purity), came to be used extensively in a group of writings traditionally referred to as the "holiness classics." In some cases it was used almost exclusively in these works. In a word, this complex of idioms became a dominant conceptuality used by the 19th century holiness movement to embody its central claim concerning the nature of entire sanctification.[142] This fact and its implications are reflected in Albert Outler's critique that there emerged among some of Wesley's successors the claim for a "perfected perfection" expressed, said Outler, in the "dubious" distinction between "a perfect heart" and "a perfect character," or between "purity and maturity," in their attempt to avoid "perfectionism," a distinction still widely defended in the holiness movement.[143]

"Holiness Classics" Interpretation of Purity

Scrutiny of the 19th century "holiness classics" as well as more recent writings[144] reveals a particular understanding of the concept of purity, one which presupposes a substantive understanding of "sin." In fact, this is true of most sanctificationist language of the period including but not restricted to the purity word group. Any claim for the elimination of "sin" from the soul, whether or not eradication terminology is used, logically entails some*thing* that is removed, thus a substantive understanding.[145] When that which is "removed" is

---

[142]Cf. Lindsey, "Radical Remedy," 127-130.

[143]Albert C. Outler, *Theology in the Wesleyan Spirit* (Nashville: Tidings, 1975), 79-80. Outler appears to assume the same meaning as the "holiness classics." When "purity" is rightly understood, *a la* the thesis of this chapter, this formula is a legitimate expression.

[144]J. Kenneth Grider, *Entire Sanctification* gives this definition: "E.S. is essentially defined as an instantaneous cleansing from Adamic sin," 11.

[145]Wood, *Purity and Maturity* in fact refers to purity as a negative rather than a positive state, "being freedom from all sin. The idea of purifying is that of the removal of something, i.e. impurity from the soul; rather than the introduction of anything into the soul. Holiness is the negation of depravity, the cleansed state—

described as "original sin," the pervasiveness of original sin is not taken seriously. If original sin is "something" within the person that can be removed, it does not describe the radical fallenness of human persons that the traditional doctrine of original sin affirms and further fails to recognize the wholeness of the human person as seen by biblical anthropology (see chapter 6 on entire sanctification). If the doctrine of original sin is taken seriously it involves the recognition that the whole person is distorted to the degree that every relational aspect of humanness is affected and not some "quantity of evil" (a sinful nature) located within the soul.[146] Paul Bassett, et. al. point out the implications of this claim: ". . . to use the Augustinian phrase "original sin", and to say baldly that entire sanctification makes us "free from original sin" (a phrase which Wesley himself never used in this precise context) is to leave ourselves open to the interpretation that we believe that entire sanctification brings "Adamic" or "sinless" perfection. A more nuanced statement of the doctrine is necessary at this point in order to make it clear that the entirely sanctified . . . remain fallible creatures in the fallen body while in 'this present evil age'."[147] A somewhat graphic refutation is made in the observation that if original sin were "eradicated," a sanctified nudist colony would be possible.

In contrast to the "ontological" implication of this "removal" of a "unitary evil" from the soul in an instantaneous moment, experience as well as scripture has demonstrated that there is no quick fix to the human condition but that a full lifetime is involved in God's gracious activity in restoring one to the image of God from which all are fallen. As we will note further on, this does not eliminate the possibility of a moment of Christian experience (even a second moment), but suggests that a different paradigm is necessary, in the

---

freedom from 'all unrighteousness,' SPIRITUAL LIFE IS 'A PURE HEART.'" In comparing purity with the health of the soul, he defines health as the absence of disease. "It is a negative state," in which "original, or birth sin . . . is totally destroyed." 15.

[146]Mildred Bangs Wynkoop attributes this development in holiness theology to the influence of a Calvinist view of human nature. *Foundations of Wesleyan-Arminian Theology*, 78-9. But see the qualification of this interpretation in chapter 6.

[147]"A White Paper on Article X."

face of biblical theology and widespread experience, in identifying the nature of that moment.

It is the thesis of this chapter that the cultic context is the basic source for the use of purity when posited of human persons. By contrast, the understanding of the meaning of purity that implies a substantive view of sin is derived in various ways, none of which takes into account the cultic concept of purity. One very interesting explanation comes from George McLaughlin who illustrates the meaning of a "clean heart" with the metaphor of dirt, defining dirt as "matter out of place."[148] This way of explaining "impurity" is similar to the way influential anthropologist Mary Douglas explains the concept of purity in the context of the Old Testament cult.[149] But McLaughlin's analogy interprets it as a substantive or materialistic concept of removing "dirt" from the human "heart," Douglas' use is "systemic."[150]

A common method of deriving the meaning of purity is illustrated by an extensive discussion found in the work of British writer Thomas Cook in his chapter on "Purity and Maturity."[151] Cook's chapter, along with the subsequent one on "The Present Tense of Cleansing," provides a rather full explanation of the use of the terminology. According to Cook the primary understanding of the

---

[148]George Asbury McLaughlin, *A Clean Heart*, 2.

[149]Mary Douglas, *Purity and Danger*, 35. "When something is out of place, or when it violates the classification system in which it is set, it is dirt." See discussion in chapter 2.

[150]Ibid. She says: "No particular set of classifying symbols can be understood in isolation, but there can be hope of making sense of them in relation to the total structure of classifications in the culture in question." vii.

[151]*New Testament Holiness*, 33-39. A brief statement from J. A. Wood reflects the same conception: "A pure heart is one 'cleansed from all sin,' hence it is morally 'clean,' unmixed, untarnished, -- free from all pollution." (14) It should be immediately recognized that this statement involves a mixture of idioms from different contexts. It must be granted that at points in his discussion of purity, Cook expresses it in a thoroughly Wesleyan way, especially in using the concept of "a single eye," which was one of Wesley's favorite, but seldom noticed, ways of expressing the substance of "entire sanctification."

concept of purity is derived from the dictionary definition, a method that is fraught with problems for biblical ways of thinking: "entire separation from all heterogeneous and extraneous matter, clear, free from mixture; as pure water, pure air, pure silver or gold."[152] This definition, with its elaboration by Cook, is materialistic in nature, informed by substantive thinking since "some*thing*" is removed. That is clearly the understanding that informs the widespread use of "purity" in the holiness classics.[153]

A potentially sounder method, but with the same outcome, is illustrated in two classical sources that propose a wide ranging survey of "scripture testimony" as justification for heart purity as the essence of entire sanctification.[154] Analysis of the proposed texts and their interpretation yields two preliminary observations: (1) numerous texts are used that make no reference to the purity word group, with the assumption imposed on them that holiness and purity are synonyms. These can be dismissed out of hand in the absence of any exegetical justification. (2) Several texts are appealed to that use the concept of purity to refer to material substances (Hebrews 10:22 [pure water]; Revelation 15:6 [linen]; 21:18 [gold]). This use implies a mixed condition that is corrected by the removal of a foreign substance but they actually have no reference to the human situation and are therefore misused to apply to "heart purity," although this meaning *is* applied to those texts that are relevant to the question at hand (e.g. Matthew 5:8; Psalm 24:3, 4; 51:2, 7, 10; Ezekiel 36:25, 29; et. al.). It should be noted that while the idea of an "unmixed" condition sounds

---

[152]It is true that the term for purity is used in this sense in scripture (e.g. Job 28:19; Ps. 21:3; Mal. 3:3) but the context is a different "language game" (Wittgenstein). See below for further discussion.

[153]Mildred Bangs Wynkoop emphasizes this substantive implication but mistakenly, in my opinion, claims that "The New Testament borrowed from, and adapted to its specific needs, the classical Greek meaning of the term *clean*. The Greek word referred to physical cleanliness, to substances having nothing which did not belong, such as clean water, wind, sunshine; metals and food which had been refined." *A Theology of Love*, 252-3. She thus recognizes the fallacy of this interpretation but fails to see its biblical source.

[154] J. A. Wood, *Purity and Maturity*, 11-27; Asbury Lowrey, *Possibilities of Grace*. 35-66;

like John Wesley's description of the distinction between the new birth and entire sanctification found in his sermon "On Patience," there is a significant difference since Wesley's description is made in terms of love, not of an ontological substance being removed. As he says in the sermon: "Love is the sum of Christian sanctification; it is the one *kind* of holiness, which is found, only in various *degrees*, in the believers who are distinguished by St. John into "little children, young men and fathers. . . Till this universal change was wrought in his soul, all his holiness was *mixed.*"[155]

These so-called proof-texts are appealed to without reference to context or other standard exegetical procedures. It is the premise of this chapter that the fundamental problem for a sound biblical understanding however is that these holiness apologists failed to take into account that this vocabulary is derived from the Old Testament cultic context and appropriated by the New without changing its basic theological significance, but filling it with new theological content by, among other things, shifting the reference from Israel and the Temple to Jesus and the Church. Brief reference is occasionally made to the cultic context but always interpreted as a type of a New Testament theme without recognizing the significance of the Old Testament background that informs the text. Hence all passages are interpreted in the light of a particular (non-biblical) world view.[156]

The problem with this approach is succinctly pointed out by P. P. Jenson: "Confusion and misunderstanding can arise when the classification system of an interpreter differs from that of the text or culture under interpretation. . . . For example, a modern interpreter will

---

[155]John Wesley, *Works*, 6:488-9.

[156]Leroy Lindsey, "Radical Remedy: The Eradication of Sin and Related Terminology in Wesleyan-Holiness Thought, 1875-1925," Ph.D. diss. Drew University, 1996. He says that "the possibility of seeing the purification as cultic or ceremonial did not enter into consideration," 74. Asbury Lowrey, *Possibilities of Grace*, says, "There is a current notion that sanctification means merely to set apart from a common to a sacred use. This we reject on the ground that it is not authorized by the Greek text. The limitation is in our theology and hearts, not in the original Scriptures." The fact is that precisely the opposite is the case as our exegesis in this chapter demonstrates.

62

be familiar with the distinction between fish and birds, but not between clean and unclean animals, except in a hygienic sense. The hygienic classification of clean and unclean may be familiar to us, but is misleading when interpreted in a society that uses purity concepts as part of a sophisticated symbol-system."[157]

An Alternate Proposal

What I am here exploring is an alternate understanding of the use of "purity" in its relation to "holiness" based on the *biblical* worldview. The hermeneutical premise that informs this analysis, as hinted at above, is that the New Testament understanding of "impurity," "cleansing" and "purity" finds its roots in the Old Testament,[158] especially in the priestly writings found primarily in the book of Leviticus.[159] This material has been the subject of intensive

---

[157]P. P. Jenson, *Graded Holiness*, 67. N.T. Wright notes this point: "As C.S. Lewis pointed out about words, when we read old books we go to the dictionaries to look up the hard words, the ones we don't know at all. The apparently easy words, the ones we use every day, pass by us without our realizing the very different meaning they may have carried five centuries ago. So it is with texts in general. If we do not make the effort to check out the underlying worldview, we will all too easily assume that the writer shared, on this or that point, a worldview we ourselves know well. The writer *must really* be talking 'about' what we assume he was talking about, and we ignore the hints within the text of a different worldview, a different underlying narrative." *Paul, the Faithfulness of God*, 1:466.

[158]For a full discussion of this hermeneutical principle see my *Grace, Faith and Holiness* (K.C.: Beacon Hill Press of Kansas City, 1988), Appendix 2. Cf. John Bright, *The Authority of the Old Testament* (Nashville: Abingdon Press, 1967), 110-140; The Petrine Epistles are a canonical illustration of a sustained application of this hermeneutical principle. Cf. H. Ray Dunning, *Partakers of the Divine Nature*. In a nutshell, this principle says that the theology of the OT is fulfilled (filled-full) by NT theology with Christological content.

[159]Other passages of this genre are found in Exodus and Numbers. It is important to understand that sanctification, and its concomitant elements are probably the only soteriological metaphors drawn from a religious context and that context is the Old Testament cult. H. Orton Wiley makes the comment that "To convey to the mind of man the riches of this grace, the entire Levitical system of the Old Testament is laid under tribute. . . . All these point to this New Testament standard of piety." But oddly he never makes use of this hermeneutical insight except for borrowing "purity" language without exegetical support or analysis and interpreting "purity" in the substantive sense consistent with western common-sense

examination in recent times. Much of this discussion focuses on the "authorship and origins of the complex text," with apparently only general agreement on the results. As Jenson comments, "Although these issues are important for an understanding of the history and theology of the text, it is not surprising that the non-specialists usually work with the 'final form' of the text."[160] For the purposes of this study I have attempted to detour around these technical and historical-critical matters and focus on the "final form of the text."

Several important refinements are needed in order to understand how the concepts may be used in New Testament theology. The first distinction that needs to be made is between "ritual purity" and "moral purity." "The relationship between these two forms of purity/impurity is of great importance for understanding the emergence of Christianity within its Jewish matrix."[161] This distinction has been defended persuasively by Jonathan Klawans.[162] "Ritual purity" is primarily described in Leviticus 1-15 and Numbers 19 (the Priestly source) and "moral purity" in Leviticus 16-27 (the holiness code). There is a significant difference in the nature of the defilement that is ascribed to each. In Klawans' summary, ritual impurity is "natural, more or less unavoidable [someone must bury the dead], generally not sinful and typically impermanent. . . . It is not sinful to be ritually impure, and ritual impurity *does not result from sin*."[163] It should also be added that this type of impurity generally includes those "impurities" classified as "unintentional" (NRSV) and may be "covered" by the "purification [sin] offering."[164] This observation

---

use as described in our analysis.

[160]*Graded Holiness*, 21.

[161]Eyal Regev, "Moral Impurity and the Temple in Early Christianity in Light of Ancient Greek Practice and Qumranic Ideology," *Harvard Theological Review*, 97.4 (2004), 383.

[162] Jonathan Klawans, *Sin and Purity in Ancient Judaism* (Oxford: Oxford University Press, 2000). See also Christine E. Hayes, *Gentile Impurities and Jewish Identities* (Oxford: University Press, 2002).

[163]Ibid. 41, emphasis added.

must be qualified by the provision that should one fail to perform the necessary ritual of purification, culpability accrues. For example, "[s]omeone who suffers corpse impurity and refuses to make use of the proper means, defiles the sanctuary, and is cut off (Num. 9:13, 20)."[165] It is instructive how "intentional" and "unintentional" interplay throughout the Levitical purity codes.

Moral impurity "results from committing certain acts so heinous that they are considered defiling. These acts include sexual sins, idolatry and bloodshed, and they bring about an impurity that *morally*—but not *ritually*—defiles the sinner, the land of Israel, and the sanctuary of God."[166] The distinction between these two forms of "sin" or "impurity" has been used to support John Wesley's full orbed understanding of the nature of sin as both intentional and unintentional, i.e., sin "properly so-called," and sin "improperly called."[167]

An additional factor must also be considered when interpreting the use of the "purity" word-group in the New Testament. Developments in the cultic laws and purity views occurred between the final redaction of the Pentateuch and the time of Jesus, the period known as Second Temple Judaism. These developments seem to have been the significant element in the conflicts between Jesus and the Pharisees. For example, Regev states that "Handwashing was not a traditional Levitical practice but an innovation of the late Second Temple period."[168] It is worth considering that possibly Jesus' statement of the 6th beatitude ("Blessed are the pure *in heart*") is meant

---

[164]Mary Douglas, "Atonement in Leviticus," *Jewish Studies Quarterly*, vol. 1 (1991-94), 109-130.

[165]Jenson, *Graded Holiness*, 54.

[166]Klawans, *Sin and Purity*, 41.

[167]Dwight D. Swanson, "Offerings for Sin in Leviticus, and John Wesley's Definition," *European Explorations in Holiness*, vol. 1.

[168]Eyal Regev, "Moral Impurity and the Temple in Early Christianity in Light of Ancient Greek Practice and Qumranic Ideology," *Harvard Theological Review*, 97.4 (2004), 388. So also Roger P. Booth, *Jesus and the Laws of Purity: Tradition, History and Legal History in Mark 7* (JSNT Sup 13; Sheffield: JSOT, 1986), 69-71; Klawans, *Impurity and Sin,* 147-148.

to distinguish kingdom life as a "righteousness that exceeds that of the scribes and Pharisees," for whom external ritual impurity was so important. Matthew 23:25-28 (par. Luke 11:38-41; Mk. 7:20-23) can be almost considered a commentary on the beatitude where the relationship between ritual impurity and moral impurity appears to be the focus. Regev notes on these passages that "it seems that the Pharisees did not hold the view that unrighteous behavior produces impurity."[169] Using a "woe oracle," Jesus condemns the Pharisees and scribes 7 times in chapter 23 (vv. 13,15,16,23,25,27,29): "Woe to you, Pharisees, scribes, hypocrites" which "drive[s] home the contrast between inner attitudes and outward behavior, a contrast found also in the Sermon on the Mount."[170] Saldarini calls attention to the fact that Matthew's account of Jesus' deeds and teaching is bracketed with a vision of a new society (cc. 5-7) and an attack on an alternate program (ch. 23) and that "it should be noted that both have succeeded quite well for almost 2,000 years."[171]

Aside from the issues of "purity" present in the conflicts between Jesus and the Pharisees as recorded in the Gospels,[172] St. Paul makes the most extensive use of "purity" themes, primarily related to the Corinthian situation.[173] Hebrews 9 implicitly addresses the subject

[169]"Moral Purity," 387.

[170]Anthony J. Saldarini, *Matthew's Christian-Jewish Community* (Chicago: University Press, 1994), 49. That Saldarini attributes these attacks to a post-70 A.D. community does not invalidate this observation. By contrast, Kenneth G.C. Newport, *The Sources and Sitz im Leben of Matthew 23* (JSNT Sup. 117; Sheffield: Sheffield Academic Press, 1995) has argued convincingly that Matt. 23:2-31 is a pre-Matthean source that has close connections with the Sermon on the Mount.

[171]Ibid. 237.

[172]These issues have to do with "ritual" defilement and purity. The Pharisees sought to impose the rigid requirements of ritual purity relevant to the priesthood based on its function in the temple upon all Israel (at least in Palestine) and attempted to observe them themselves. Jesus ignored much of this restriction and thus created a conflict with them. While Jesus did not totally reject all cultic regulations (he sent the cured leper to the priest) he subordinated them to moral purity. Paul, on the other hand, apparently rejected the entire concept of ritual purity (or at least radically marginalized it) in favor of an exclusive emphasis on moral purity. This would obviously be important for his Gentile mission.

by way of its reference to the sin offering which was actually a "purification" offering dealing with "ritual defilement,"[174] and contrary to popular interpretation having nothing to do with establishing a relation to God, since it functions within the covenant relation. Rather it concerns the maintaining of that covenantal relation previously established by grace.[175] Paul's thought (and that of Hebrews as well) is informed by the Old Testament (Hebraic).[176]

In the Old Testament purity is defined in relation to "place," which centrally includes the sanctuary (tabernacle/temple) as the dwelling place of God, but also the entire camp.[177] The New

---

[173]Cf. Michael Newton, *The concept of purity at Qumran and in the letters of Paul* (Cambridge: University Press, 1985); and Sarah Whittle, "Purity in Paul," in *Purity in Bible & Theology*, eds. Andrew Brower Latz and Arseny Ermakov, (Eugene, OR: Wipf and Stock, 2014); Kor Yong Lim, "Paul's Use of Temple Imagery in the Corinthian Correspondence: The Creation of Christian Identity" in *Reading Paul in Context: Identity Formation* (London: T & T Clark, 2010).

[174]Jacob Milgrom, "Sin-Offering or Purification-Offering?" *Vetus testamentum*, 21 no 2 Ap 1971, 237-239.

[175]Cf. H. Ray Dunning, *Superlative Christ*, 79-85. Dwight D. Swanson, "Offerings for Sin in Leviticus, and John Wesley's Definition," *European Explorations in Holiness*, vol. 1; Victor P. Hamilton, "Recent Studies in Leviticus and Their Contribution to a Further Understanding of Wesleyan Theology," *A Spectrum of Thought*, ed. Michael Peterson (Wilmore, KY: Asbury Pub. Co., 1982)

[176]Kathy Ehrensperger, "'Called to be saints'–the Identity-shaping Dimension of Paul's Priestly Discourse in Romans," in *Reading Paul in Context: Explorations in Identity Formation* ed. Kathy Ehrensperger and J. Brian Tucker (N.Y.: T & T Clark International, 2010), 90-112 argues that ritual and cult are not only significant aspects of a Jewish way of life but were key aspects of life for all Mediterranean and Near Eastern cultures in antiquity. This does not seem to invalidate the claim that Paul's thought is primarily shaped by his Jewish heritage even though there were parallels in other cultures. As Eyal Regev says, ". . . a profound legacy of Jewish thought about moral impurity was inherited by early Christian communities," "Moral Impurity," 391.

[177]Eyal Regev has argued that not all purity laws relate to the "Temple cult or to holy things in general," to which he ascribes the term "non-priestly purity." ("Moral Impurity," 368ff.) Thus it is the case that Yahweh required purity in the camp as well as in the sanctuary in order to assure the divine presence.

67

Testament, especially Paul, sees the Church as the New Temple, now the dwelling place of God through the Holy Spirit.[178] This is most fully spelled out in the Corinthian correspondence (1 Cor. 3:16-17; 6:19; 2 Cor. 6:16). As in the Levitical laws, moral impurity defiles the "sanctuary," (church) which must be "cleansed" and in extreme cases the source expelled from the community to assure the purity of the "temple."[179] Immediately we see that "purity" is a corporate concept, as is holiness. This does not deny, however, that there is a personal aspect involved since biblically one's relation to God is personal but not individualistic. Jo Bailey Wells argues that the use of "holy nation" and "holy people" of Israel are intended to emphasize this dual emphasis.[180]

Relation of Sanctification and Purity

A good place to focus in attempting to understand the relation between sanctification and purity is with Leviticus 10:10 where the Lord says to Aaron: "You are to distinguish between the holy and the common, and between the unclean and the clean" (NRSV). The two pairs to be distinguished are antitheses, i.e. the holy is the antithesis of the common and the unclean is the antithesis of the clean, which basically implies purity. Gordon J. Wenham's explanation makes their relation quite clear: "Everything that is not holy is common. Common things divide into two groups, the clean and the unclean. Clean things become holy, when they are sanctified. But unclean objects cannot be sanctified. Clean things can be made unclean, if they are polluted.

---

[178]Michael Newton, *The concept of purity at Qumran and in the letters of Paul* (Cambridge: University Press, 1985); R. J. McKelvey, *The New Temple* (London: Oxford University Press, 1969); B. Gästner, *The Temple and Community in Qumran and the NT* (Cambridge: University Press), 1965); L. Cerfaux, *The Church in the Theology of Paul* (N.Y.: Herder & Herder, 1959). The Gospels also clearly imply that Jesus himself replaces the temple as the embodiment of the presence of God thus introducing an additional and significant element to the picture.

[179]Cf. Newton, *Concept of Purity*, 86-97.

[180] Jo Bailey Wells, *God's Holy People: A Theme in Biblical Theology* (EBSCO Publishing: e-book collection), 39.

Finally, holy items may be defiled and become common, even polluted, and therefore unclean."[181] The implication of these distinctions may be further clarified by the use of the logic of immediate inference. We may say that "all holy things [or persons] are clean," but we cannot logically infer that "all clean things [or persons] are holy" by converting the proposition.[182] Only that which is clean can be sanctified or made holy. As Wenham says, "Anyone or anything given to God becomes holy. . . . A person dedicated to the service of God is holy."[183] In illustrating this point Kathy Ehrensperger notes that "animals that are deemed fit for the purpose of sacrifice are pure, but profane until the moment when they are actually offered as a sacrifice; only then are they considered to be holy."[184] There are no degrees of "purity" but there are degrees of uncleanness (cf. different cleansing rituals reflecting this distinction) and also degrees of holiness determined by the proximity to the temple, and its heart, the holy of holies.[185] This further implies that *holiness and purity are not synonyms but that purity is the prerequisite for "being sanctified."* The narrative of the divine-human encounter at Sinai in establishing the covenant demonstrates this theological order. The people must prepare themselves by rituals of purification prior to coming into the presence of Yahweh and consecrating (sanctifying) themselves to a covenant relation with him. Based on her exegesis of 1 Cor. 6:9-11,

---

[181]Gordon J. Wenham, *The Book of Leviticus* (Grand Rapids: William B. Eerdmans Pub. Co., 1979), 29.

[182]To convert a universal affirmative proposition invalidly infers a universal from a particular.

[183]Wenham, *Leviticus*, 22.

[184]"Called to be Saints," 101. "Common" and "profane" are synonymous. Profane literally means "outside the temple," which conforms to the OT source of holiness with its prerequisite of purity. Cf. Richard Bauckham, "The Holiness of Jesus and His Disciples in the Gospel of John," *Holiness and Ecclesiology in the New Testament* ed. Kent E. Brower and Andy Johnson (Grand Rapids: Wm. B. Eerdmans Pub. Co., 2007) for a discussion of the antonyms profane/holy and impurity/purity, 95-98.

[185]P. P. Jenson, *Graded Holiness: A Key to the Priestly Conception of the World.*

Sarah Whittle concludes: "E. P. Sanders' claim . . . that 'in their present life, Christians have been sanctified in the sense of cleansed,' does not do justice to Paul's soteriology, conflating these important and distinct aspects. To be washed is to be purified from the defilement acquired by participating in the activities set out in the vice list [moral rather than ritual impurity]; to be sanctified is to [be] brought into the realm of the holy God; to be justified is to be placed into right relationship."[186]

The bottom line thus appears to be that the use of "purity" as a synonym for "entire sanctification" is exegetically questionable[187] and to do so, when the understanding of purity is defined as the absence of a foreign ontological substance rather than from Biblical thought, is to set up the problem of "perfectionism" that has plagued the holiness movement since the 18th century. Biblically, it appears exegetically sound to affirm that "purity," understood in the cultic sense as transformed via the Christ event, is the prerequisite for sanctification[188] which is the consecration of whatever or whoever is "cleansed" by the establishing of a covenant relation with God (which includes the forgiveness of sins [moral impurity]), thus becoming a part of the "community of faith" through "baptism" (viewed as a rite of purification; cf. 1 Cor. 6:11[189]). The metaphors of cleansing or washing are thus more appropriately used of the forgiveness of sins, the "washing of regeneration," thus producing purity from moral impurity rather than ritual impurity.[190] At least in one passage, John

---

[186]"Purity in Paul," 144.

[187]Ibid..

[188]Jenson, *Graded Holiness* says: "Purity is a necessary but not sufficient condition for consecration. For example, potential priests must first of all be legitimate heirs of Aaron." But this restriction is transcended under the new covenant with the "universal priesthood of all believers."

[189]This is not to suggest baptismal regeneration but that baptism symbolizes the cleansing of moral impurity effected by the blood of Christ. Sarah Whittle rightly notes that Paul's thought "may also have the purification of Christ's atonement in view." *Purity in Paul.*

[190]Paul appears to have abandoned, *as critical*, the entire concept of ritual

Wesley comes very close to affirming the same understanding in his sermon on "Sin in Believers:"

> We allow that the state of a justified person is inexpressibly great and glorious. . . . He is washed, he is sanctified. His heart is purified by faith; he is cleansed 'from the corruption that is in the world,' the love of God is shed abroad in his heart by the Holy Ghost which is given unto him.' And so long as he 'walketh in love,' he worships God in Spirit and in truth. He keepeth the commandments of God, and doeth those things that are pleasing in his sight; so exercising himself as to 'have a conscience void of offence, toward God and toward men:' And he has power both over outward and inward sin, even from the moment he is justified.[191]

Paul's admonition to the Romans (6:12-13) draws out the practical implication of this relationship of grace: "Therefore, do not let sin exercise dominion in your mortal bodies, to make you obey their passions. No longer present your members to sin as instruments of wickedness, but present yourselves to God as those who have been brought from death to life, and present your members to God as instruments of righteousness." The point is that one who has now been "cleansed" from moral impurity resulting from "presenting their members as instruments of wickedness" is in a position to consecrate themselves to God with a view to ethical holiness. W. M. Greathouse

---

purity and impurity but it was considered an important issue in the context of the Gentile mission, an issue that appears early in the Cornelius incident (Acts 10:1— 11:18). The widespread use of Acts 15:9 in the holiness classics to demonstrate the secondness of "entire sanctification" fails to take into account the fact that the context of the question is the relation of Gentiles to Jewish law. Some sources deny that Gentiles were considered ritually unclean but were generally viewed as unclean in the moral sense (cf. Romans 1:18-32; ref. Jonathan Klawans, "Notions of Gentile Impurity in Ancient Judaism," *AJS Review* 20/2 (1995), 285-312) so that "purifying their hearts by faith" refers to the removal of this barrier to full participation in the new age. It further fails to recognize the context of Acts 10 where the language explicitly refers to an initial entrance into the new covenant. Cf. Chris Miller, "Did Peter's Vision in Acts 10 Pertain to Men or the Menu," in *Bibliotheca Sacra* 159 (July-September 2002): 302-17; J. Julius Scott, Jr., "The Cornelius Incident in the Light of its Jewish Setting," *Journal of the Evangelical Theological Society* 34 (December, 1991): 475-484; Robert W. Wall, "The Acts of the Apostles," in *The New Interpreter's Bible* (Nashville: Abingdon Press, 2010).

[191]John Wesley, *Works*, 5:146-7.

implies the relation to consecration we are suggesting: "Emancipated from the old life of sin, we face a new possibility. We may return to the old life, or we may put our redeemed selves at the disposal of God."[192]

In this sense of entering into a right relation to God, one may be sanctified and enjoy a *status* of holy (1 Cor. 1:2).[193] This then becomes the condition that qualifies one to "consecrate" herself or himself to God completely as in Romans 12:1.[194] Thus Paul's word that "Christ loved the church and gave himself up for her, that he might sanctify her, *having cleansed her by the washing of water with the word*" (Eph. 5:25-6, RSV, emphasis added) reflects this *ordo*. Thus it may be that "entire consecration" may be the substance of what could be called "entire sanctification," what Wesley occasionally referred to as "the single eye" and clearly that to which St. Paul was referring in his commitment to the upward call in Phil. 3:12-16.

Sam Powell essentially concurs with this understanding except he emphasizes a most important qualification. This "consecration" is an ongoing, recurring commitment to this "telos." In describing the nature of Christian perfection he says:

> No single decision determines our character. On the contrary, character is constructed through a multitude of momentary acts and commitments. Christian perfection thus begins with choosing to walk

---

[192]*Romans 1-8*, 186.

[193]In her study of Paul's use of "purity," Sarah Whittle suggests that his primary antithesis is "holy/impure" rather than purity/impurity as in the OT and the former is used to describe the means by which Gentiles are brought near to God. Gentiles are impure and in the washing of regeneration they are made holy, a status of relationship characterized as belonging to God. Thus she concludes, "In Paul's scheme unbelievers are characterized as impure, and believers characterized as holy." She apparently does not notice that this holiness is a status to be distinguished from ethical holiness.

[194]Ehrensberger argues that this verse has clear indications of a holiness discourse: "Thus similar to Israel at Mount Sinai, these, as the called in Christ, are now in the realm of God, the Holy One, who calls them to be holy," and relates the call to their being addressed in 1:7 as "called to be saints." *Called to be Saints*, 102.

with the Spirit. This choice, however, is not a once-for-all event—it must be renewed and reaffirmed. Christian perfection is a life that, over time, is given over to God in such a way that transformation occurs and freedom from sin is achieved. Christian perfection, consequently, is not a permanent *state* but instead requires our continuous resolve to remain walking with the Spirit.[195]

If this conclusion is valid, it may be legitimately inferred that what has traditionally been called entire sanctification is a "second" aspect of the dynamic of the Christian life and implies support for Mildred Bangs Wynkoop's assertion that "second" means "depth" rather than a chronological secondness.[196]

Entire sanctification then refers to one who has been made holy (a *status* resulting from a relation to the holy God) and pure by the "washing of regeneration" consecrating herself to the single minded pursuit of God's ideal as embodied in the image of God in which humanity was originally created. An exception to our analysis of purity is suggested by James 1:7, echoed in 4:8. It carries the implication that a pure heart is one that is "single minded." Thus, in this sense, one may refer to this volitional aspect of purity in the terms made popular by Sören Kierkegaard: "purity of heart is to will one thing." The explanation of Eugene Boring integrates this concept with a major emphasis of both Wesley and scripture:

"Purity of heart" is not only the avoidance of "impure thoughts" (e.g. sexual fantasies), but refers to the single-minded devotion to God appropriate to a monotheistic faith. Having an "undivided heart" (Ps. 86:11) is the corollary of monotheism, and requires that there be something big enough and good enough to merit one's whole devotion, rather than the functional polytheism of parceling oneself out to a number of loyalties. Faith in the *one* God requires that one be devoted to God with *all* one's heart (Deut. 6:4; cf. Matt. 22:37). This corresponds to the "single eye" of 6:22, the one pearl of 13:45-46, to Paul's "this one thing I do" (Phil. 3:13) and Luke's "one thing is needed" (Luke 10:42, NIV)—not one *more* thing. The opposite of a pure heart is a divided heart (James 4:8), attempting to serve two

---

[195]Samuel M. Powell, *Holiness, Why It Matters Today*, 28.

[196]Wynkoop, *A Theology of Love*, 347.

masters (6:24), the "doubt" (*distazō*, lit. "have two minds") of 14:31 and 28:17, and the conduct of the Pharisees (23:25).[197]

A Synergistic Interpretation of Consecration

The 19th century holiness theology, following Phoebe Palmer, made consecration a prerequisite of entire sanctification but interpreted it as a human action whereas the latter is exclusively the work of God.[198] Maddox explains this emphasis as the result of the early American Methodist's switch from Wesley's moral psychology to a "Reidian moral psychology" which "pushed them back toward the Western Christian tendency of posing God's agency and human agency as mutually exclusive in the process of salvation. . . . Holiness writers did not escape this impact."[199] Properly understood, in the light of scripture and John Wesley's understanding, the nature of the "consecration" or sanctification that characterizes the cleansed person's focused pursuit of the image of God is an interplay between divine and human elements. If it is true, as Paul says in 1 Cor. 12:3 that "no one can say 'Jesus is Lord' except by the Holy Spirit," it is equally true that no one can commit herself or himself to the holy life apart from the enablement of the Spirit. Drawing on the Levitical perspective, Jenson emphasizes this synergism:

". . . since the normal state of earthly things is purity, it requires a special act of God to make a thing or person holy. God ultimately consecrates or sanctifies, although he may make use of persons and material means. Moses anoints both the sanctuary and the priests with the holy anointing oil but this is in strict accord with the divine instruction, and the infilling by the glory of God at the consecration

---

[197]Quoted in W. M. Greathouse, *Wholeness in Christ* (K.C.: Beacon Hill Press of Kansas City, 1998), 178.

[198]In discussing the terminology of holiness, J. B. Chapman said: "Generally speaking, consecration is human sanctification, while divine sanctification is purification." *Terminology of Holiness*, 8. See also Thomas Cook, *New Testament Holiness*, 124f.

[199]"Reconnecting the Means to the End," 54.

74

emphasizes the limitation of the purely human construction. The consecration consists of a double movement, since the initiation of a new relationship with the divine realm entails a corresponding separation from the earthly sphere."[200]

In commenting on Paul's exhortation to the Corinthians (2 Cor. 7:1) to "cleanse themselves," in order to "perfect holiness," Sarah Whittle's observation is pertinent to this issue:

> Paul is not instructing the Corinthians to make themselves holy, but to make themselves pure as a requirement for God to make them holy. Paul's acknowledgement of the sanctifying role of the Spirit along with his acknowledgement that believers must avoid defilement makes it clear that he does not have in view the idea of perfecting holiness as personal achievement. . . Perfecting holiness is contingent on their self-cleansing. But, this avoidance of defilement in and of itself does not result in making one's self holy. Rather, if one is pure or clean, consecration, as a work of the Spirit, is able to take place."[201]

Hoo-Jung Lee's conclusion in summarizing his dissertation research that included an analysis of the Eastern Fathers on John Wesley's theology declared that

> Wesley's *synergistic* view of sanctification and perfection, that is somewhat alien to Western theology, owes a lot to Macarius' Eastern doctrine based on ascetic praxis. However, Macarius also represents

---

[200]Jenson, *Graded Holiness*, 48. In a meaningful note, he adds "Separateness is often thought to be the basic meaning of holiness, but it is more its necessary consequence. Consecration is a separation to God rather than a separation from the world [ref. Norman Snaith, *Distinctive Ideas of the Old Testament*, (London: Epworth Press, 1955), 30: "A person or a thing may be separate, or may come to be separated, because he or it has come to belong to God. When we use the word 'separated' as a rendering of any form of the root *q-od-sh*, we should think of 'separated *to*' rather than of 'separated *from*." and holiness has a positive content."] Wells affirms the same: ". . . it is always God who ultimately consecrates or sanctifies (piel or hiphil of קרש), even though the transition may be prescribed through ritual means." *God's Holy People*, 82.

[201]"Purity in Paul." This explanation implies that one means of dealing with the defilement of moral impurity is to discontinue the defiling practices as well as emphasizing the synergistic character of the process.

Syriac spirituality that underscores the seriousness of the fall and the total dependence on grace in salvation. In this profound dialectic, human efforts or striving for perfection, in the theology of Macarius and Wesley, are not regarded as sufficient or independent from grace but should be construed as the response *enabled* or empowered by divine grace.[202]

Conclusion

This theological model, based on biblical exegesis, maintains the central emphasis on the importance of the holy life but avoids the tendency toward perfectionism that is indigenous to the 19th century tradition and has been the major factor in the problems which many sensitive Christians have found with the paradigm to which they have been exposed. Up to this point I have implicitly utilized three of the aspects of the so-called "Wesleyan Quadrilateral." The element of experience has also been explored in a limited way. In a number of sessions with deeply dedicated Christians, I have found that this proposed paradigm resonates with their experience. Some of these groups were composed chiefly of older folk with long tenure in a holiness church, a group that one would think would be most resistant to a changing paradigm, but the opposite was the case. The frustrations of their early experience were freely expressed and the present proposal gave them a sense of liberation and reality.

The same response has been found among candidates for the ministry. In addition, thanks to the help of Rev. Jeff Sexton, the secretary of the district where I serve, I was able to examine the testimonies of candidates to the ministry on my local district concerning their experience of sanctification and found an interesting pattern. While this certainly makes no claim to scientific accuracy, it demonstrates that experience at this level gives a measure of credence to a new paradigm. Only two candidates used traditional language and concepts. There was an almost unanimous recognition that what they described as "entire sanctification" was the initiation of a process that

---

[202]"The Doctrine of New Creation in the Theology of John Wesley," Ph.D. dissertation, Emory University, 1991, 255-6.

was characterized by an increasing conformity to an ethical ideal. Only a very few recognized the nature of this process to be informed by the image of God although this was implicit in the identification of the ideal in terms of Christlikeness. There was clearly an identification of their experience of "entire sanctification" with a commitment, or surrender, or consecration. Over several years of interviewing ministerial candidates, I have noticed that many of them identified their response to a call to ministry with their entire sanctification. Since a call to ministry implicitly entails a total commitment of one's future to the service and worship of God, such an understanding could be a legitimate identification. In a very real sense, although usually not articulated with clarity and specificity, their experiential reality correlated with the exegetical proposal of this study.

Chapter 4
Sanctification and the Image of God

Thesis: The goal of salvation broadly understood is the renewal of humanity in the image of God with a view to the new creation.

Both John and Charles Wesley consistently emphasized the centrality of the image of God as the redemptive goal of God's restoration process in the light of the Fall. Patrick Eby demonstrates that the restoration of the image of God was the theme that persisted from the earliest days throughout all his life in the thought of Charles Wesley.[203] In his sermon on Original Sin based on Genesis 6:5, John concludes:

> Ye know that the great end of religion is, to renew our hearts in the image of God, to repair that total loss of righteousness and true holiness which we sustained by the sin of our first parent. Ye know that all religion which does not answer this end, all that stops short of this, the renewal of our soul in the image of God, after the likeness of Him that created it, is no other than a poor farce, and a mere mockery of God, to the destruction of our own soul.[204]

Hoo-Jung Lee demonstrates that "even for the young [John] Wesley, the *restoration of the image of God* in accordance with the scheme of the original creation, and the overcoming of the fall is the *central* element in the understanding of genuine Christianity."[205] Thus, like Charles, this emphasis was consistent throughout his entire life.

John refers to every aspect of grace in the total salvation process as a manifestation of this intention. This included the purpose of prevenient grace, regeneration, growth in grace and entire sanctification as well as final glorification. Thus the broader

---

[203]"The One Thing Needful: The Development of Charles Wesley's Theology of the Restoration of the Image of God ," Ph.D. diss, Drew University, 2010.

[204]*Works,* 6:64-5. Quotes similar to this could be multiplied.

[205] "New Creation," 29.

significance of "sanctification" involved the entire scope of salvation, including as we shall see, the whole creation.

Ben Witherington, III explored the theme of the image of God in scripture in 2 volumes of over 800 pages each. But he rather simply summarized his research in the introduction: "Salvation history could be described as the story of the attempt to restore human beings so that they once more properly reflect the image of God on earth, which they were always intended to do."[206] It thus appears that the Wesleyan and biblical focus are on the same page.

The key to understanding the full meaning of sanctification, broadly conceived, thus requires a careful study of the meaning of the biblical teaching concerning the image of God. On the surface this might seem a difficult task since the Old Testament says very little about the subject. Following the creation stories that focus on the origin of humanity the text seems to be silent on the subject except for two brief references (Gen. 5:2; 9:6). But if we identify the substance of the concept, we will find that its meaning informs the entire scripture in terms of the content even if the explicit language is scarce.[207] A number of relevant passages are found in the New Testament, most of which imply that the image was lost and in need of restoration. Romans 3:22b-23 is the summation of Paul's argument in 1:18—3:20: "For there is no distinction, since all have sinned and fall short of the glory of God." C. H. Dodd comments that "The glory of God is the divine likeness which man is intended to bear. In so far as man departs from the likeness of God he is sinful."[208] This means that the term "glory" is essentially a synonym for "image" here as it clearly is in 2 Corinthians 3:18—"And all of us, with unveiled faces, seeing the *glory* of the Lord as through reflected in a mirror, are being transformed into the same *image* from one degree of glory to another; for this comes from the Lord, the Spirit." As here, Paul's reference to "the Lord" is

---

[206]*The Indelible Image*, 2 vols. (Downers Grove, Ill.: IVP Academic, 2009-2010), 1:20.

[207]David J. A. Clines remarks on this: "Yet we become aware, in reading these early chapters of Genesis and in studying the history of the interpretation of these passages, that the importance of the doctrine is out of all proportion to the laconic treatment it receives in the Old Testament." "The Image of God in Man," 54.

[208]*The Epistle of Paul to the Romans* (Fontana Books, n.d.).

generally to Jesus who is the bearer of the "image" or "glory" in contrast with the law that also reflected the "image" but only in a preliminary way. Romans 8:29 states in a straightforward way God's redemptive purpose to restore humanity to the lost image, as embodied in Jesus: "For those whom he foreknew he also predestined to be conformed to the image of his Son, in order that he might be the firstborn within a large family." As N.T. Wright comments, "This is the point, at last, to which the long argument beginning with 1:18 was looking forward. The image of God, distorted and fractured through idolatry and immorality, is restored in Jesus the Messiah, the Son of God."[209]

The doctrine of the *imago dei* has occupied the attention of theologians from the beginning of Christian theologizing, with varying understandings. Our purpose permits only a cursory survey of this material, with brief looks at certain theories that have implications for an understanding of sanctification.

From early in Christian history, apparently beginning with St. Irenaeus, theologians have recognized a 2 fold dimension to the image of God. Irenaeus derived his understanding from Genesis 1:26 as a result of misunderstanding the use of two terms (image and likeness) to refer to two different things. Since the Protestant Reformation most scholarship has recognized that this is an example of Hebrew parallelism, which repeats one thought a second (or more) time using different terms.[210]

Eastern and Western Christendom developed the theme of the *imago* in different directions. In the Eastern interpretation a distinction continues to be made between the image and the likeness. The *image* denoted the universal human potential for life in God. The *likeness* was the progressive realization of that potentiality. Unlike the West, the eastern theologians believed that Adam and Eve were created innocent but not complete or "perfected." Thus the continued response to God in their freedom and resulting participation in the divine nature

---

[209]*The Letter to the Romans*, 602.

[210]Mildred Wynkoop followed the Eastern tradition in interpreting the image of God in terms of this paradigm, *Theology of Love*, 119-121.

(divinization) would develop the *likeness*. For the Western church, the Fall introduced death and corruption with the result that human beings can "no longer hope to attain the Likeness of God on our own,"[211] however Eastern theologians "did not hold that the Fall deprived us of all grace, or of the accountability for responding to God's offer of restored communion with Christ."[212]

The Western understanding came to its fullest expression in the Medieval Synthesis, as articulated by St. Thomas Aquinas (1225-1274), while still retaining the dual meaning of the terms. His theological anthropology was part of his larger vision that there were two dimensions to human existence that could be roughly envisioned as a two-storied house. The lower "story" was the "image" whereas the "likeness" was a superadded gift, the second story. Consistent with this vision, human beings have a two-fold end or *telos*: a natural end and a supernatural end. The "image" includes the capacity of freedom along with the intellectual ability (reason) to pursue and actualize the natural virtues, which constitute mankind's natural good. At this level, Thomas followed closely the ethics of Aristotle. The supernatural virtues of faith, hope and charity constituted the supernatural end with its consummation in the ultimate vision of God. They were the result of grace and faith. In the Fall, the "likeness" was lost or removed while the image remained although somewhat debilitated. Humans could still achieve their "natural telos," which was good but incomplete. It required the restoration of the likeness to achieve mankind's supernatural *telos*. Much of medieval Catholic piety was shaped by this vision.

With Protestantism, the image continued to be interpreted as two-fold in terms of the *natural image* and the *moral image*. The natural image referred to those characteristics that identified the determinative qualities of personhood, qualities such as reason, freedom, immortality and the capacity for self-transcendence. The "moral" image refers to those qualities that reflect the nature of God (his communicable attributes). G. C. Berkouwer's comment about the natural image demonstrates the inadequacy of this way of explaining it:

---

[211]St. Augustine gave classic expression to this position.

[212]Maddox, *Responsible Grace*, 66.

It is regrettable that the valid emphasis on the dogma of the image of God in the wider sense [natural image] has often taken on the form of an analysis of the ontic structure of man, e.g., as defined by person, reason and freedom. For it is undeniable that Scripture does not support such an interpretation. Scripture is concerned with man in his relation to God, in which he can never be seen as man-in-himself, and surely not with man's "essence" described as self or person.[213]

John Wesley, at times, interpreted the image of God in a three-fold sense, adding to the natural and moral image the political image by which he intended mankind's relation to the animal creation. Of greater significance for our purposes is Maddox' observation that "Wesley's anthropology recognized four basic human relationships: with God, with other humans, with lower animals, and with ourselves. A holy (and whole!) person is one in whom all of these relationships are properly expressed."[214]

As referred to in chapter 1, a relational understanding of the image has become a dominant way of describing it in recent times. While this perception may have been introduced into contemporary scholarship by Dietrich Bonhoeffer[215] and Karl Barth, it actually finds its source in the Genesis account of creation. The primary relation—to the Creator—is implicit in the narrative in terms of the communion between the Lord God and the first pair, a relation Bonhoeffer refers to as "freedom for," suggesting the idea of a relation of "openness." There was nothing that interfered with an uninhibited fellowship so long as each partner in the relation maintained their proper role, which meant Adam's recognition of himself as creature and subject to the sovereign.

Explicit in the narrative is the recognition of a relation of freedom for or openness in the male and female relation. The absence of clothes signified this radical openness marked by intimacy based on integrity, honesty and trust. The relation to the earth and other aspects

---

[213]*Man: The Image of God* (Grand Rapids: Wm. B. Eerdmans Pub. Co., 1962), 59-60.

[214]*Responsible Grace*, 68.

[215]Dietrich Bonhoeffer, *Creation and Fall* (London: SCM, 1959).

of the natural creation has a different dimension. The word translated "dominion" was not intended to suggest exploitation but responsible stewardship. As God's representative, which meant the role of a king, Adam was to care for the environment in which he and Eve were placed. His prerogative of naming the animals signified the function of a king. Implicit throughout, and determinative of the other relationships, was the humans' understanding of themselves, who they were and their role in God's creation. All the other relations were distorted when this role was rejected. Ultimately it is the case that each relation informs and is informed by the other three relations.

Recognition of this complex of relations as constituting the image of God is pervasive with both biblical and theological scholars. Even if obliquely, numerous interpreters represent the image of God according to either this 4-fold pattern or a 3-fold one that is virtually the same. One of the big Old Testament words for God's ideal for humanity is *shalom*, which Elmer Marten's defined in terms of the pre-fall condition depicted in Genesis: "in Eden, as the opening chapters of Genesis describe it, . . . man is in tune with God, Adam and Eve are unashamed with each other; they live in harmony with themselves as well as with animals. Not only their needs but their desires are fully met. Here is the perfect state."[216]

Christopher J. H. Wright depicts the ethical structure of the Old Testament using the analogy of a triangle. The apex of the triangle he identifies as the theological angle (relation to God); the other two are the social angle (relation to the community) and the economic angle (relation to the land)." These three are mutually influential and encompass "the covenantal basis of Old Testament theology."[217]

N.T. Wright, speaking somewhat informally in a lecture about humans made in the image of God said: "Human being know in their bones that they are made for each other, human beings know in their bones that they are made to look after and shape this world and human beings know in their bones that they are made to worship someone

---

[216]Elmer Martens, *Gods' Design* (Grand Rapids: Baker Book House, 1981), 28.

[217]Christopher J.H. Wright, *An Eye for an Eye*, 19-20.

whom they resemble." In a word, human beings are made for relationship, worship and stewardship.[218]

In summarizing the Sermon on the Mount, John Wesley declared: "It is the eternal Wisdom of the Father, who knoweth whereof we are made, and understands our inmost frame; who knows how we stand related to God, to one another, to every creature with God hath made, and, consequently, how to adapt every law he prescribes, to all the circumstances wherein he hath placed us."[219]

These references all concur in the significance of the image of God as involving a complex of relations that provides the framework for the theology and ethics of the Old Testament embodied in the law. We noted previously how Christopher Wright depicted this complex using the imagery of a triangle. My proposal is to add a smaller triangle in the middle of the larger one with the angles corresponding to the outer one. This triangle refers to the "self" to suggest that each of the angles involve the relation God intended so long as the "self" is appropriately related to each of them. In a word, that relation is the key to both an appropriate embodiment of the *imago* and at the same time the key to a distortion of each.

It is significant that the relation to God occupies the peak position in the triangle since that is the primary one while the others are subsidiary but essentially involved in the full complex of elements that constitute the image of God.

The image of God as described in this chapter is not only a "fact" of human nature, it is also a vocation. Abram and his descendents were chosen to live that vocation and thus demonstrate to the world the greater blessedness of serving the true and living God. The Torah addressed each of these relations and gave guidance concerning how they should be implemented. Repeatedly however they failed in this vocation with the result that God sent his son as the

---

[218]N.T. Wright, "Jesus and the World's True Light," Intervarsity Press Conference, January 1999. This way of describing these relations implies what could be legitimately understood by the so-called "natural image," but more appropriately as the function of prevenient grace as a barrier to the total deconstruction of the characteristics that mark humanness, a reflection of the image of God even in fallen humanity

[219]*Works*, 5:248.

one faithful Israelite (Rom. 3:22)[220] to carry out Israel's vocation and through his death and resurrection inaugurate the beginning of the new creation in which God's initial purpose for the human race began to become actualized through the power of the Holy Spirit released into the world for those who would confess Jesus as Lord of the world. That vocation now devolves upon "the children of Abraham," whom Paul defines as those who have faith in Jesus (Galatians 3:7), namely the church.

The understanding of the image of God that we have briefly explored here provides a clue to the meaning of sin. The central word used for sin in the New Testament is *harmartia*, which means "to miss the mark." C. H. Dodd's interpretation of Romans 3:23 resonates with the overall emphasis of scripture: "'The glory of God' is the divine likeness which man is intended to bear. In so far as man departs from the likeness of God he is sinful. To 'come short of the glory of God' is to sin. This definition, simple, broad, and profound, should be borne in mind whenever Paul has occasion to speak about sin."[221] Gustav Aulén makes the same point: "From the point of view of sin the concept of the 'image of ' sets forth the lost destiny of man, and from the point of view of salvation it reveals the divine purpose in creation."[222]

Theologians have offered several proposals as to the essential nature of sin. When sin is interpreted in terms of the image of God, it can be seen that each of them has validity in terms of one or more of these relations, each indicating an aspect of the broken relation between the Creator and his creature. Since the *imago Dei* is what identifies mankind as human,[223] whatever distorts or destroys the *imago* is dehumanizing. In commenting on Paul's indictment of the fallen race in Romans, N. T. Wright says, "Paul's view of sin . . . is that it is not the breaking of arbitrary divine rules, but that it is subhuman or nonhuman behavior, deeds that are unfitting for humans

---

[220]This is exegetically preferable to the traditional translation as "faith in Jesus Christ." See footnote in NRSV. Cf. also W.M. Greathouse, *Romans 1-8*, 122.

[221]*The Epistle of Paul to the Romans*, 75.

[222]Gustav Aulén, *The Faith of the Christian Church*, trans. Eric H. Wahlstrom & G. Everett Arden (Philadelphia: The Muhlenberg Press, 1948). 267.

[223]See Dunning, *Grace, Faith and Holiness*, 159-61.

to perform."[224] This implies that whatever--whether deed, attitude, affection, or motive—violates the structure of humanhood as defined by the *imago Dei* is sin.

The Genesis narrative makes it clear that the primary relation—to God—was disrupted when the first pair made the choice to assume the role that belonged to the Creator. The serpent had enticed Eve with the proposal that if she ate the forbidden fruit, she would become like God (Gen. 3:5) and when she and Adam had done so the Lord God declared "See, the man has become like one of us." (v. 22) There were two aspects to this disastrous choice: the first was *unbelief* in the sense of trust since the pair failed to believe that God's provision for them was for their well-being, that they knew better than he. The result was *idolatry*, the worship of an aspect of the creation (in this case, themselves) rather than the Creator. Elmer Martens points out that "if [Adam and Eve's disobedience in the garden] is to be described theologically by a root word, it must be described as transgression understood as a fractured relationship between God and man."[225] Oswald Chambers highlights this aspect of sin: "The essential nature of sin is my claim to my right to myself, and when sin entered in, the connection between man and God was instantly severed; at-one-ness was no longer possible."[226]

In describing the result of idolatry in the pagan world (Romans 1:18-32) Paul points out how idolatry leads to dehumanizing behavior, particularly in relation to homosexual practice, which impinges on the second *imago* relation. Regardless of contemporary tolerance of so-called "alternate life-styles," as N.T. Wright says, "We cannot isolate these verses from Paul's large argument, both in this paragraph and in Romans as whole. From this it is clear that he regards homosexual practice as a dangerous distortion of God's intention. . . . What we cannot do is pretend that it means something other than what it says."[227]

---

[224]Wright, *Romans* in *New Interpreters' Bible*, 434.

[225]*God's Design*, 49.

[226]*Psychology of Redemption*, 11.

[227]*Romans*, 435.

Thus we see that the disobedience that disrupted the divine-human relation also radically altered the interpersonal relation so that the "openness" that had characterized the first pair in their created condition was lost. This loss was symbolized by the covering of the body with fig leaves and the sense of shame that emerged (3:10). St. Augustine, although mistakenly making sexuality the essence of original sin, highlighted the results of this apostasy by pointing to the shame that attaches to conception so that while everyone knows its cause, it always occurs in the greatest possible secrecy.

What now intrudes itself into the male-female relation is the motive of self-gratification. All men now tend to do as Augustine confessed he had done: "I polluted the spring of friendship with the lust of concupiscence." This is the significance of *sensuality* as a fundamental expression of sin. The sexual relation becomes the most obvious instance of the dominance of self-gratification in interpersonal relations. It is what, *per se*, makes sexual activity outside of marriage sinful. Since the marriage bond entails self-commitment to the other person, seeking the benefits of marriage outside that commitment cannot avoid the primary motivation of self-gratification. It is true, as Martin Luther suggested when he spoke of the "rape of the wedding night," that marriage does not necessarily preclude the dominance of self-gratification but this becomes a different sort of expression and does not justify extra-marital sexual behavior. In a word, what happens is that the primordial "I-Thou" relation degenerates into an "I-It" relation., In terms of the Kantian categorical imperative, other persons are not treated as "ends-in-themselves" but as means to an end.

The elevation of self to the seat of authority likewise perverts man's relation to nature or the earth. His original mandate was to cultivate the created world for the glory of God. The Fall twisted this around so that the task of tilling the earth (developing culture) became motivated by greed and self-advantage. The practical results in terms of the "rape of the earth" are appalling. Exploitation, irresponsibility and greed all paint a gloomy picture for the future of the environment because man has sought to exploit the earth for his own pleasure in ways that far exceed his needs.

From thiss it may be seen that while the "essence" of sin may be legitimately identified as "idolatry," "pride," "sensuality," or "unbelief," each of them is a distortion of the divinely created role of the human race, thus suggesting that the most overarching concept, that encompasses all the rest, is *alienation*. Humanity, in the condition of fallenness is alienated from God, each other, the earth and from one's authentic self. This can take numerous forms of distorted humanness.

Chapter 5
Sanctification and the Image of God
(continued)

It is one thing to derive an understanding of the meaning of the *imago Dei* and another to implement it in lived experience. Up to this point, we have attempted to make certain points that impinge on this issue. We have stressed that sanctification should be generically understood as the renewal of human persons in the image of God and emphasized that sanctification is a thoroughgoing ethical concept. Christian conversion is described by such scriptural metaphors as justification, regeneration, the new birth and adoption. But these represent the establishing of a relation that is at least initially transforming, which is why the terminology of "initial sanctification" is appropriately applied to these, as John Wesley did (he did not use the terminology of initial sanctification) by emphasizing that sanctification begins at justification.

While God accepts us on the basis of "faith alone," and without prior qualifications, he does not intend to have us remain at that level of relationship. This truth is captured in the trenchant words of N.T. Wright as he reflects on Romans 6:

> This chapter shines a bright spotlight on the dangerous half-truth, currently fashionable, that "God accepts us as we are." Indeed, the question of 6:1 could be read as raising exactly this question: Will "God's acceptance" do as a complete grounding of Christian ethics? Emphatically not. Grace reaches where human are, and accepts them as they are, because anything less would result in nobody's being saved. Justification is by grace alone, through faith alone. But grace is always *transformative*. God accepts us where we are, but God does not intend to leave us where we are."[228]

The point to be emphasized here is that the ethical life that God intends his people to pursue is embodied in the concept of the image of God. The paradigm that we have derived exegetically is that entire sanctification is a whole person commitment or consecration to the pursuit of this ideal, not the full realization of it at any point in the journey.

---

[228]*Romans*, 548.

Another element that should be considered in exploring this subject, is the eschatological dualism that informs the New Testament, especially as it is utilized by St. Paul in Romans and Galatians. The point here is that while the Torah provided guidance in living out the various aspect of the *imago*, it did not provide the inner resource to live it out. This is the contrast Paul draws between Romans 7 and 8. As a result of the death and resurrection of Christ providing for the enabling power of the Holy Spirit, the New Testament's call to a Spirit-filled life is essentially a call to reflect the image of God (cf. our chapter 7). Even though the epistles of the New Testament are occasional in nature, that is, they were written to address particular problems in particular contexts, underlying their message are the various aspects of the *imago*. Hence we shall seek to briefly emphasize how life in the Spirit is ethical in nature focusing on the relevant relationships as vocation.

Relation to God. The relationship to God that is foundational to the image of God is described in scripture in terms of love, as did John Wesley. The central text of the Hebrew faith in Deuteronomy 6:4-5 (shema) and Jesus' summation of the law in Matthew 22:35-37 emphasize this point. This quality of relatedness marked by whole-being love is conditioned on obedience. This was true in the pre-Fall state as described in the creation story in Genesis. It was not obedience in general or in the abstract but a specific point of obedience was identified. It should be emphasized that the emphasis on obedience does not imply a legal relation. The failure of the first pair to obey was more profound than simply breaking a law. It was the betrayal of a relationship of trust. Furthermore the call for obedience after the Fall was not the requirement for restoring the relation but rather, as in the garden, describes the manifestation of a relation of trust, a "response to grace." Although obedience is strongly emphasized in Deuteronomy as well as by Jesus in John 14:15 it is not to be interpreted in a legalistic fashion but as the response out of love for the Creator who prescribes what is for our happiness or well-being—"If you love me you will keep my commandments."

This implies that the purpose of this requirement of unconditional obedience is to maintain communion, not merely obedience. The contrast can be illustrated by the relation between parent and child. When the child questions why she should obey her parent's instruction or prohibition, and the parent's response is "Because I said so!" that implies obedience for obedience's sake. But in the ideal relation (which realistically is rare, if ever) the parent is always right and when the response is "because it is for your well-being!" and the child trusts the parent implicitly, the result is a relation of communion, openness.

Martens makes this point in relation to the Ten Commandments:

> There is some reason to be squeamish about the commandment language, partly because the Old Testament designation is not "commandment" but "words" . . . and partly—this is more crucial—because "commandment" inaccurately describes these statements as legalistic and harsh, so that disobedience brings inevitable punishment. But if Exodus 20 is viewed against the ancient Near Eastern covenant stereotype, the harsh colour of "commandment" is quickly softened to "rightful response".[229]

The basis for this aspect of the image is who God is, the sovereign Creator but perhaps more importantly, because as the Creator, "He knows how we were made; he remembers that we are dust" (Ps 103:14). On the grounds of both his holiness and his wisdom, the Lord has the "right" to ask for unconditional obedience. No aspect of the creation, human or otherwise, has the right to ask for such unconditional love and obedience. Sören Kierkegaard emphasizes this point: "A man must love God in *unconditional obedience* and love him in *adoration*. It would be ungodliness if a man dared love himself in this way, or dared love another person in this way, or dared let another person love him in this way."[230]

This unconditional love provides a principle of discrimination to which Paul is referring in Colossians 3:15—"And let the peace of Christ rule in your hearts. . ." Thomas Cook refers to this criterion as "the arbiter of the heart," and points out that it is far more significant in guiding behavior than the conscience, which, he says "guarantees

---

[229]Martens, *God's Design*, 71.

[230]From Søren Kierkegaard, "Works of Love," in *A Kierkegaard Anthology*, ed. Robert Bretall (New York: Modern Library, 1946), 286.

only good intentions." He describes the function of the *peace of God* like this:

> When this peace becomes the paramount consideration, everything that disturbs that profound rest of the soul will be instinctively avoided, and every act that would weave the thinnest veil between us and the face of our adorable Saviour, we shall instantly shrink from. A man who is exploring an old well lowers a candle before him, knowing that where that can live, he can live. If the light goes out, he knows that it is not safe to go farther. The peace of God is the Christian's test-flame.[231]

Susanna Wesley's definition of sin, which she gave to her children, sounds the same note: "Whatever weakens your reason, impairs the tenderness of your conscience, obscures your sense of God, or takes off the relish of spiritual things, whatever increases the authority of your body over your mind, that thing for you is sin." The ideal nature of this relation is such that I acknowledge God as absolute sovereign and loving Father with the result that any activity, attitude or disposition that compromises that relation must be avoided.

If we were to focus exclusively on this relationship, we could easily slip into a mysticism that is narcissistic, devoid of compassion for others and perhaps "so heavenly minded as to be of no earthly use." So it is important to recognize that no matter how pivotal the relation to God is, it is foundational to the other relationships that entail responsibility in relation to others and the environment. It is not without significance that the scripture speaks more about our love for others and responsibility for earthly goods than about our love for God. To those we now give attention.

Relation to Others. One of the intriguing features of the Genesis creation narratives is the use of the plural form for Deity. Genesis 1:1 declares: "In the beginning *Elohim* (plural for the singular *El*) created the heavens and the earth." The plural pronouns become both pronounced and prolific when the writer comes to speak of the origin of human being. Up to that point, the first creation narrative (1:1—2:4a) records "then God said" in connection with each day's

---

[231]*New Testament Holiness*, 147, 149.

92

creative activity with the originating fiat immediately following. But in 1:26 it is followed by an "in-house" consultation concerning this particular potentiality: "Let *us* make man in *our* image, according to *our* likeness." The plural is then transferred to the proposed created being: "Let *them* have dominion . . ." In the 27ᵗʰ verse, the creation of mankind is stressed to be in the form of "male and female," a plural creature. Certainly all other "animals" also had male and female species but the structure clearly indicates something special is implied by this characteristic of human being.

This corporate characteristic of humanity may be further emphasized by W.M. Greathouse's description of the corporate use of the name, "Adam," in both Genesis and Romans: "'man' in Romans is the *'adam* of the OT—'humankind.' . . . The Hebrew word for 'humankind' is *'adam,* a generic term that embraces not only male and female but also all humanity. The transition from the generic *'adam* to the personal 'Adam' does not occur until 4:25. In ch. 5[:1-2] we find the corporate significance of the term. . . . The dual sense of Adam is preserved in Rom 5:12-21.²³²

Traditionally, biblical scholars have had difficulty with the plural forms used of God in these passages. Some have argued that it indicates the idea of a "heavenly court" where the Supreme Deity gathers his "court" of lesser beings around him and together they plan the strategy for the apex of the creative work. Evidences of this idea may be found elsewhere in the Old Testament. Conservative students have many times suggested that we have here a foregleam of the Trinity. As long as this is not taken to be an explicit teaching, it can be properly recognized as pointing to an important truth. The New Testament revelation of God's trinitarian nature is here found to be not in conflict with Old Testament monotheism. More to the point of the Hebrew mind is the suggestion that the plural indicators reflect the fullness of being of Yahweh that involves no compromise of "monotheism" but does support the theology of God as a social being.

St. Augustine was groping for a basic truth about humankind in his efforts to identify a trinitarian structure within human nature on the assumption that the *imago* would entail the same ontological structure in humanity as revelation disclosed about the divine nature. His basic

²³²W.M. Greathouse, *Wholeness in Christ* (K.C.: Beacon Hill Press of Kansas City, 1998), 34-35.

error, however, was in seeking to confine the "social" structure within the individual. The truth to which these biblical affirmations point is an interpersonal ontological structure. Modern understandings of the self have brought this more clearly to light but it was a truth that the biblical mind grasped all along.

As in the case of the divine-human relation, the person-to-person relation can also be described as "openness." It was an "I-Thou" relationship marked by the absence of shame. The reference (Gen. 2:25) to the fact that "they were both naked . . . and were not ashamed," symbolizes this kind of openness. The absence of desire as "lust" that has self-gratification as the primary element in its motivation make such unashamed openness possible in this picture of almost naïve unselfconsciousness.

Again, this relation can be summarized in the concept of love. Love for God and others is inseparable. In the prayer Jesus taught his disciples, the only petition about which he makes comment is the prayer for forgiveness as we forgive those who trespass against us. Our forgiveness of others is a condition for our forgiveness by the heavenly Father (Matthew 6:14). And furthermore this love is not restricted but is to be extended to enemies as well. The holiness tradition has informally adopted as its key text Hebrews 12:14 but unfortunately has usually failed to recognize the two-fold condition for "seeing God." "Pursuing peace with everyone" is just as much a condition as "pursuing holiness."

Gustav Aulén provides an excellent description of the nature of this love for the other: "'Loving God' means primarily . . . obeying the will of God. 'Loving one's neighbor' means neither infatuation or sentimental compassion, but a caring and attentiveness which expresses itself in practical deed, whose basis is man's open heart toward one another and toward the demands for a life together. The decisive thing was that God's ethical demands were to be fulfilled within the human community."[233]

This aspect of the *imago* is the theological foundation for the people of God being seen as a body of believers in an organic relation with each other and not a collection of individual having a private

[233]Gustav Aulén, *Jesus in Contemporary Historical Research* (Philadelphia: Fortress Press, 1976), 138.

relation to God. Seen from this perspective this relation manifests itself in the corporate body by the characteristic of unity. Where the body—the church—is an authentic Spirit-originated and Spirit-filled entity, it manifests this quality. In Jesus' prayer for his disciples in John 17:17-24 the correlation between unity and vocation is explicitly made. The distinguishing mark of the early days of the church following the Pentecostal outpouring was their mutual love manifested in a caring community. This explains why the unity of the church was such a burning issue in the Pauline epistles. On the surface, as already suggested, the problems to which they were addressed were different but underneath the surface, the unity of the church was at stake.

That this was the issue with the Corinthian congregation was quite obvious. There were a number of issues that contributed to the disruption of unity, all of which were expressions of a distorted understanding of the Spirit-filled life lived out as if they were still functioning in terms of the "present age" from which they had been delivered in principle but not in practice. Some perceived themselves to be a "spiritual aristocracy" as a result of their spiritual gifts so they were looking down on those who did not manifest those spectacular gifts. Some were possessed of superior theological understanding relating to the status of idols which other did not have, so they were snobbish about that. For Paul, all this falls short of reflecting the image of God, a shortfall that could be remedied by the "more excellent way" of love.

The problem with the Galatian churches was two-fold. The fundamental issue concerned the identity of the children of Abraham. What were the identifying marks of the community of faith? This was the watershed between the "gospel" Paul preached and the "non-gospel" being propagated by his Judaizing opponents (1:6-9). They were insisting that to be a part of the authentic community Gentiles should accept the marks of the children of Abraham according to the flesh, including particularly circumcision. Paul, on the other hand, argued that the authentic mark of the Christian community was faith in Jesus as Messiah and the presence of the Holy Spirit.[234]

One can now see that Paul's polemic at Galatia may best be understood as a polemic regarding identity symbols. Shall the people of God be identified by Torah or by Christ? Which symbol is

---

[234]This was the basis of Paul's insistence that there is no distinction between Jew and Greek, bond or free, male or female in Galatians 3:28-29.

appropriate for the present redemptive-historical circumstances? The polemic is not in the first place soteriological (that is, faith or works as instruments of justification) but eschatological (whether God has fulfilled the promises to Abraham by means of the Christ-event) and, by consequence, ecclesiological (whether the believing Gentiles are in fact full members of the covenant community).[235]

The second aspect of the problem was the question of the most effective norm for controlling behavior, whether the Torah or the Spirit. Paul's argument was that the Torah had served the temporary function of being a custodian for Israel (3:23) but was now superceded by Christ and the Spirit. Actually, as he had demonstrated in Romans, the Torah had been unable to accomplish its purpose due to the debilitating effects of "the flesh."

Underlying these issues as an implicit concern is the unity of the people of God. If Torah (circumcision, kosher food and Sabbath keeping) is the defining norm, it excluded the Gentiles.[236] As Jacob Neusner, a Jewish scholar said, "the most important meaning of the Torah lies in its defining who is Israel and who is not."[237] Paul is arguing for the principle of love so beautifully expressed in Edwin Markham's poem:

> "He drew a circle that shut me out-
> Heretic , rebel, a thing to flout.
> But love and I had the wit to win:
> We drew a circle and took him In !
>
> From the poem " Outwitted"

But there is a further implication for community life that Paul emphasizes. This implication comes to expression in his description of

---

[235]T. David Gordon, "The Problem at Galatia," *Interpretation* 41 (1987), 40.

[236]This speaks directly to the question of how Jesus fulfilled the law and his answer here invalidates the traditional distinction between the ceremonial and moral law as a means of explaining the matter.

[237]Quoted in Gordon, "Problem at Galatia," 38, n. 14.

the conflict between "flesh" (*sarx*) and "spirit" (*pneuma*). As Russell describes it: "He now rips back the curtain to reveal how the community of the *sarx* [flesh] will really function in the absence of the empowering work of the Spirit. Such a community stands in stark contrast to the functioning of the community of the *pneuma [Spirit]*."[238] Essentially it becomes a picture of how a legalistic understanding of the holy life is the seed bed for drawing distinctions between person in the community and thus disrupting the unity of the body. He describes the results of this in terms of animal behavior, "you will eat each other up" (5:15).

The drawing of boundaries based on legalistically applied behavioral standards has hounded the holiness movement from the beginning.[239] Many divisions that have occurred, rending the body of Christ and the witness of holiness, have been over issues of matters like dress and entertainment. In no sense is Paul promoting a position that leads to antinomianism. He makes that point explicitly. The essence of the Spirit-filled life is described as "faith working through love" (5:6) and is manifested in the fruit of the Spirit, all of which are expressions of love. Love will foster a relationship of serving one another that is the summation of the whole Mosaic law (5:13-15). Thus, as Russell sums up: "Ironically the end of the true gospel and its manifestation is the fulfillment of the basic purpose of the whole Mosaic law: loving edification of one's neighbor. In other words the law's fulfillment ultimately can be distilled into relational terms."[240]

That this is one essential aspect of what sanctification is all about makes it is a most disturbing fact that there is so much dissension within the ranks of those who identify themselves as a holiness church. From my earliest Christian life, I have had the unfortunate experience of observing what can only be characterized as "carnal" behavior among too many professors of the "second blessing." There have been too many cases of holiness churches racked with controversy over trivial issues, including fighting and

---

[238]Walter Bo Russell, "Does the Christian have 'Flesh' in Gal. 5:13-26," *Journal of the Evangelical Theological Society* 36/2 (June 1993), 184.

[239]Dunning, "Nazarene Ethics as Seen in a Theological, Historical and Sociological Perspective."

[240]Russell, "Does the Christian Have Flesh," 185, n. 27.

squabbling among church members and between congregations. Does this invalidate the truth of sanctification? God forbid! What it does is to highlight the necessity of a sounder understanding of what is involved in the sanctifying grace of God other than the expectation of an automatic removal of an internal entity that results in automatic saintliness.

Relation to the Earth. Included in the divine intention in creating humanity is the charge to "have dominion" over the natural order. This was a mandate to exercise responsible stewardship over the earth and all its non-human products and inhabitants. The basis for this responsibility is the goodness of creation, which stands in contradiction to all forms of Gnosticism, a teaching that flourished in the 2nd century but still poses a threat to authentic biblical faith. Its basic premise was that matter (including the body) is evil, only spirit is good. This means that the physical universe is of no consequence so you can either ignore it or indulge it without consequence to the spirit. Since the body is the shell of the spirit, salvation is seen as escape from history and this world. Since it is evil, this world is destined for the trash can and thus there is no need to exercise particular care for it, precisely the opposite of what the Creator intended for his good creation.

This relation reminds us that holiness is a very earthly reality. As William Temple stated in a classic passage: Christianity "is the most avowedly materialist of all the great religions."[241] This explains why the land plays such a prominent role in the Old Testament. Abraham is promised a land, a promise renewed to the Israelite slaves in Egypt and eventually given to them in the conquest of Canaan. But it was given to them with conditions and if those conditions were not kept the result would be the loss of the land. This is, of course, what eventually happened in 587 B.C. in the Babylonian captivity.

The central question for us here concerns the purpose for the gift of the land. Since Israel's election involved living out the Creator's intention for the human race in their corporate life as embodied in the image of God, they were to demonstrate in their relation to the land how God intended the stewardship to be carried out

---

[241]William Temple, *Nature, Man and God* (London: Macmillan & Co., 1935), 478.

and the law gave numerous instructions to that end. Actually, the rabbis came to understand the gift of the land to be more than a small strip of real estate along the coast of the Mediterranean Sea, it included the whole earth. This is one reason the land disappears as a factor in the New Testament, its meaning doubtless summarized in Jesus' eschatological statement that "the meek shall inherit the earth." In one sense the responsibility for the earth appears to be assumed in the New Testament by ones relation to his or her possessions. On that subject, Luke T. Johnson says, "The way we use, own, acquire and dispense material things symbolizes and expresses our attitude and responses to ourselves, the world around us, other people, and, most of all, God."[242]

The failure to observe the mandate of stewardship has resulted in environmental difficulties and other problems that have caused this dimension of humanity's God-appointed destiny to force itself upon modern consciousness. Holiness people should be particularly sensitive to this issue since it is native to the *telos* they are (or should be) pursuing.

Relation to Self. It should now be clear how interwoven in all three of the other relations is the place of the self. Implicit in each of the other relations is a focus upon God and his glory so that the Lord is the determinative partner in the divine-human relation and this gives character to the others. This is not, however, a relation that is impersonal, arbitrary or forced but free. The logical consequence is that the relation can be upset if the free partner (*'adam*) decides to dissolve the situation of the Lordship of the creator and assume an equal partnership or usurp the prerogatives of the Creator. This possibility was actualized in the Fall, which basically takes the form of a "revolt against heaven."

Analysts of contemporary culture tell us that the prophets of the modern world are Friedrich Nietzsche, Karl Marx and Sigmund Freud. For them, instead of relationship, worship and stewardship being the norm of human life, the new normal is money (Marx), Sex (Freud) and Power (Nietzsche).

N.T. Wright makes the astute observation that these three philosophers describe a fallen world. It is the world in which we live in the 21st century, a world that is marked by forces that dehumanize mankind because those forces are antithetical to the elements that

---

[242]*Sharing Possessions*, (Philadelphia: Fortress Press, 1981), 40.

characterize the image of God which embodies the nature of true and authentic humanity. How important it then is for those who claim to be holiness people, sanctified by consecration through the power of the Holy Spirit to "reflect the divine image," to be shining examples of what the Creator God intended his creation to be, in a word, be the "light of the world."

Chapter 6
Entire Sanctification

Thesis: While not a biblical term, entire sanctification may be an exegetically sound designation of an aspect of Christian experience when referred to the whole person rather than to the act/process of renewing humanity in the image of God.

We observed in the Introduction that the ultimate criterion of claims about Christian experience must be the exegesis of relevant Biblical texts seen in the context of the whole tenor of scripture. It is in this light that we propose to explore the central claim of the modern holiness movement beginning with John Wesley, which is the possibility of a spiritual experience referred to as entire sanctification or Christian perfection.[243]

While reference to "perfection" (without a qualifier) is found in several texts in both Old Testament and New Testament, the term "entire sanctification" is not. In fact the one passage that can be cited in support of this terminology is 1 Thessalonians 5:23-4: "May the God of peace himself sanctify you entirely; and may your spirit and soul and body be kept sound and blameless at the coming of the Lord Jesus Christ. The one who calls you is faithful, and he will do this." It

---

[243]John L. Peters points out that on occasion Wesley seemed to distinguish between these terms, "a distinction which he generally fails to maintain." *Christian Perfection and American Methodism*, 52. Hoo-Jung Lee, "The Doctrine of New Creation in the Theology of John Wesley," argues that Wesley's cosmic vision militates against an individualistic interpretation of sanctification and in that context implies that Christian perfection is a *telos* fully actualized only in the eschaton. Mildred Wynkoop's critique of Wesley at this point is telling. She points out that when Wesley identified full sanctification and Christian perfection he created considerable ambiguity. The reason: "All the *practical* advice he gave weakens his own position at this point. That is, when he related perfection to the human situation, the 'absolute' of sanctification was no longer 'perfect'." Her conclusion was that "we could be justified in concluding that it is not quite accurate to equate the fullness of sanctification with Christian perfection." *Theology of Love*, 270, 300. R. Newton Flew's classic work, *The Idea of Perfection in Christian Theology: an historical study of the Christian ideal for the present life* (N.Y.: Humanities Press, 1968), as the full title suggests, demonstrates that throughout Christian history, Christian perfection has been viewed as the *telos*, rather than a full attainment, in the pursuit of the deeper life.

appears that the meaning of the concept hangs on the proper exegesis of this passage.[244] The first thing to note is that this is a prayer. Paul's prayers for his converts, it has been suggested, embody his theological understanding of the sanctified life.[245] If we place this prayer in the larger context of the first letter to the Thessalonian church we may get a reasonably clear idea of its intention. The exhortation in 4:1-8 strongly suggests that what Paul had in mind was the ethical dimension of the life of the church. The believers at Thessalonica had been immersed in a culture characterized by idolatry (1:9), and sexual immorality (4:3). Whether 4:3-4 is translated (or interpreted) as referring to ones own body (NEB) or to marital fidelity to one's wife (RSV) the concern is sexual purity in either case. Unlike converts from Judaism, who generally lived by high moral standards, converted pagans were in need of intensive instruction in Christian ethical mores.

In the light of this central emphasis of the letter, his prayer in 5:23-24 logically implies this same ethical concern. The language used, ("wholly" [holoteleis] and "entire" [holoklaron]), clearly indicates that his prayer has in view the entirety of both the church's life,[246] and the whole person. The New English Bible captures this significance by its rendering, "May God himself, the God of peace, make you [ethically] holy in every part." Luther's translation, adopted by the New International Version, of "through and through" likewise emphasizes the wholeness that Paul has in mind. Unfortunately in too many cases, tradition has taken precedence over sound exegesis and claimed that the passage teaches entire sanctification as "a complete

---

[244]Wayne McCown, "God's Will . . . For You; Sanctification in the Thessalonian Epistles," *Wesleyan Theological Journal*, vol. 12, Spring 1977, 26-33, points out that the sanctificationist texts in these letters have been widely used by holiness scholars but their use is "generally incidental and/or supportive. One senses that they are regarded as important texts, comprising part of the biblical basis for the doctrine of sanctification. However, they are seldom accorded an extended expositional treatment."

[245]Cf. W.E. McCumber, *Holiness in the Prayers of St. Paul* (K.C.: Beacon Hill Press of Kansas City, 1955). A prayer similar to this one is found in Philippians 1:9-11, where the essence of the holy life is viewed as love.

[246]The second person pronouns are plural but obviously each individual is involved in the corporate life of the church.

[and final] cleansing from all sin."[247] To the contrary John Wesley soundly comments on this passage: "every part and all that concerns you; all that is of or about you."[248]

The reference to the "God of peace" further carries the idea of wholeness in relation to the entire scope of life's relations. The Greek word *eirēnē* is informed by the Hebrew *shalom*. This term, though commonly used as a greeting, is pregnant with meaning. It carries the significance of "harmony of an individual with himself, with nature, with the world of people, and clearly with God, the Creator."[249] Kent Brower describes this peace as "the wholeness and completeness of the individual centered on God. It contrasts with the disorder, disintegration, and chaos that characterize all of humanity's relationships since the Fall."[250]

The theme of wholeness that pervades the entire passage is self-consciously emphasized by Paul's reference to "spirit, soul and body." This reference, and its relation to the concept of sanctification, implies that we must do a brief survey of Paul's anthropology. James D. G. Dunn reminds us that "We . . . will never begin adequately to appreciate Paul's theology unless we understand his anthropology" and points out that all the most relevant anthropological terms are found in "the first main theme of Paul's exposition in Romans: *sōma* [body] (1:24); *sarx*[flesh] (2:28; 3:20); *kardia* [heart] (1:21, 24; 2:5, 15, 21); *nous* [mind] (1:28); *psychē* [soul] (2:9); *pneuma* [spirit] (2:29); and *syneidēsis* [conscience] (2:15).[251]

---

[247]Ralph Earle, *Sanctification in the New Testament*, 45.

[248]*Notes on the New Testament* (London: Epworth Press, 1954), 763.

[249]Elmer Martens, *God's Design*, 28. It should be recognized that these relations constitute the image of God. (cf. chapter 4)

[250]Kent E. Brower, "1Thessalonians," *Asbury Bible Commentary* ed. Eugene E. Carpenter & Wayne McCown (Grand Rapids: Zondervan Publishing Company, 1992), 1103.

[251]James D. G. Dunn, *The Theology of Paul the Apostle*, 51, 51.n. 1. Cf. also W. David Stacey, *The Pauline View of Man* (London: MacMillan, 1956); D. E. H. Whiteley, *The Theology of St. Paul* (Oxford: Basil Blackwell, 1964), 38ff; N.T. Wright, "Mind, Spirit, Soul and Body: All for One and One for All, Reflections of Paul's Anthropology," Lecture given to the Society of Christian Philosophers, March

W. D. Stacey, comparing the Pauline anthropology with other options in the ancient world, is willing to allow the possibility of some Hellenistic influence, basically in the use of certain terms, but concludes:

> Paul's approach to anthropology was synthetic, not analytic. The Hebrew did not see man as a combination of contrasted elements, but as a unity that might be seen under a number of different aspects. Behind each aspect was the whole personality. Platonism, Orphism, and the Greek view generally, provide the opposite point of view. In this matter, Paul was in the Hebrew tradition. Every word in Paul refers to the whole man. *Sarx*, the usual term for man as a fallible creature, can, when man is viewed under a different aspect, become a means of serving God, for that other aspect will include the whole man and, therefore, the *sarx*. In the same way, *pneuma* could become involved in sin. The use of *psychē, pneuma, sarx, soma* and *kardia*, to describe man as a unity under various aspects is conclusive evidence of the Semitic cast of Paul's mind, and further proof is not necessary.[252]

The consensus of New Testament scholars soundly rejects both a dualism and a trichotomy of the human person.[253] Whiteley suggests

---

18, 2011.

[252]Stacey, *Paul's View of Man, 222-3.* Stacey offers an additional caveat by suggesting that some of Paul's anthropology is derived from neither Hebrew nor Greek sources but revelation, thus unique: "Pauline Christianity does not appear to be either Hellenism or Judaism or a mixture of the two. Some other dominant influence is clearly at work. May it not be that this influence was revelation? It may well prove that the driving power of Paul's faith was an understanding of God that was hidden from the Greeks, and not revealed to the prophets or the Rabbis, but was revealed to Paul. In the life, trial, and death of Jesus, some of which Paul may well have observed, in the Resurrection, and above all, in the encounter near Damascus, a revelation was made to Paul which, in due time, was followed by the appearance, in the form of letters, of a faith which we know as Pauline Christianity," 55.

[253]David J.A. Clines stated that "recent biblical scholarship has been well-nigh unanimous in rejecting the traditional view of man as a 'composition' of various 'parts,' and has emphasized rather that in the biblical view man is essentially a unity. When this insight is applied to the doctrine of the image, it is difficult to resist the conclusion that the whole man is in the image of God." "The Image of God in Man,"

that the contrast between the two anthropologies (Hellenistic and Hebrew) can be made by the terms *aspectivally* (Hebrew) and *partitively* (Greek) and adds, "It is fair to say that the anthropological language of the Biblical writings is aspectival, not partitive.[254] Simply put, following Plato, Hellenism held that the human person is composed of parts. If this anthropology were to be taken as definitive for 1 Thessalonians 5:24, there are three parts to the person. It thus becomes possible to articulate a doctrine of holiness by defining the function of each part in isolation from the whole person. But no contemporary biblical scholar would agree with this interpretation of Paul's anthropology. As Whiteley observes, "The language is trichotomistic, it is true: the thought is monistic, both in the anthropological and in the metaphysical sense. The threefold formula may be due to some liturgical tradition, but St. Paul employs it to express the prayer that the whole man will be preserved and kept holy."[255] Or as Wright says, it is "a multi-faceted description of the whole."[256] H. Wheeler Robinson affirms the same perspective: "this is not a systematic dissection of the distinct elements of personality; its true analogy is such an Old Testament sentence as Deut. vi.5, where a somewhat similar enumeration emphasizes the totality of the personality."[257] It is common knowledge that this Old Testament passage and its repetition by Jesus in the New is John Wesley's standard definition of "entire sanctification," or "Christian perfection."

The summative commandment includes two additional pertinent anthropological terms: heart *(kardia)* and soul *(psychē)*. The

---

57.

[254]*The Theology of St. Paul*, 36.

[255]Ibid. 37. Mildred Bangs Wynkoop, in commenting on this passage, says "Paul was not teaching that man is composed of these unrelated elements of personality. He was telling them that God's grace brings purity to the entire human personality." *Foundations of Wesleyan-Arminian Theology*, 76-7.

[256]"Mind, Spirit, Soul and Body," 13.

[257]H. Wheeler Robinson, *The Christian Doctrine of Man* (Edinburgh: T. & T. Clark, 1972), 108. Mildred Wynkoop affirms this position in her critique: "Ontological trichotomy, a recent revival of Gnostic thought in some Christian circles, undermines a concept of the unity of personality so basically assumed in Hebrew thought." *Theology of Love*, 50.

New Testament use of these terms is quite fluid but a general understanding can be derived from Stacey's detailed analyses.[258] "Heart" is used figuratively as the "seat of the emotions" and is sometimes equivalent to love (Philippians 1:8 and 2:1). As with all anthropological terms, heart refers to one aspect of the whole person and "tends to express the inward and hidden in contrast to the outward and revealed," as for instance the distinction Paul makes between two types of circumcision, "one formal and outward, and one of the heart, which is inward." "From the heart springs conduct, both good and bad. Emotions, decisions, intentions or judgments, seated in the heart, may be praiseworthy or otherwise." In the light of these functions, Rudolf Bultmann concludes, "Clearly the heart is not a higher principle in man . . . but just the intending, purposing self—which decides within itself or is moved from without—which can turn to either the good or the bad." It would be fair to say that the "heart" refers to the volitional aspect of the person. Stacey concludes from this that Paul diverges from the teaching of the Rabbis who held that the heart is the seat of the "evil impulse." For Paul, he says, "evil is at home in the flesh, not the heart." The implication of this analysis, in light of Paul's understanding of *sarx* (see below and Appendix A) is that one cannot identify a separable aspect of the person to be "removed," but as with other anthropological terms, in its ethical use *sarx* refers to the whole person as fallen.

Psychē is used by Paul, in continuity with the Old Testament, to refer to the animating principle of man; it designates man as a living being. He does not use it to refer to "life" in general but rather to "that specifically human state of being alive which inheres in man as a striving, willing, purposing self." It is important to note that the Greek view of the soul cannot be found in Paul, which is reflected in the fact that he never uses soul and body together for the whole man. *Psychē* is not used extensively, because, as Stacey concludes, "Paul, with his theocentric faith, saw man in relation to God, and realized that the highest and best [*pneuma*], was derived from God," resulting in his

---

[258]The entire discussion here is dependent on Stacey, *Pauline View of Man*, 194-197; 121-127.The quote from Bultmann is from his *New Testament Theology*, 1:221.

making *pneuma* central with *psychē* having a lesser function. This, says Stacey, is derived from his own experience of the Spirit, which is the distinctive feature of life in the "age to come," and became the "basis of his anthropology." *Pneuma* thus may be simply identified as referring to the whole person in relation to God through the Spirit.

This understanding has extensive implications for the biblical interpretation of the doctrine of original sin. In discussing the understanding of original sin in the Protestant reformers, Luther and Calvin, Thomas Noble points out that both have a holistic understanding of man, various references, such as "flesh" and "spirit," being descriptions of the whole person from different aspects. This implies that original sin is "not simply something *in* us, not even a kind of disease or tendency." It means that, "although there is much that is good ethically in us, nonetheless we are fallen as a whole."[259]

This concept of wholeness that informs both biblical anthropology and the classical Protestant reformers has significant implications for the claim of traditional holiness theology that entire sanctification entails the "eradication" of original sin. The typical defense of this claim is based on an argument that contradicts the wholeness of the human person. One way of doing this is to differentiate the body from the soul, implying a Platonic dualism. Even John Wesley seems to take this course as the result of his empiricist epistemology. He identifies the "fallenness" or source of "sin improperly so-called" with the effects of the Fall on the body. Since these "sins" are the result of ignorance and misunderstanding, not intention, he explains this by what to contemporary thought is a strange theory to demonstrate how the understanding became distorted and darkened. His commitment to an empiricist theory of knowledge (*a la* John Locke) led him to say that since the understanding is informed by the bodily senses, the body was first corrupted leading to distorted communication to the understanding. As a result "it mistook falsehood for truth, and truth for falsehood."[260]

---

[259]T. A. Noble, "Doctrine of Original Sin in the Evangelical Reformers," *European Explorations in Christian Holiness*, Summer, 2001. Although inconsistent with his larger discussion, H. Orton Wiley refers to original sin as "a privation of the image of God." And concludes that "This is more in harmony with the tenor of the Scriptures than the notion of an "infusion of evil qualities into the soul as a result of the divine degree (sic)." *Christian Theology*, 2:123.

[260]Wesley proposed the theory that the forbidden fruit contained a "juice"

The defense commonly made by the 19th century holiness theologians used "depravity" to cover the consequence of the Fall for both body and soul but a distinction is made between the physical consequences that will continue until death and the "residue of sin in the moral nature of the regenerated believer" which is separable. The claim is then made that "it is only the moral taint, the virus in the blood stream of the spiritual man," which can be separated and eradicated. The separable element has also been referred to as a "nature" not inherent in created humanity and is "separable" from the person whose condition it represents. The argument is that "if . . . the term *original sin* is to be stretched to include man's total ab- or sub-normalities, then we must distinguish between an inner spiritual core that is eradicable and an 'outer layer' that is ineradicable but will only yield to the spiritual disciplines of growth in grace. Rather than so extending the term *original sin*, it would seem more consistent to differentiate it from the amoral scars of sin."[261]

How did this understanding arise? What was its origin? We are apparently faced with a curious anomaly. There is considerable evidence that the references to "sin" in terms suggesting a "substance," as well as the prominent use of "eradication" and similar terms, in the late 19th century holiness movement is the result of the influence of the emergence (or re-emergence) of a "two-nature" interpretation of the Christian life in the early 19th century. According to this theory, in regeneration a "new nature" is transplanted within the believer that continues to co-exist with the "old nature" until ended by death. These two natures are present in such a way that they function independently

---

that when ingested into the human body began a process that in modern terms would be termed the hardening of the arteries and the accumulation of cholesterol in the bloodstream. This is what distorted the instrument of the body so that it could not contribute true information to the "soul." In a sense he was really ahead of his day in recognizing these factors as limiting the human life span. Albert Outler, Ed., *The Works of John Wesley, The Sermons*. 4 vols.(Nashville: Abingdon Press, 1984-85), 4:298

[261]A summary of James B. Chapman, *The Terminology of Sin*, 32-35; H. Orton Wiley, *Christian Theology*, 2:119f; Richard S. Taylor, *Exploring Christian Holiness*, 3:92-93.

of each other. For all practical purposes, the believer is a "split personality." The "new nature" is the basis of the believer's acceptance by God while the old "sinful nature" is the source of the sinfulness of the believer. There is a lifelong struggle between these two natures with the "sinful nature" sometimes dominating the ethical life of the believer. This in no way affects the believer's relation to God since there is no necessity of a holy life. Thus sanctification is significantly disparaged. In fact, the idea of sanctification is referred to negatively as being an attempt to earn acceptance with God by good works. It is obvious that this opens the door to rampant antinomianism.

Academic research has demonstrated rather conclusively that this two-nature theory was introduced and popularized in the modern world by John Nelson Darby (1800-1882) and the Plymouth Brethren, also the source of the new version of premillenialism called Dispensationalism.[262] Walter Russell confirms this chronology in noting that "Throughout most of the history of the Christian church, theologians have not spoken of human beings possessing a 'sin nature' or a 'new nature,' but only of possessing *human* nature. However, within the last century or so the behavior of humans has been attributed by certain Christian writers to the possession of either a 'sin nature' or a 'new nature'"[263] This teaching exerted a wide influence among evangelical preachers and teachers including Dwight L. Moody, A.J. Gordon, H. A. Ironside, and through the Bible edited by C.I. Scofield, multitudes of both clergy and lay people. It was this teaching that influenced the choice of the translation commitee of the 1973 version of the New International Version to translate *flesh (sarx)* as "sinful nature" in various New Testament passages.[264]

---

[262]Juan Ramon Sanchez, Jr., "The old man versus the new man in the doctrine of sanctification: A critique of the two-nature theory," M.Th. thesis, Southern Baptist Theological Seminary, 2002; Brian K. Sandifer, "A Critical Analysis of the Two Nature View of Regenerate Man: Toward an Understanding of the Cause of Sin in the Life of the Believer," Ph.D. diss, Southeastern Baptist Theological Seminary, 2010.

[263]Walter Russell, "The Apostle Paul's View of the 'Sin Nature'/'New Nature' Struggle," in *Christian Perspectives on Being Human: a Multidisciplinary Approach to Integration* ed. J. P. Moreland and David M. Ciocchi (Grand Rapids: Baker, 1993), 207-8.

[264]Prior to the appearance of the NIV, a group of holiness theologians

One of the early holiness scholars, Daniel Steele, wrote an extended attack on this two-nature theory with the title *Antinomianism Revived* (1887). The connection with Darby and the Plymouth Brethren was emphasized and their teaching clearly articulated. Steele referred to their divisive character resulting in splits into several Brethren groups but observed: "But in the worst of their theological tenets they are quite generally agreed -- their Antinomianism. We have heard Mr. Darby say that if any man had anything to do with the law of God, even to obey it, he was a sinner by that very act."

The following excerpts make Steele's concerns quite clear as he reflects considerable acumen in theological debate:

Their primal error seems to be in their conception of the Atonement. They teach that sin, as a kind of personality, was condemned on the cross of Christ and put away forever. Whose sins? Those of the believer. All his sins past, present, and future, are "judged" and swept away forever in the Atonement, and the believer is to have no more concern for his past or future sins, since they were blotted out eighteen hundred years ago. Here is their most mischievous tenet respecting faith and its relation to the Atonement and to eternal life: In regeneration, the new man is created in the believer, and the old man remains with all his powers unchanged. Mr. Darby asserted to the writer that after more than fifty years of Christian experience he found the old man in himself worse than he was at his regeneration. Says McIntosh: "It is no part of the work of "the Holy Spirit to improve human nature, -- that seems to be past praying for, -- but to make a brand new man to dwell in the same body with the old man till physical death luckily comes and kills the old Adam who had successfully defied all power in heaven and earth effectually to crucify him.[265]

---

protested this rendering, pointing out that translating the term *sarx* this way was a commentary (technically, a *gloss*) rather than a translation. A modest concession was made but the terminology remained. Because of this, W.M. Greathouse in his commentary on Romans pointed out that the (pre-2011) NIV's rendering "makes it virtually impossible to use it as the basis for a faithful interpretation of the original Greek. . ." *New Beacon Bible Commentary*, 218. This translation was changed in the 2011 revision of the NIV to *flesh*.

[265]Daniel Steele, *Antinomianism Revived*, digital reproduction, NNU website. The second part of this book was an attack on the new version of

A somewhat later holiness writer, Henry E. Brockett, likewise wrote a book challenging the two-nature theory as taught by H.A. Ironside in his book, *Holiness the False and the True*, a classic attack on Christian perfection. Brockett's concern was the same as Steele's, the implication for the holy life. The explicit antinomian implications of the teaching was his central point of attack.[266]

However, neither Steele nor Brockett challenged the two-nature teaching on either philosophical or exegetical grounds. They merely opposed the antinomian implications of the teaching. Perhaps this was largely because of the period of time in which they wrote when scientific biblical studies had not developed (or their ultra-conservative attitude removed it from their purview[267]) or partly because the holiness proponents were largely dependent on proof-text defenses of their beliefs. But the soundest refutation of the two-nature theory would have been to call attention to biblical anthropology. The wholeness of the human person in biblical thought would have decisively refuted the possibility of a dualism of the human person suggested by the Darby theory.

A further result of this study suggests that the 19th century holiness theologians accepted the two-nature theory but responded differently.[268] The chronology of the period implies that this acceptance was the catalyst for the emergence of the prominent

premillenialism taught by Darby, known as Dispensationalism. Steele was himself, a post-millenialist.

[266]Henry E. Brockett, *Scriptural Freedom from Sin* (K.C: Beacon Hill Press, first printing 1941).

[267]Cf. Wesley Tracy, "Foreword," H. Ray Dunning, *Becoming Christlike Disciples*, 4.

[268]Henry Brockett is an example of one who, though attacking the antinomian implications of the two-nature theory (see above) retained it and argued that the "old nature" was eradicated. *Scriptural Freedom*, 54-59. In his more recent theology of sanctification, Richard S. Taylor devoted an entire section in defense of the "two-nature theory," following the so-called "Augustinian-Dispensational" interpretation as taught by C.I. Scofield, Lewis Sperry Chafer and John Walvoord, including arguing for its validity on the basis of the creedal interpretation of the Person of Christ as involving "one person in two natures." Unfortunately this both misunderstands the Creed and implies the Christological heresy of Nestorianism.

emphasis on the "eradication" of the "carnal nature," which implicitly referred to the "old nature" as seen by the two-nature theory, virtually treated as an entity within the believer. Leroy Lindsey, in his Ph.D. dissertation, has demonstrated that it was in this period when such language began to be used by holiness writers. During what he designated as the "First Generation" (1837-1875) the "Holiness writers did not see the destruction of sin in the human heart as an end in itself. Sin had to be removed in order for the heart to be filled with love, which was the actual goal."[269] The controversy with which they were primarily concerned was whether entire sanctification was gradual or instantaneous. They did, however, use seminal language anticipating the later more radical language of "eradication." The "common terms American Methodists of that era employed to describe the 'deliverance' from sin they believed to be inherent in sanctification" were "purify," "destroy," and "cleanse."[270] The first direct use of the term "eradicate" appears to be in the mid-thirties by a Methodist preacher named John Lindsey of Connecticut in a sermon at the New England annual conference.

During the "second generation" (1875-1900), the "eradication" of inbred sin tended to become an end in itself. One of the more significant factors in creating a polemical situation regarding the issue was the emergence of the Keswick movement in England. Rather than emphasizing the "eradication" of sin, Keswick spoke about the "suppression" of sin by the power of the Holy Spirit. This clearly reflected the "two nature" understanding as did the "second blessing" wing of the holiness movement. Both theologies would have been better served with a biblical anthropology that might have provided them with a sounder vehicle for dealing with the issue of sin and its relation to sanctification.[271]

---

[269]Leroy E. Lindsey, "Radical Remedy: The eradication of sin and related terminology in Wesleyan-Holiness thought, 1875-1925, Ph.D. diss. Drew University, 1996, 55. It is evident in this dissertation that the author is concerned throughout to defend the "radical remedy" for sin embodied in the concept of "eradication." As a result he does not come to terms with the real theological or biblical issues.

[270]Ibid. 62.

[271]For a clear-cut assumption of the two-nature theory arguing for the

A tremendous advance is reflected in the comments of W. M. Greathouse on Romans 6:5-6—"The traditional KJV translation, 'our old man is crucified with him,' is problematic on several counts. If the conviction Paul expressed in Gal 2:20 are presumed here, the 'old man' cannot refer to some 'thing' or 'nature' within us that must be extracted. It is not an alien, cancerous tumor living metaphorically within us that dies—*we* die in some real, yet figurative, sense. We cannot identify 'the old man' with 'carnality' or 'the sinful nature,' as some nineteenth-century Holiness interpreters did. "Our 'old man' must be the sinful persons we once were, our former pre-Christian selves, the old Adam that once defined our existence as humans."[272] (For an exegetical analysis of terms, such as "old man/new man," used to refer to the "two-natures" in the 19th century holiness teaching, see Appendix A.)

To understand further the wholeness for which Paul prays, we will seek to examine the several additional terms he uses to refer to the human person. But each of these must be considered as referring to various aspects of the whole person. Whiteley's illustration of the *aspective* way of reference makes this clear: "we speak of [man] aspectively when we call him an Englishman, not a German, or a Methodist, not a Congregationalist; the whole man is Methodist, so that Methodism is not a part of the man, but an aspect of him."[273] It should further be noted that all the anthropological terms are relational in nature, i.e. they refer to one aspect of the complex of relations that constitute the nature of the human. In particular, as John A. T. Robinson points out, Paul discusses anthropological issues in terms of mankind's relation to God: "All Hebrew thinking [Paul was a Hebrew, not a Greek philosopher] was done, as it were, in [the] vertical dimension of man's relatedness to God as a creature and as a fallen creature. . . . Consequently, all words pertaining to the life and constitution of man are to be seen as designating or qualifying this fundamental relationship of man to God."[274]

"destruction" of the sinful nature, see Brockett, *Scriptural Freedom from Sin*, 54-63.

[272]*Romans 1-8*, 182.

[273]Whiteley, *Theology of St. Paul*, 36.

[274]John A. T. Robinson, *The Body* (Philadelphia: Westminster Press, 1952), 16.

Paul's use of anthropological terms, however, cannot be reduced to a textbook type analysis since there is a certain looseness about his use of them, with overlaps and duplications. As Stacey states succinctly, "Paul was not always precise in his use of words."[275] N.T. Wright offers this warning: "Paul uses over a dozen terms to refer to what humans are and what they do, and since he nowhere either provides a neat summary of what he thinks about them or gives us clues as to whether he would subsume some or most of these under two or three heads, it is arbitrary and unwarranted to do so on his behalf or claim his authority for such a scheme."[276] This suggests that the most appropriate way of getting at Paul's understanding is by looking at the use of the relevant terms in particular texts. One of the most fruitful of such texts is Romans 12:1-2. Wright describes this passage as "dense as any passage in Paul."[277] The Apostle here urges his audience to "present their *bodies* as a living sacrifice" (emphasis added).

John A. T. Robinson asserts that "The concept of the body forms the keystone of Paul's theology. In its closely inter-connected meanings, the word *sōma* knits together all his great themes."[278] This term, like many others, has a spectrum of meaning. Dunn suggests using the term "embodiment" meaning that *sōma* refers to the embodiment of the person. In this sense it is a relational concept. "It denotes the person embodied in a particular environment. It is the means by which the person relates to that environment, and vice versa." It "means more than my physical body: it is the embodied 'me,' the means by which 'I' and the world can act upon each other."[279] "In short, *sōma* gives Paul's theology an unavoidably social and ecological dimension."[280] Wright's summary captures this perspective:

---

[275] *Pauline View of Man*, 123.

[276]Wright, "Mind, Spirit, Soul and Body," 5.

[277]*New Interpreter's Bible*, 10:703.

[278]Robinson, *The Body*, 9.

[279]Dunn, *Theology of Paul, 56.*

". . . the point of 'body' is not that it refers to one part only of the human totality, but that it refers to the complete person seen from one point of view: the point of view in which the human being lives as a physical object within space and time."[281] John A. T. Robinson emphasizes this point by contrasting the Hebrew concept of the body with the Greek. For the latter the body is the "principle of individuation, that which marks off and isolates one man from another." The Hebrew, on the contrary, saw the body as "what bound him in the bundle of life with all men and nature, so that he could never make his unique answer to God as an isolated individual, apart from his relation to his neighbor."[282]

In understanding the Pauline use of *sōma*, it is important to explore a brief analysis of the use of *sarx*, literally translated *flesh*. Like other terms Paul uses in his references to humanity, this one also has a variety of implications. For our purposes, we focus only on what can be referred to as the moral or ethical use. In this sense, "man as *sarx* is thus involved in an order of creation which is, at one and the same time, of God's willing and yet in antagonism to Him. . ." *kata sarka*, in this use, describes the "state of opposition to God and Christ" and is referred to in Romans 8:5 as "living according to the flesh" and is opposed to living "according to the Spirit."[283] John A. T. Robinson summarizes the relation between *sarx* and *sōma*: "*While sarx stands for man, in the solidarity of creation, in his distance from God, sōma stands for man, in the solidarity of creation, as made for God.*"[284] Consistent with the Hebraic understanding of how anthropological language is holistic in its reference, W.M. Greathouse says that "by 'flesh' [*sarx*] Paul means the total person alienated from the life of God and therefore under the control of sin."[285] Or as Stacy says, "sarx

---

[280]Ibid. 61.

[281]*New Interpreter's Bible*, 10:704.

[282]*The Body*, 15.

[283]Ibid. 23.

[284]*The Body*, 31. Emphasis his.

[285]W.M. Greathouse, "A Pauline Theology of Sanctification," *Biblical*

represents the whole man in his proneness to sin."[286] It can be used adjectivally of all the other anthropological terms.[287]

Paul's appeal in Romans 12:1 is to "present your bodies a living sacrifice" The use of sacrificial language is derived from the cult and implies the understanding of the relation between purity and sanctification developed in chapter 3. The sacrifice that is "pleasing to God" is one that has been qualified by cleansing through the blood of Christ, and validated by the witness of the Spirit that the one who presents him or her self to God has been vindicated as a child of God, i.e. justified. In a word, this exhortation is a call for sanctification as a consecration to an ethical lifestyle based on the merciful action of God. This is why the following ethical teaching in Romans 12-15 takes the form of the relation between the indicative and imperative mood.

Verse 2 adds to this appeal by introducing the element of the "transformation of the mind." One of the most significant anthropological terms used by Paul is *nous*, translated as mind. It is the word Paul uses for man when the reasoning aspect is determinative, for man using his powers of judgment. Its importance in the context of sanctification along with *sōma* comes to expression in this pivotal passage. The Greek word translated "transformed" is *metamorphoo* from which we get our term *metamorphosis*.

What is the role of the "mind" and its transformation in Paul's soteriology? Mind (*nous*) like the other anthropological terms is a way of referring to a particular "aspect" of the whole person. As N. T. Wright notes, "In the New Testament "mind"—*nous* or *dianoia*—is

---

Resources for Holiness Preaching, 2 vols. Ed. H. Ray Dunning and Neil B. Wiseman (K.C.: Beacon Hill Press of Kansas City, 1990), 1:37. Also in "Sanctification and the Christus Victor Motif," *Wesleyan Theological Journal*, vol. 38, No. 2, Fall, 2003, 221, n. 18.

[286]*Pauline View of Man*, 202.

[287]Cf. Richard E. Howard, *Newness of Life* (K.C.: Beacon Hill Press of Kansas City, 1975), 29: "It will help us to better understand the term *flesh* if we realize that it has a strong *descriptive* significance, which we normally associate with an adjective. For all practical purposes it is used as an adjective—in an absolute sense. The object which it modifies is not stated but is provided by the context. Thus you need to ask first—flesh *what*?"

not the name of a superior or more 'real' element. The mind and the understanding can be 'darkened,' distorted, unable to grasp reality and so encouraging all kinds of dehumanizing behaviour."[288]

It is that latter aspect of mind to which Paul refers in Romans 1:18-32. It is also the reason why he exhorts his readers in 12:2 to "be transformed by the renewal of your minds." In the context of the eschatological dualism that informs his theology, he is concerned that the directing, controlling aspect of the person be no longer conformed to "the present evil age" but now conformed to "the age to come." N.T. Wright's commentary captures the radical significance of this exhortation:

> . . . as Paul insisted in 1:18-32, the human mind and heart are, in their natural state, dark and rebellious, full of wickedness and evil. What is required is not for people simply to learn to live authentically, without external pressure, but for them to be renewed, so that what proceeds from the transformed mind does indeed reflect the image of God. . . . Paul holds out a vision of a mind renewed, able now at last to think for itself what will please God, instead of being darkened by the deceitfulness of sin."[289]

The nature of the transformed mind is seen in Paul's repeated reference to "the mind of Christ" (1 Cor. 2:16; Phil. 2:5-11; cf. also 1 Peter 4:1). Having the "mind of Christ" results in a relationship within the community of faith likewise characterized by "the same mind" (Rom. 12:16; 2 Cor. 13:11), which is the basis of unity in the Spirit. As Stacey explains: "Whether in individual or community, the result of the Spirit's ministrations is always the strengthening of ethical life, the imparting of spiritual gifts, and, supremely, the cultivation of faith, love and unity."[290]

N.T. Wright's summary of Romans 12:1-2 is instructive:

---

[288]"Mind, Spirit, Soul and Body," 10.

[289]*New Interpreter's Bible*, 10:705.

[290]*Pauline View of Man*, 131.

Paul seems to be saying three interlocking things. First, offering your body (by which he here means your whole self) to God is the utterly fitting thing to do, since God has redeemed you and will transform that body to be like the risen body of Jesus Christ, a transformation which you must anticipate in appropriate behavior here and now. Second, this self-offering is not merely of your body, but of your body as *directed by your reasoning mind.* Third, when you worship God in this way, with your whole self, you are not (of course) actually lying down on an altar and cutting your own throat, but you are doing so 'spiritually'—not just metaphorically, but in the realm of spiritual reality.[291]

This transformation is for the purpose of not being "conformed" to "this present age." Thus we are placed squarely in the most pervasive perspective of New Testament theology. New Testament theology, particularly the theology of St. Paul, is informed by the apocalyptic dualism that was characteristic of much rabbinic theology of the Second Temple period. Paul had come to believe that the death and resurrection of Jesus had signaled the end of the old age ("the present age") and marked the inauguration of the new age ("the age to come"). Thus the church is living in the "time between the times," in the power of the Spirit made available to those who have experienced "the powers of the age to come" (Heb. 6:5). This perspective is embodied in 2 Corinthians 5:16-17: "From now on, therefore, we regard no one from a human point of view; even though we once knew Christ from a human point of view, we know him no longer in that way. So if anyone is in Christ, there is a new creation: everything old has passed away; see, everything has become new!"

The theme of "new creation" is somewhat obscured by most translations of verse 17, which appear to suggest that Paul is referring to personal transformation (which is a glorious truth) whereas he is referring to the new age of the Spirit launched into this present age by Jesus' death and resurrection and the gift of the Holy Spirit. As some scholars suggest, the text really says, "If anyone is in Christ—new creation!"[292] The Revised English Bible has this illuminating

---

[291]N. T. Wright, *After You Believe* (N.Y.: Harper Collins, 2010), 149-50.

[292]N. T. Wright, lecture; Richard B. Hays, *The Moral Vision of the New Testament* (N.Y.: Harper Collins, 1996): "The sentence in Greek, . . lacks both

118

translation: "For anyone united to Christ, there is a new creation: the old order is gone; a new order has already begun."[293]

The use of "according to the flesh" in this context gives us a significant clue as to the meaning of *sarx* in relation to the apocalyptic dualism of the ages. Living *kata sarka* is the indication that one is still living existentially and ethically in "the present age" with its values and world view, which is passing away. With the death and resurrection of Jesus, a new era with different values and world view is inaugurated. Hence Paul's ethical appeals are appeals to order one's life and experience in terms of the death and resurrection of Jesus. This implicitly implies that the life of the "age to come" as lived out in the present takes a cruciformed shape.

Two very practical implications follow from the perspective that holiness of heart and life is being lived out in a tension between the no longer and the not yet. It is possible to distort the significance of this by the claim that one has experienced a grace that grants one what can be called "realized eschatology." In a word, it is the claim of faultlessness or perfectionism. John Wesley encountered this claim among some of his followers, to which he referred as "enthusiasm" (fanaticism).

Peter, in his first letter, describes the holiness to which the "new Israel" is called (1 Peter 1:16) as lived out in a tension between the grace that was made available at the first advent and the grace that will appear at the Second Advent (1:10-13).[294] This warns against making extravagant claims regarding any experience of grace, while at the same time avoiding diminishing the transforming effectiveness of the grace made available in the present time by the work of Christ. It suggests the necessity of recognizing that there is a relationship of victory over the "flesh" that should be characterized by the ongoing pursuit of the "glory" that will be fully actual only in the consummation.

This brings us back to 1 Thessalonians 5:23-24. This prayer is offered in the light of this eschatological dualism with the coming (*parousia*) of Christ in view. In the light of a repeated emphasis

subject and verb:", 20.

[293]Quoted in Greathouse, *Romans*, 161.

[294]Cf. H. Ray Dunning, *Partakers of the Divine Nature*, 38f.

throughout the letter (1:3; 3:6, 12-13;4:9-10) Richard H. Hays summarizes the import of its ethical implications: "The Thessalonians are not being told to do something; rather, Paul is asking that God act in their lives to increase their love for one another and to sanctify them in preparation for the *parousia*. Paul conceives the church as a people being prepared by God for the fullness of God's kingdom; the holiness that will make them ready for the final judgment finds expression in the love that abounds within the community."[295]

In the light of this brief analysis of the biblical material, it seems quite sound to affirm that "entire sanctification" may be reasonably identified as the consecration of the "whole person" to the focused pursuit of the image of God as manifested in every aspect of ones human nature, body, soul, spirit, heart, and mind. It implies that it begins the constantly evolving process of appropriating the power of the Holy Spirit to "put off" the "old man," which, as W.M. Greathouse interprets, is the resident of the "present evil age" and the correlative "putting on" the "new man" who is the embodiment of "the age to come." It further implies, what is the same thing, that there is a lifetime of eliminating the "flesh" [*sarx*] from every aspect of human functioning since living according to the flesh is characterized by self-centered existence. It is this latter aspect of the sanctified life that J.O. McClurkan, leader of one of the southern branches of the early holiness movement referred to as "a deeper death to self," which in reality should be occurring throughout the Christian life.[296]

As we have noted in other sections, this understanding provides an interpretation of sanctification that is based on scripture as interpreted by the best of biblical scholarship and clearly retains the essence of the holiness message. It provides a rationale that makes both exegetically sound and existentially livable both a "crisis" and a "process" without appealing to question begging distinctions.

---

[295]*Moral Vision*, 22.

[296]Cf. William J. Strickland and H. Ray Dunning, *J.O. McClurkan: His Life, His Theology, and Selections from His Writings* (Nashville: Trevecca Press, 1998), 118ff. McClurkan's teaching placed him in some tension with the holiness movement of his day but kept him in touch with real life. From experience he recognized that all of life cannot be compressed into one moment of experience.

Chapter 7
The Holy Spirit and Sanctification

Thesis: The relation of the Holy Spirit to sanctification in the New Testament is a fulfillment of the Old Testament hope for inner transformation and is the enabling Agent in the pursuit of the image of God as embodied in Jesus Christ.

In his monograph on the Holy Spirit, William Barclay comments that "our thinking about the Spirit is vaguer and more undefined than our thinking about any other part of the Christian Faith."[297] Granted the validity of this observation, there may be three reasons for this phenomenon: first, it is difficult to conceptualize the reality of "spirit," with the result that the average person probably thinks about the Holy Spirit as a quasi-material entity like "Casper the ghost." And this may have been exacerbated by the KJV translation of *pneuma* as Ghost. Second, without reference to an objective criterion, claims about the guidance, revelation or manifestations of the Spirit are so susceptible to subjectivism that if we are critically sensitive, we find it extremely difficult to distinguish our feelings, inclinations and even personality quirks from the Spirit's influence. Third, and most significant, if we do not interpret the meaning and function of the Spirit within the larger context of the biblical world view, our understanding will almost unavoidably be skewed by other factors.

The first two of these issues are addressed in the New Testament by identifying the Spirit and his work with the person of Jesus. The terminology (*ruach* in the OT and *pneuma* in the NT) connotes a variety of meanings and within themselves do not identify a specific content. While the concept of Spirit in the Old Testament reflects the ways in which God, who is transcendent, related to human existence and experience, the accounts of such relations suggest that the Spirit of the Lord was viewed as an "influence" without any essential ethical content (e.g. Num. 11:24-30; Judges 13:25; 14:6). As George Lyons says, "the Old Testament and intertestamental Judaism alone cannot account for many of the distinctively Christian assumptions concerning the Spirit. The tendency in Judaism toward a

---

[297]William Barclay, *The Promise of the Spirit* (Philadelphia: The Westminster Press, 1960), 11.

personalization of the Spirit was firmly in place before the time of Jesus, but it was the early Christian conviction that the Spirit was the Spirit of Jesus which was the greatest single contributing factor in the process that led to the fourth-century understanding of the Holy Spirit as the third person of the Holy Trinity."[298]

Similarly, Paul W. Meyer says that "While there is little, if anything, distinctively Christian about either the language about the Holy Spirit or the notions of Spirit found even in Paul, *these become distinctively Christian precisely when they are related, and by virtue of being related, to the figure of Jesus Christ*—in Paul's terms, to the pattern of death and resurrection that is central to his credo."[299]

The second reason is likewise addressed by the near identification of the Holy Spirit with the Spirit of Jesus, thus giving a high measure of objective content to the nature and work of the Spirit. This becomes quite clear in the Paraclete sayings in John 14:15-31. Jesus' promise to his disciples of "another Helper" oscillates between reference to himself and the "Helper." A.M. Hunter puts it pointedly: "Paul does not identify Christ with the Spirit. The truth is rather that it is through the Spirit that Christ comes to Christians. Theologically, Christ and the Spirit are distinguishable; experientially, they are one."[300]

This third reason implies that the first step in understanding the biblical teaching about the Holy Spirit is to take a wide-angle view of the Biblical narrative especially focused on the history of Israel in the Old Testament. God's choice of Abram to be the progenitor of a redemptive race (Gen. 12:1-3) began coming to fruition with the Exodus and the Sinai Covenant. Israel was chosen and "sanctified" by these events, which involved the giving of the law, to be the agents through whom God would bring justice to the world. In their corporate life they were to be a paradigm of God's creative

---

[298]George Lyons, "The Spirit in the Gospels," *The Spirit and the New Age* ed. Alex R.G. Deasley and R. Larry Shelton (Anderson, IND: Warner Press, Inc., 1986), 36.

[299]Paul W. Meyer, "The Holy Spirit in the Pauline Letters," *Interpretation* 33 (1979), 5. Emphasis his.

[300]A. M. Hunter, *The Gospel According to Paul* (Philadelphia: Westminster Press, 1966), 35-36.

intention for the human race and the law incarnated the essence of what that entailed. But scarcely had this vocation been launched and the law given when the people recapitulated the sin of Adam in the golden calf incident. The later rabbis referred to this event as the "fall of Israel." The entire subsequent history became a litany of failure culminating with the Babylonian Captivity in 587 B.C., which was preceded by the departure of the "glory [shekinah, presence] of God" from the Temple (Eze. 10). This sad picture reflected the fact that those who were supposed to be the solution to the problem had become a part of the problem themselves. The indictment of the Jews by Paul in Romans 2:17-29 reflects their failure to be the light of the world. N.T. Wright perceptively points out that "His point is . . . that the national boast of ethnic Israel, that of being the creator's chosen people, is falsified if theft, adultery, and so forth are found within the nation. . . . Paul is not so interested in demonstrating that 'all Jews are sinners . . . as in showing up Israel's failure [as a whole] to be the light of the world."[301]

The glowing pictures of return from exile--including the restoring of Israel's glory predicted by the prophets--did not materialize resulting in a national spirit of despondency that God had forsaken them and this "present age" was under the dominion of alien forces, as they themselves were under the dominion of pagan nations. In a word, the "captivity" had never come to an end. As an aspect of this, "many Jews during the intertestamental period came to regard the present age as one devoid of the Spirit. They believed that prophetic inspiration departed from Israel with the death of the last canonical (i.e. Old Testament) prophets. This view arose because of the widely held rabbinic conviction that the Holy Spirit was first and foremost 'the prophetic spirit,' the instrument of divine revelation and inspiration."[302]

All this raises the question as to how this failure could have occurred. What was missing or perhaps more pertinent, what was present? The prophets Jeremiah and Ezekiel provided the most incisive analysis of the problem in the Old Testament. They recognized that the Old Covenant did not explicitly provide for a heart transformation and

---

[301]N.T. Wright, *Romans*, 445, 447.

[302]Lyons, "Spirit in the Gospels," 35.

thus expressed a hope that the coming of the Spirit in the eschatological age would bring moral renewal. "In Ezekiel 36:26ff., the priest-prophet implicitly recognizes the inadequacy of a restored ritual and, along with Jeremiah (31:31ff.), anticipates an eschatological time of heart transformation. He explicitly attributes this to the operation of the Spirit: 'I will put my spirit within you, and cause you to walk in my statutes' (36:27)."[303]

The fulfillment of this hope is celebrated by Paul in Romans 8:3-4 – "For God has done what the law, weakened by the flesh, could not do; by sending his own Son in the likeness of sinful flesh, and to deal with sin, he condemned sin in the flesh, so that the just requirement of the law might be fulfilled in us, who walk not according to the flesh but according to the Spirit." The law had promised to give life but because of "sin" [the "hidden Adam" in each of us] it had only brought to consciousness the presence of sin (7:7-11). The law was good but "the problem lay elsewhere: in the 'flesh'—not the physicality of human nature, which was God-given and will be reaffirmed in the resurrection, but in the present rebellious and corruptible state of humankind, within which sin had made its dwelling."[304]

God has addressed this problem through the death and resurrection of his son, the one faithful Israelite (Rom. 3:22). Paul says that what was done at the cross was the "'condemnation' of sin, the real culprit all along . . .and stresses that what was done there was the act of God in Christ, not (as it were) the action of Christ upon God."[305] While this has tremendous implications for understanding Paul's view of the Atonement (see ch.8), the central point being made in Romans is the gift of life through the Spirit made available through the work of Jesus. These dual truths, argues N.T. Wright, stands at the heart of Pauline theology. As a Pharisaic Jew Paul understood that the twin truths of Jewish theology were monotheism and election, God and

[303]Dunning, *Grace, Faith and Holiness*, 403-4.

[304]Wright, *Romans*, 577.

[305]Ibid. 575.

Israel. Wright's underlying argument in all his work is that Paul's theology "consists precisely in the redefinition by means of Christology and pneumatology of those two key Jewish doctrines.[306]

The relation between the cross and the sending of the Spirit is clearly expressed in John 7:37-39 where John makes the parenthetical point that the Spirit's coming is dependent on the completion of Jesus' vocation. This implies that the nature and work of the Spirit is integrally related to the cross, which itself implicitly introduced a new understanding of power from the dominant one found in the Old Testament having to do with enduement for service. Thus fundamentally, "Paul's experience of the Spirit is one of being conformed to Christ and his cross: that is, for Paul the Spirit is the Spirit of cruciformity. . . . Thus the criterion of the Spirit's activity is cruciformity, understood as Christ-like love in the edification of others rather than oneself."[307]

With this background, we need to briefly examine John Wesley's understanding of the Holy Spirit. I am in full agreement with Donald Dayton's summary statement that "for Wesley the Holy Spirit is understood primarily as the instrument by which this whole process of salvation and sanctification is achieved. . . . and [it is] . . . very Christocentric in character."[308] Wesley himself makes this abundantly clear in his sermon on "Scriptural Christianity" based on Acts 4:31— "And they were all filled with the Holy Spirit." The question is the purpose for this "filling." Wesley's answer is:

It was, therefore, for a more excellent purpose than this [the gifts of the Spirit] that "they were all filled with the Holy Ghost." It was, to give them (all Christians in all ages) the mind which was in Christ, those holy fruits of the Spirit which whosoever hath not, is none of his; to fill them with "love, joy, peace, longsuffering, gentleness, goodness;" (Gal. v.22-24) to endue them with faith, with meekness and temperance; to enable them to crucify the flesh, with its

---

[306]N.T. Wright, *Climax of the Covenant*, 1. This point is the key to unlocking the significance of Romans 7 & 8, which we shall explore in Appendix A.

[307]Gorman, *Cruciformity*, 57, 60.

[308]Donald Dayton, "Pneumatological Issues in the Holiness Movement," *The Spirit and the New Age,* ed. Alex R.G. Deasley and R. Larry Shelton (Anderson, IN: Warner Press, 1986), 253.

affections and lusts, its passions and desires; and, in consequence of that inward change, to fulfill all outward righteousness; to "walk as Christ also walked," in "the work of faith, in the patience of hope, the labor of love." (I Thess. i.3.)[309]

But Dayton further points out that, as in a few other areas (see Introduction), Wesley left a measure of ambiguity to his successors. While it is clear (re. above quotation) that his dominant emphasis was Christological, Dayton argues that his doctrine of "assurance" or "the witness of the Spirit" "breaks [the Christological] pattern to a certain extent." One emphasis was oriented toward Christology, the other toward pneumatology.[310]

The latter emphasis began to develop within Wesley's lifetime, chiefly under the influence of John Fletcher who was Wesley's designated successor to leadership of the revival. Wesley disagreed with Fletcher on this emphasis. Dayton points out that there was "more at stake in this difference than either realized." Although Fletcher generally maintained the theme of moral transformation like Wesley, his emphasis on the Spirit, "had the potential of moving in the direction that Wesley feared—to give more autonomy to the Holy Spirit in such a way as to separate the work of the Spirit from the work of Christ and to separate the coming of the Spirit in the life of the individual from initiation into Christian life."[311] Although probably not widespread, but nonetheless taught by many folk theologians of the holiness movement, this resulted in the view that the believer did not receive the Holy Spirit until the experience of entire sanctification.

One of the most significant and far-reaching developments in the 19th century holiness movement was the almost universal equation of entire sanctification with the "baptism with the Holy Spirit." This meant that there was a shift of focus in biblical interpretation, moving now from the Johannine and Pauline material to the Book of Acts. This move, along with the central emphasis on "cleansing" as the

---

[309]*Works*, 5:38.

[310]Dayton, "Pneumatological Issues," 255.

[311]Ibid. 257.

function of Spirit baptism, became the primary apologetic foundation for the "secondness" of entire sanctification.[312] The next step, both logically and historically, was the emergence of Pentecostalism with its emphasis on tongues-speaking as evidence of the Spirit baptism along with other themes such as divine healing and millennial eschatology. As Dayton concludes from his research, "By the late nineteenth century the holiness movement was immersed in these themes and had adopted doctrines of divine healing and had shifted from a post-millennial eschatology to a pre-millennial eschatology.[313] The "right-wing" holiness movement attempted to remain grounded in its Wesleyan roots by rejecting the distinctive emphasis of the Pentecostal movement but having bought into the theology that led inevitably in this direction, the only recourse was institutional pronouncement.

Since the references to the Spirit in Acts are in the context of narrative recounting the story of the early church, they are subject to a variety of interpretations.[314] Because this subject has been explored *ad infinitum*, I will only offer 4 hermeneutical suggestions: 1. The nature of the book of Acts--recounting the spread of the gospel throughout the ancient world in fulfillment of Jesus' final instruction to his disciples--naturally lends itself to an emphasis on power for witnessing (Acts 1:8). The Old Testament hope for the age to come was that the Spirit of the Lord would provide an empowering presence but would also bring moral renewal. When Peter explained the meaning of the outpouring of the Spirit on the 120 who had gathered in the anteroom of the temple,[315] he quoted Joel 2:28-32, a passage that emphasized the gift of prophecy as divine enablement rather than moral renewal. The

---

[312]We have already seen that equating "cleansing" with "sanctification" is exegetically questionable. See Chapter 3.

[313]Ibid. 259. The early holiness camp meeting associations would not allow the preaching on these two themes from their platforms.

[314]See Chad Owen Brand, ed., *Perspectives on Spirit Baptism, Five Views* (Nashville: Broadman and Holman Pub., 2004).

[315]Since the text doesn't say, I agree with F.F. Bruce that this makes much better sense than the general assumption that they were in an "upper room" for this event. F.F. Bruce, *Commentary on the Book of Acts* (Grand Rapids: Wm. B. Eerdmans Pub. Co., 1973), 56.

early chapters in Acts, in particular, emphasized the effectiveness of the disciples' witness to Jesus, but even here, it was their witness to Jesus, which points us to my second suggestion.

2-The central emphasis surrounding the Day of Pentecost was actually upon Jesus rather than the experience of the Spirit. After briefly answering the onlookers' question, Peter focuses his message on Jesus, particularly his resurrection. He is specifically addressing his Jewish audience (2:22) and zeroes in on one major point, the evidence that the Jesus whom they had crucified had been exalted to lordship and messiah-ship by the resurrection. It is "this [same] Jesus" that God has approved, in contrast to the judgment conventional wisdom had pronounced upon him. Thus the conclusion of his sermon is stated as a logical conclusion: "Therefore let the entire house of Israel know with certainty that God has made him both Lord and Messiah, this [same] Jesus whom you crucified." (2:36). Having been "convicted" by Peter's apologetic, the listeners wanted to know how they were to respond. To their question Peter responded "Repent, and be baptized every one of you in the name of Jesus Christ so that your sins may be forgiven; and you will receive the gift of the Holy Spirit." In the light of this context, repentance here carries its literal meaning of "change your mind." The prevailing understanding of who and what the promised messianic figure was to be has now to be abandoned and replaced with a vision informed by the figure of the Suffering Servant of Isaiah 40-55. We now are able to see more clearly the import of the words from heaven at Jesus' baptism and on the Mount of Transfiguration: "This is my beloved Son, *in whom I am well pleased/ hear ye him.*" (Matt. 3:17; 17:5). The blessings to be received by this change of mind were the anticipated blessings of "the age to come:" forgiveness of sins and the gift of the Spirit. Thus the whole scenario brings the understanding of the Holy Spirit under the aegis of the Son. This is what validates William Barclay's conclusion that "There is no book in the New Testament in which the Holy Spirit becomes so personally vivid as He does in the Book of Acts," since "What gives the Spirit His personal vividness in Acts is the fact that the work of the Spirit and the presence of the Risen Lord are one and the same thing."[316]

---

[316]*The Promise of the Spirit*, 61-62.

A third important consideration is the corporate nature of the giving of the Spirit. In contrast to the emphasis on individual (even private) religious experience prevalent since the 18th century Enlightenment, Luke records no instances in Acts where the Spirit is bestowed upon an individual qua individual. It is always described or portrayed as a corporate gift. The nearest to an exception is the "conversion" of Saul of Tarsus. But this is not really an exception since he receives the gift of the Spirit only when the "church" came to him in the person of Ananias who greeted him with the hand of churchly fellowship: "Brother Saul."

This phenomenon raises questions about the meaning of the holiness of the church in relation to the holiness of the individual. Under the influence of the Enlightenment, the latter has dominated the popular religious mind where religion has been privatized and described as what one does with their solitariness. With the rise of postmodernism, an especially slippery idea, the mood in many quarters has gone in the opposite direction. John Wesley is well known and often quoted for saying that "Christianity is essentially a social religion; and that to turn it into a solitary religion, is indeed to destroy it."[317] But he also balances it with an emphasis on the holiness of the individual believer in a discussion of the affirmation of the Apostles' Creed, "We believe in the holy, Catholic church." Various rationales for the holiness of the church have been offered but "the shortest and the plainest reason that can be given, and the only true one, is: the church is 'holy' because it is holy; though every member thereof is holy, though in different degrees, as he that called them is holy."[318]

This observation has implications for the renewal of humanity in the image of God that we have explored as including, among other relations, a relation to others. This is why it is exegetically legitimate to refer to the original Pentecost as "the birthday of the Church."[319]

---

[317] *Works*, 5:296.

[318] Ibid. 6:400.

[319] Wiley, *Christian Theology*, 3:107; Charles W. Carter, *The Person and Ministry of the Holy Spirit* (Grand Rapids: Baker Book House, 1974) in supporting the 19th century tradition of interpreting Pentecost as the "second blessing of entire sanctification" of the disciples rejects the designation of Pentecost as the "birthday of the church." Richard S. Taylor rejected this interpretation of Pentecost for the same reason. *Exploring Christian Holiness*, 3:133.

What we have in Luke's picture of the early church is a portrayal of a sanctified body of believers constituted as such by the infilling of the Holy Spirit. It is more than a group of individually sanctified persons enjoying fellowship of the "coke and cookies" variety. What we see here is a binding together of Spirit-filled persons into an organic unity of love created by the "community-creating Spirit" who abides within. This is actually a fulfillment of Jesus' prayer for his followers in John 17:17.

This interpretation is further illustrated by the gift of tongues-speaking, which may legitimately be described as an "inaugural manifestation" of the beginning of the "age to come." Its significance is highlighted by F.F. Bruce who, with many others, makes the point that "The event was surely nothing less than a reversal of the curse of Babel."[320] This incident as recorded in Genesis 11:1-9 depicts the crowning evidence that the "original sin" disrupted the image of God as relation to the other.

Alex R.G. Deasley emphasizes this same point concerning the corporate nature of the gift of the Spirit in the Pauline epistles. He says that this is why Paul treats the "place of the Spirit in the Christian community before the place of the Spirit in the life of the Christian individual." Deasley quotes as support of his discussion the words of W.D. Davies: "for Paul the Spirit is, or at any rate should be, profoundly the possession of every individual Christian," but "to isolate this individual nature of its activity is to distort Paul's whole conception of the Spirit. It is not this which is most characteristic of his thought. More noticeable is his emphasis on the Spirit as the source of Christian fellowship and unity."[321]

The fourth interpretive suggestion is that the narrative structure of Acts detailing the major transition in salvation history makes it difficult to use it to identify a structure of Christian experience. This difficulty is exacerbated by the fact that there is no uniformity of

---

[320] *Acts*, 64.

[321] Alex R.G. Deasley, "The Spirit in the Pauline Epistles," *The Spirit and the New Age* ed. Alex R.G. Deasley and R. Larry Shelton (Anderson, IN: Warner Press, 1986), 125-129.

experience, thus it does not present us with a "normative sequence of Christian experience."[322] The variety of experience is evidently related to the particular situation thus suggesting the significance of Laurence Wood's question: "Does not the Spirit deal with each person according to his own personal salvation history?"[323]

The mature expression of the fully developed New Testament view of the normative Christian experience of the Spirit is found in Paul's epistles. To explore the Pauline corpus would take us beyond the constraints of space. The following references reflect my own interpretation of Paul's theology of the Holy Spirit. They demonstrate the central point needing to be emphasized for the paradigm of sanctification I am exploring, namely the correlation of the Holy Spirit and his work with the person and work of Jesus.

Alasdair I.C. Heron observes that "in returning from the Synoptics and Acts to Paul, we find a richer conception and deeper exploration of the nature of the Spirit, of its activity, and of *its inherent connection with Jesus Christ.*"[324] James S. Stewart evaluated Paul's contribution to be in his understanding that "Not in any accidental and extraneous phenomena, . . not in any spasmodic emotions or intermittent ecstasies . . . but in the quiet, steady, normal life of faith, in power that worked on moral levels, in the soul's secret inward assurance of its sonship of God, in love and joy and peace and patience and *a character like that of Jesus.*"[325]

---

[322]McCown, "Holy Spirit in Acts", 112.

[323]Laurence W. Wood, "Exegetical-Theological Reflections on the Baptism with the Holy Spirit," *Wesleyan Theological Journal*, 14 (Fall 1979), 55.

[324]*The Holy Spirit* (Philadelphia: Westminster Press, 1983), 44. Emphasis added.

[325]*A Man in Christ* (N.Y.: Harper and Row, Pub., n.d.) 308. Emphasis added.

Chapter 8
Sanctification and the Atonement

Thesis: Certain Atonement metaphors from the New Testament have significant implications for the experience of sanctification.

Traditional evangelical thought has always interpreted the work of Christ as a remedy of the sin problem resulting from the Fall. Western Christian thought generally understood the problem to be guilt, understood in a legalistic sense, with the death of Christ dealing with that guilt. The Eastern Church usually saw the consequence of the fall as loss of immortality and emphasized the Incarnation as the means of transforming human nature, to which they applied the term, *divinination*. The degree of completeness with which the atonement dealt with the sin problem varied from one theological tradition to another, especially in Protestant thought. The Protestant Reformers emphasized the atonement as providing for the forgiveness of sin but did not see it as addressing the full problem. This is encapsulated in Luther's formula describing the believer as *simul justus et peccator*, at the same time justified and a sinner. Calvin was a bit more optimistic (see chapter 11) but still stopped short of affirming a full deliverance from sin, thus insisting on repentance as an essential part of the Christian life. He wrote,

> We have not a single work going forth from the saints that if it be judged in itself deserves but shame as its just reward . . . For since no perfection can come to us so long as we are clothed in this flesh, and the law moreover announces death and judgment to all who do not maintain perfect righteousness in works, it will always have grounds for accusing and condemning us unless, on the contrary, God's mercy counters it, and by continual forgiveness of sins repeatedly acquits us.[326]

John Wesley, on the contrary, insisted that the provision of the work of Christ availed for the full problem of sin. He relied on such passages as 1 John 3:8—"The Son of God was revealed for this

---

[326]*Institutes of the Christian Religion*, III, xiv, 10.

132

purpose, to destroy the works of the devil." He sharply commented in the *Notes*, "all sin. And will He not perform this in all that trust in Him?" Wesley's emphasis on the necessity for Christ's priestly work for the "entirely sanctified" believer results in some ambiguity about this straightforward claim. His successors in the next century concurred in this judgment and strongly insisted on affirming a "radical" remedy for the sin problem by ignoring his emphasis on Christ's priestly work.

Systematically, Wesley's central claim calls for an interpretation of the atonement that is consistent with the claim. Oddly enough, Wesley himself reflected a form of the atonement that was inconsistent with his emphasis on the possibility of full sanctification in this life.[327] Harald Lindström highlights one of the possible reasons for this: "Wesley never took up the Atonement for special consideration in any of his treatises or tracts. Nor is it the main theme in any of his sermons. His views on it will be found primarily in scattered remarks bearing on his exposition of sin, justification, and sanctification. Yet it was undoubtedly a pivotal and essential theme in both his preaching and his thought."[328]

The holiness writers in the 19th century spent little time with systematic theology and thus did not generally explore the doctrine of the atonement. One exception is Richard S. Taylor who, in his early monograph on the doctrine of sin (1939), devoted two chapters to a discussion of the relation between the atonement and sin. He insisted:

> It is vitally important that we consider, carefully, those passages which indicate provision in the atonement for perfect and present cleansing from original sin. For, if heart purity is God's plan for every Christian, then most certainly complete freedom from actual sin would be required. Furthermore, a provision in the atonement so momentous and far-reaching as this would point distinctly to the belief that God's one method of redemption is by saving man, here and now, from all sin; it would certainly not lead one to believe that God proposed to save man in his sin on the merits of Christ.[329]

---

[327]H. Ray Dunning, *The Whole Christ for the Whole World* (Eugene, OR: Wipf & Stock, 2008).

[328]Harald Lindström, *Wesley and Sanctification* (London: The Epworth Press, n.d.), 55.

The final statement of this reference has profound implications. It implicitly rejects, as logically inconsistent with the claim for full deliverance from both actual and original sin, any version of a satisfaction theory of the atonement.[330] The concept of *merit* implies the imputation of the ethical righteousness of Christ to the believer while the believer remains as sinful as before.

It is not illogical in the context of a satisfaction theory to correlate the concept of *merit* with an understanding of the atonement as it relates to justification, since justification has to do with one's relation to God. It is logically and theologically inconsistent, on the other hand, to apply the concept of merit to sanctification when this doctrine is understood biblically. If one believes that sanctification refers to the attribute of the person that qualifies him or herself for eschatological acceptance, then the concept of merit may consistently be used, but it implies positional holiness rather than a real transformation. The result, in any case, is confusion between justification and sanctification. Oddly enough, in the light of this theological anomaly, the holiness writers of the 19th century tradition rather consistently used the concept of merit to refer to the relationship between sanctification and the atonement. J. A. Wood seems to conflate all the soteriological metaphors under this rubric when he says, "Justification, God's act, and sanctification, God's work, are experimentally by faith, meritoriously by the blood of Christ, instrumentally by the word of God, and efficiently by the Holy Ghost. See John xvii. 17; 1 John i.7; Rom. xv.16; 1 Timothy iv. 5."[331]

J.B. Chapman's statement is more to the point and illustrates a repeated refrain in all the "holiness classics:"

---

[329]*A Right Conception of Sin*, 96.

[330]Oddly, 60 years after this statement, the author published a defense of the theory that he here implicitly rejected as inconsistent with holiness theology. *God's Integrity and the Cross* (Nappanee, IN: Francis Asbury Press, 1999).

[331]*Purity of Heart*, 9. None of the cited texts are relevant to the issue of merit.

Christian perfection, perfect love, the baptism with the Holy Ghost, Christian purity, and other such terms imply the same work and state of grace. That work is wrought in the hearts of believers subsequent to regeneration, on the basis of the merits of the blood of Jesus, on condition of faith, and by the efficient agency of the Holy Ghost."[332]

H. Orton Wiley, also, in one brief statement states that the meritorious or procuring cause of entire sanctification is the blood of Christ and quotes 1 John 1:7, which has no relation to the issue of merit. In defining the "Wesleyan" view of sanctification, Melvin E. Dieter refers to entire sanctification as the result of "the same faith in the merits of Christ's sacrifice for sin that initially had brought justification and the new life in Christ."[333] No writer that we could find makes any effort to identify a logical, biblical or theological basis for making such a claim.

It is true that John Wesley used the terminology of *meritorious* in referring to the blood of Christ, but he never used the concept of *merit* in relation to sanctification as such. When he spoke of the meritorious work of Christ, it was always in relation to justification in the sense that he held to no experience of perfection that eliminated the need for the continuing gracious acceptance based on the work of Christ. This was expressed frequently as reflected in the following quote from a letter to Mr. Alexander Coates: "Keep to this: Repentance toward God, faith in Christ, holiness of heart and life, a growing in grace and in the knowledge of Christ, the continual need of his atoning blood, a constant confidence in him, and all these every moment to our life's end."[334]

It is theologically sound to relate the biblical understanding of sanctification to the work of Christ, but not by the concept of *merit*.

---

[332]*Terminology of Holiness*, 36. Cf. also Daniel Steele, *Love Enthroned*, 112, 116; Asbury Lowrey, *Possibilities of Grace*, 66, 90. A carefully nuanced understanding of the term "merit" might legitimately be used here if it is interpreted as meaning "adequate provision," and used in tandem with the metaphor of "the blood of Christ," which relates to the sacrificial imagery applied to the atonement. But no writer in this tradition has made such a carefully developed analysis.

[333]Melvin E. Dieter, "The Wesleyan Perspective," in *Five Views of Sanctification*, ed. Stanley N. Gundry (Grand Rapids: Zondervan, 1987), 17.

[334]Wesley, *Works*, 12:241.

Hence, we propose to briefly address this matter. It is important to note first that the New Testament uses several metaphors to refer to the work of Christ, three of which have special significance for the relation between the atonement and sanctification. No one metaphor can capture fully the many splendored truth of the work of Christ and the aspects we propose to explore could doubtless be multiplied. As Richard B. Hays notes, "The cross is a complex symbol in Paul's thought-world, encoding a rich variety of meanings."[335]

The Atonement as Victory (Christus Victor motif). From the first use of salvation language in Exodus 14:30 in connection with the escape from Pharaoh through the Red Sea, the meaning of salvation has carried the connotation of deliverance from bondage. The term means "to be wide, spacious, free." "Both language and the Exodus events define this word as the gift of freedom by the hands of God."[336] Throughout the Old Testament this was popularly understood as political in nature. The implication of the idea of deliverance is that there is a force that enslaves God's people that must be broken before deliverance can occur. In its first use, the power of Egypt had to be broken. In 587 B.C. Israel "returned to Egypt" and in the subsequent years of domination by pagan powers from Babylon to Rome the Israelites longed for deliverance and looked forward to Yahweh's intervention on their behalf in a New Exodus. The notes of hope for deliverance that sounded forth from the lips of Zechariah (Luke 1:67-79) in his Spirit-inspired celebration reflected the long anticipated deliverance he perceived God was now about to bring to pass: "Blessed be the Lord God of Israel, for he has looked favorably on his people and redeemed them. He has raised up a mighty savior for us in the house of his servant David, as he spoke through the mouth of his

---

[335]Richard B. Hays, *The Moral Vision of the New Testament* (N.Y.: HarperCollins, 1996), 27.; Likewise N.T. Wright notes "God's action to rescue humans and the world is such a constant topic in Paul's letters, and he says so many different things about it in so many different contexts, [that it results in] the multi-faceted nature of his thought." *Redemption from the New Perspective*, 81. See my book, *The Whole Christ for the Whole World* for a more extensive examination of the various ways of explaining the atonement.

[336]Arnold B. Rhodes, *The Mighty Acts of God* (Richmond, VA: CLC Press, 1964), 80.

holy prophets from of old, that we would be saved from our enemies and from the hand of all who hate us." What Zechariah no doubt thought to be a deliverance from Rome and other political powers that had for years frustrated Israel's hopes of being the free people of God turned out to be far more and quite different than he envisioned.

In Jesus, God did indeed return to his people, and break the power that held them in bondage but that power was not political or military. And the means was not by force but by way of the cross, a way they had never anticipated and had great difficulty getting their minds around. Even Jesus most intimate followers could not grasp it and apparently never did until after the Resurrection. The enslaving power was the power of evil that Jesus met on its own turf and defeated in a mighty conflict, thus becoming Christ the Victor. In N.T. Wright's trenchant words, "The cross of Jesus, instead of being as one might suppose the place where the powers celebrated a triumph over him, stripping him naked and holding him up to public contempt, is to be seen as the place where Jesus celebrated *his* triumph over *them*."[337]

Paul celebrates this victory in Gal. 1:3-4: "Grace to you and peace from God our Father and the Lord Jesus Christ, who gave himself for our sins *to set us free from the present evil age*, according to the will of our God and Father, to whom be the glory forever and ever. Amen" (emphasis added).

This Galatian passage reflects the substructure of New Testament theology derived from a transformation of the dominant rabbinic eschatology. The "present age" is under the dominion of demonic "powers" with Satan as the "prince of the powers of the air." The rabbinic hope was that the "age to come," the kingdom of God, would break into history and disrupt the social order bringing the "present age" to an end. The New Testament writers came to see what was implicit in Jesus' ministry, that the "age to come" had broken into the present with his work even though the "present age" had not been brought to a close. However, the point was that the powers that controlled the "present age" have been broken and those who experience the benefits of the victory of the cross now, as it were, live in the "age to come." This is what Paul meant in referring to himself and his contemporaries in 1 Corinthians 10:11 as those "on whom the ends of the ages has come."[338]

---

[337]"Redemption from the New Perspective," 99.

In Colossians 2:15 Paul[339] refers to the victory of the cross in terms of a common practice of ancient armies to demonstrate the defeat of their enemies: "He disarmed the rulers and authorities and made a public example of them, triumphing over them in it [the cross]." Reference to such a practice is probably reflected in Nahum 2:7 describing the defeat of Nineveh, the capital of Assyria, by the Babylonians: "its mistress is stripped, she is carried off, her maidens lamenting, moaning like doves, and beating their breasts" (RSV). "It had been Assyria's custom to lead away captive the gods of her victimized nations. Now her own chief goddess is to be brought up and carried away without dignity. In this case her maids would be the 'sacred' harlots moaning as doves and beating their breasts in anguish."[340]

With this eschatological dualism in the background, Paul explores the "victory of Christ" in Romans 6 in terms of "dominion" using the imagery of a dichotomy of "old master/new Master." As Robert Tannehill describes it, "The term 'two dominions' is chosen because Paul sees man's situation as characterized by two sets of powers which 'reign' or 'have dominion over' men. However, we can also speak here of two 'aeons.'" The term "aeon" is not explicitly used "but it has the advantage of making clear the eschatological setting of this pattern of thought."[341]

The old aeon is dominated by a lord or master that Paul personifies as "sin." Tannehill explains, "Here it is clear that sin is not merely a series of separate acts nor an abstract principle, but a

---

[338]Cf. Gordon D. Fee, *God's Empowering Presence* (Peabody, Mass: Hendrickson, 1994) for an excellent summary of this "framework" of Paul's worldview, 804.

[339]Many scholars dispute the Pauline authorship of Colossians as well as Ephesian. N.T. Wright, on the contrary, finds no compelling reason for doing so. He repeatedly refers the material to Paul, e.g. "Redemption from the New Perspective: Towards a Multi-Layered Pauline Theology of the Cross," et. al.

[340]H. Ray Dunning, "Nahum," *Beacon Bible Commentary,* 10 vols. (K.C.: Beacon Hill Press, 1966), 5:255.

[341]Robert C. Tannehill, *Dying and Rising with Christ* (Berlin: Verlag Alfred Töpelmann, 1967), 15.

demonic power, a world ruler who claims the obedience of men just as God does."[342] The new aeon is under the dominion of Christ. What Paul is primarily concerned with in this passage is the change that takes place when men are freed from their slavery to sin and become slaves of a new master. The implication is that, as illustrated by his reference to baptism (6:1-3), they cannot continue to live a life of sin because the new master, like the old, has a total claim to their service and holds them in his power, but it is the power of love and a slavery that is perfect freedom—from sin.

But any liberation from an "old master," can result only if the "new master" has broken the "old master's" hold on the slaves by conquering him (the idea of "purchasing" the freedom is far from this vision thus contradicting any literalising of the ransom motif of the atonement). And this reality is implicitly referred to in vv. 13 and 18. It is to this victory that W. M. Greathouse refers: "Because of what Christ has done for us, we are no longer helpless slaves to sin. In fact, the enslaving power of sin in our lives is broken. Sin no longer reigns as our master. Through the liberating power of Christ's saving death we are free not to sin."[343]

N.T. Wright, in his Romans commentary, argues that the Exodus motif hangs over the entire book, especially Romans 8 and also in Galatians 4 "which speaks of "God's people as being enslaved, and then, at the right time, God sending forth his Son and his Spirit to rescue those who are 'under the law.'" On this point he adds further, "Paul tells the story of Israel being redeemed from Torah as though Torah were a new sort of Pharaoh, an enslaving power. Torah has become, in fact identified as one of the *stoicheia tou kosmou*, the 'elements of the world,' which I take to mean the shabby line-up of tutelary deities of the nations, the sub-divine beings to whom the world has been entrusted until the time of fulfillment." Furthermore, "Perhaps the most obvious point [of contact with the Exodus motif] is Romans 6, where those in Christ come through the waters of baptism, symbolizing the dying and rising of and with Christ, and so pass from the slavery of sin to the new life of sanctification."[344]

---

[342]Ibid. 16.

[343]*Romans 1-8*, 174.

[344]"Redemption from the New Perspective," 82, 88.

This understanding of the atoning work of Christ dominated Christian thinking for the first one thousand years of Christian history. It has been reintroduced into the modern world by Swedish theologian Gustav Aulën.[345] It offers a significant alternative to certain dominant ideas that have informed much evangelical theology, ideas that make it logically difficult to relate the atonement to sanctification. In relating the *Christus victor* motif to sanctification, W.M. Greathouse says, "Christ's victory *for* us becomes his victory *in* us by the indwelling Spirit (Romans 8:1-11). Christ's victory is reproduced in us. In the Holy Spirit, Christ for us becomes Christ in us, recapitulating in our history his triumph over sin. This is the meaning of Christus Victor for sanctification."[346] Or as C.H. Dodd comments, "By his life of perfect obedience, and his victorious death and resurrection the reign of sin over human nature has been broken."[347]

The Atonement as Sacrifice. Much of Israel's relation to Yahweh revolved around the matter of sacrifice. The theological understanding of sacrifice in that context informs one major interpretation of Jesus' death in the New Testament. While the book of Hebrews contains the major discussion of the sacrificial understanding of the work of Christ, it is present in other passages as well, both Pauline and Johannine. The central question concerns how sacrifice is understood to function. The major problem here is that there is no explicitly stated rationale in the Old Testament; we must infer its meaning from more indirect references. Since I have discussed the issues involved more fully in other places, I will here only summarize those conclusions and make some application to the point at issue in this discussion.[348]

---

[345]Gustav Aulën, *Christus Victor*, trans. A.G. Hebert (N. Y.: Macmillan Co., 1951).

[346]"Sanctification and the Christus Victor Motif," *Wesleyan Theological Journal*, vol. 38, No. 2, Fall, 2003, 223.

[347]C.H. Dodd, *The Epistle to the Romans* (N.Y.: Harper and Bros., 1932), 93.

[348]Dunning, *Grace, Faith and Holiness*, 354-360; *The Whole Christ for the*

The two major theories about how sacrifices functioned in the Old Testament are encapsulated by the two terms by which *hilasmos* may be translated: propitiation and expiation. These terms represent two distinctly different understandings of the atonement.[349] In order to avoid prejudicing the issue either way, the NIV wisely translated it as "atoning sacrifice." How one interprets the Greek word is a theological issue, not a linguistic one. Propitiation suggests an offering directed to the deity to pacify or satisfy him (or her). By means of a gift, the deity is persuaded to overlook the sin of the guilty one. Expiation deals with the estrangement between the human and deity by "removing" the cause of the alienation, namely sin. The total picture in the descriptions of sacrifice in the Old Testament leads me to the conclusion that the latter is the most exegetically and theologically consistent meaning.

But for our purposes it is important to recognize a fact that is too often overlooked. There is a 2-fold function of sacrifice. One is a covenant establishing sacrifice and examples of this (Genesis 15; possibly the Passover) involve no offering given to God. Rather it is God himself who initiates the offering. Once the covenant is established, the sacrificial system in the cult[350] serves to maintain the covenant relation by providing cleansing for *inadvertent sins*. This is the provision made in Leviticus 1-7, particularly with the sin-offering.[351] There is no sacrifice for *willful sin*. This is why the writer to the Hebrews, basing his (or her) appeal on the covenant maintaining sacrifices of the Israelite cult can say, "For if we willfully persist in sin

---

Whole World, 96-98; "Sacrifice," *Beacon Dictionary of Theology*, ed. Richard S. Taylor, et. al. (K.C.: Beacon Hill Press of Kansas City, 1983).

[349]Some have attempted to integrate these two but trying to "work both sides of the street" this way tends to become special pleading.

[350]By "cult" is meant all forms and acts ritually performed in a worship setting where the people's dealings are with deity and is to be distinguished from cults, which are aberrant religious groups.

[351]N.T. Wright suggests that this understanding of sacrifice is the clue to Paul's claim in Philippians 3:6—"as to righteousness under the law, blameless." He suggests that Paul is not claiming moral perfection but that in case of inadvertent violations of the law he took advantage of the sacrifice for such and that his claim is that he has not committed high handed sin. This makes perfect biblical sense.

after having received the knowledge of the truth, there no longer remains a sacrifice for sin" (Hebrews10:26). Willful sins may be reduced to inadvertent sins by repentance and thus capable of being cleansed by sacrifice.[352]

It is in connection with this second function of sacrifice that the relation of the atonement to sanctification becomes relevant. If the result of a single experience would result in "sinless perfection," then this function would be irrelevant but, as John Wesley insisted, there is no such experience in this life. That is the implication of his statement in the mature expression of his views in *The Plain Account of Christian Perfection*:

> The holiest of men still need Christ, as their Prophet, as "the light of the world." For he does not give them light, but from moment to moment; the instant he withdraws, all is darkness. They still need Christ as their King; for God does not give them a stock of holiness. But unless they receive a supply every moment, nothing but unholiness would remain. They still need Christ as their Priest, to make atonement for their holy things. Even perfect holiness is acceptable to God only through Jesus Christ. . . . The best of men may therefore say, "Thou are my light, my holiness, my heaven. Through my union with Thee, I am full of light, of holiness, and happiness. But if I were left to myself I should be nothing but sin, darkness, hell.[353]

The significance of the atonement in its sacrificial aspect provides both for the establishing of a covenant relation between God and mankind based solely on the grace and mercy of God and once that relation is made, it provides for the continuing cleansing from those inadvertent behaviors, attitudes, disposition and "tempers" that continue to plague us as finite fallen creatures until the final resurrection.[354] The glory and greatness of this sanctifying aspect of

---

[352]Jacob Milgrom, "Sacrifices and Offerings, OT," *Interpreters Bible, supplementary volume* ed. Keith Crimm (Nashville: Abingdon, 1976).

[353]John Wesley, *A Plain Account of Christian Perfection* (K.C.: Beacon Hill Press of Kansas City, reprint), 62.

the work of Christ is celebrated by the Hebrew writer: "And every priest stands day after day at his service, offering again and again the same sacrifices that can never take away sins, But when Christ had offered for all time a single sacrifice for sins, 'he sat down at the right hand of God,' . . ." (10:11-12).

The Atonement as Paradigm. In the early part of the 20th century, during the heyday of the social gospel, Charles M. Sheldon wrote a popular and influential book titled *In His Steps* that depicted the revolutionary results of a group of church people living by the principle of asking "What Would Jesus Do?" That motto reemerged in the late 20th century as a popular phrase. But as my college professor of theology used to say, the real question is "What would Jesus have me to do?" In either case Jesus is seen to be the model of the Christian life. Unfortunately, there is a significant difference both between Jesus and us and between his day and ours. However, there is a sense in which the New Testament indicates that following Jesus means "imitating" him but this is seen in relation to the cross. As George Eldon Ladd asserts: "It is true that Paul does not hold up the *earthly life* of Jesus as a standard of moral excellence."[355] Likewise Robert C. Tannehill says, "Paul seldom concerns himself with the ethical quality of Jesus' life. Instead he focuses his attention on the saving events of the cross and resurrection."[356]

---

[354]J.A. Wood, as a representative spokesman for the 19th century holiness movement, disagreed with this understanding. He said: "In an important sense we hold with Mr. Wesley that the fully purified soul can say, 'Every moment Lord I need the merit of thy Blood." But, it is not in the sense that . . . His blood is cleansing the heart all the time as when He cleansed it from all sin when He entirely sanctified it. This is Plymouth Brethren doctrine, and is a strange *state* of purity which needs or admits a constant cleansing. . . . A continuous cleansing would imply a continuous impurity, or there would be nothing to be constantly cleansed. . . when the heart is entirely sanctified, purity becomes a normal *state* or condition of the soul which is in exact adjustment with the divine will, and the Holy Spirit can pervade and sustain it in every part. The Christian graces exist without alloy, and they remain so unless the heart becomes polluted again by actual sin." (emphasis added) From *Mistakes Respecting Christian Holiness*, quoted by Leland Lindsey, "Radical Remedy," 211.

[355]George Eldon Ladd, *A Theology of the New Testament*, revised edition (Grand Rapids: Wm. B. Eerdmans, 1993), 560.

[356]Robert C. Tannehill, *Dying and Rising with Christ* (Berlin: Verlag Alfred Töpelmann, 1967), 26-7.

In the two cases in which Paul enjoined his converts to "imitate Christ" as he did, the context points to "affliction" and "sacrificial service" (1 Thess. 1:6; 1 Cor. 11:1). The classic passage in Philippians 2:5ff. refers to Jesus' submission to the death on the cross as the paradigm for the corporate life of the church. In a word, Paul interprets the Christian life in an analogy with Jesus' self-giving of himself. As Richard B. Hays summarizes, "to be in Christ is to have one's life conformed to the self-giving love enacted in the cross."[357] This is no doubt the experiential significance of Paul's testimony, "I have been crucified with Christ; and it is no longer I who live, but it is Christ who lives in me. And the life I now live in the flesh I live by the faith of the Son of God who loved me and gave himself for me" (Gal. 2:19-20).

Jesus, from his baptism, self-consciously carried out his vocation in terms of the Isaianic vision of the Suffering Servant. When he called folk to be his disciples he invited them to share this vocation, to take up their cross and follow him. It is not strange that when the early church attempted to come to terms with who Jesus was, in the light of his death and resurrection, they turned to Isaiah 53.

It was the anomaly of the early church's identification of the crucified Jesus with Israel's Messiah that was the source of Saul of Tarsus' vigorous opposition to this new sect. After all, a crucified messiah is a failed messiah. When Saul was encountered by the "risen Christ" on the Damascus road, the result was a "Copernican revolution" in his understanding of God's program. It was in the light of this "blinding" revelation that he could say in 2 Corinthians 5:16— "From now on, therefore, we regard no one from a human point of view; even though we once knew Christ from a human point of view." The phrase "from a human point of view" is an interpretation. What Paul says is "according to the flesh." When we recognize that here, as elsewhere, *flesh* is a shorthand way of referring to the "present age" that has now been invaded by the "age to come" we can easily see that Paul is referring to the way of thinking about the Messiah and the kingdom of God that has been transcended by the radically transforming vocation of Jesus.

---

[357]Hay, *The Moral Vision of the New Testament*, 32. See Hay's extended discussion of this theme, 27-32.

When Paul came to express his own vocation and that of his converts, this vision became the focal point of all his ethical instruction. He saw it implied in the believer's baptism since this experience was an identification with Jesus' baptism that was itself a proleptic event prefiguring his death on the cross. How then could one "continue in sin" since being identified with Jesus in *his* baptism was, like his, a declaration of intent to die, i.e. put to death the old now that the new has come. (Romans 6:1ff.) Living in the light of the inauguration of the "age to come" meant replicating, in a finite sense, the event that sounded the death knell to the "present age." This is really the significance of 2 Corinthians 5:17.

When we survey the central passages of Paul's ethical instruction to his churches, we find that they reflect a "cross-shaped" pattern. When he enjoined the Philippians to "Let the same mind be in you that was in Christ Jesus," it was the submission to the "death on a cross" that defined that "mind." (Philippians 2:5-9)

Chapter 9
Theology and Experience

Thesis: The varieties of human personality, understanding and situations requires great latitude in prescribing patterns of experience, allowing the Holy Spirit freedom in leading seekers of spiritual development in a diverse pattern of experiences.

We have already seen how developments in the holiness tradition have virtually forced faithful theologians to rethink some of the traditional formulations and claims of the early preachers and evangelists who articulated the folk theology that became dominant during the post-Civil war period.[358] I have already suggested several major paradigm shifts that might help preserve the message in the 21st century. Another way forward in this task is to take a careful look at the nature of experience. It is one thing to formulate a sound (and biblical) understanding of what "sanctification" is all about and another to actualize that understanding in experience. We have always emphasized the fact that a correct doctrine does not really make a holiness church, but its embodiment in the life of the people. How we approach this fact is crucial.

The almost infinite variety of factors that shape experience makes it hazardous to attempt to base a theology of experience upon a particular "experience" to which the religious experience of all must conform. While there are distinctive elements in the *ordo salutis* that may be precisely analyzed theologically, individual experience seldom conforms to academic theology. In attempting to close the "credibility gap" between theology and experience, Mildred Bangs Wynkoop concludes that "When abstract technical words are wedded to psychological terminology, confusion always results. . . . Holiness theology suffers from this possible ambiguity when it insists that textbook doctrine must become a part of human experience."[359] She

---

[358]Cf. Quanstrom, *A History of Holiness Theology.*

[359]Wynkoop, *A Theology of Love*, 187.

also observed that "if one approaches Scripture inductively, . . .it is not so clear that a chronological order can be detected. Rather there seems to be a spiritual 'complex' of interrelated elements partaking so much of each other that it is difficult to isolate any one for examination apart from the others."[360] Actually, the nature of scripture, as Wynkoop here implies, is such that it does not yield itself to inductive analysis at all.

A careful study of John Wesley's sermons will demonstrate that his use of scripture does not reflect an inductive approach. He utilizes texts without regard for any pattern of Christian experience. In a word, the Christian life is viewed in a holistic fashion with passages applied to that holistic vision without distinction. Wesley would apparently seldom if ever ask of a particular text, "does this apply to the regenerated but not entirely sanctified person?" or "does this text describe the life of the entirely sanctified?" in contrast to other phases of the Christian pilgrimage. This clearly reflects his emphasis on the continuity of the Christian life. He thus avoids a kind of dispensational "rightly dividing the word of truth" with regard to experience.

By contrast theology is an intellectual enterprise that seeks to formulate in an internally consistent fashion beliefs about a god and his or her relation to the world. This is normally done as an effort to state in formal propositional ways the implications of the authoritative source or sources recognized by the theologian or the religion she represents. *Christian* theology undertakes this task as an effort to articulate the implications of the Christian gospel, understood as the proclamation that the crucified and risen Jesus Messiah is Lord of the world, as witnessed to by the Hebrew-Christian scriptures.

When theological reflections on these implications have reached a measure of consensus, they are often formulated into a creed. In the broadest sense, this explains the existence of the so-called ecumenical creeds. They are doctrinal statements arrived at by the official representatives of the undivided church prior to 1054, when the Eastern and Western churches officially parted company. Subsequently other groups of Christians have developed their own creeds that reflect their own distinctive emphases regarding Christian beliefs. Of considerable interest and significance is the fact that there was no ecumenical creed concerning soteriology, or the doctrine of salvation. However, it is true the creeds that were formulated had as

---

[360] Ibid. 226.

their underlying concern the soteriological significance of the issues at stake. This comes explicitly to expression in the words of the Nicene Creed, "for us men and our salvation." The point being that the doctrines that were at stake (Trinity, Incarnation, Christology, Creation, etc.) were essential to salvation. Not that to believe them effects salvation but salvation is possible only if they are true.[361] Rightly understood this is the meaning of any creed that insists its affirmations are "essential to salvation."

The New Testament speaks of several salvation metaphors such as regeneration, new birth, adoption, sanctification, justification, etc. and theologians have sought to organize these into an order of salvation, commonly referred to as the *ordo salutis*. The nearest to an explicit statement in scripture of an *ordo* is found in Romans 8:30.[362] These metaphors can be organized *theologically* into a pattern but *existentially* it is rare—if ever—that a person will intellectually recognize and identify these elements in their experience until they have attained a level of theological maturity. They just know that their lives have been impacted in a transformative way. As noted in an earlier chapter, scholars have often pointed out the variety of experiences in Acts thus suggesting that one cannot derive a uniform pattern from the accounts recorded there. In similar fashion it is difficult and unwise to pin down John Wesley's understanding because he takes quite seriously the fluidity of Christian experience. This aspect of his understanding is clearly reflected in his observation that

[361]The exception to this is the Athanasian Creed, but John Wesley took exception to its assertion that salvation is dependent on believing its deliverances: "I am far from saying, he who does not assent to this 'shall without doubt perish everlastingly.' For the sake of that and another clause, I, for some time, scrupled subscribing to that creed." *Works*, 6:200.

[362]Greathouse comments on this verse: "Predestination concerns the church, not just individual persons. . . . *Called* implies a summons or invitation of God and the Spirit. *Those he called, he also justified*, because they responded in faith to his call. Justification here comprehends both justification and sanctification, the entire process of salvation from its outset to its consummation." *Romans 1-8*, 277. N.T. Wright concurs and adds: "Justification thus points forwards to 'glorification,' Paul's larger term for the eventual goal. I note that this is a larger category than 'sanctification,' though it includes it en route." "Redemption from the New Perspective," 93.

"several states of the soul are often mingled together, and in some measure meet in one and the same person." [363] Ultimately, this statement points to the Achilles heel of Wesley's understanding, which he bequeathed to his 19th century followers, namely the concept of "states of the soul." As Rob Staples says, "This 'wooden' schematization colors all of Wesley's thinking regarding the doctrines of salvation. His theology cannot really be understood in all its facets without keeping in mind such a scheme."[364] However, says Staples, his own experience and that of his followers led to a realization that this way of describing experience was 'too neat and too rigid,' which led to the above concession and later to the statement that, in principle, rejects the idea of "state": "Does not talking, without proper caution, of a justified or sanctified state, tend to mislead men; almost naturally leading them to trust in what was done in one moment? Whereas we are every moment pleasing or displeasing to God, according to our works; according to the whole of our present inward tempers and outward behaviour.[365]

Nonetheless, Wesley does attempt to develop a kind of taxonomy of spiritual states, such as "faith of a servant, faith of a son," etc. but these are not presented with the rigidity of a fixed *ordo*. They are more of an attempt to recognize the diversity and validity of Christian experience. Many of Wesley's successors, particularly in the 19th century holiness revivals tended to develop a fixed pattern of experience that has been characterized as a "reification" of experience.[366] This phenomenon resulted in a Procrustean bed to which many were forced to conform, or at least imposed upon themselves. I observed this consequence early on in my Christian experience. I became a Christian while a young teenager, with little or no real church background to provide an understanding of what I had embraced. During those early days, our local church was engaged in a very fruitful method of evangelism by holding tent meetings in outlying

[363]"The Spirit of Bondage and Adoption," *Standard Sermons*, 1:196.

[364]Staples, "John Wesley's Doctrine of Christian Perfection," 225.

[365]*Works,* 8:338.

[366]Al Truesdale, "Reification of the Experience of Entire Sanctification in the American Holiness Movement," *Wesleyan Theological Journal*, vol. 31, No. 2, Fall, 1996, 95-117.

communities with the result that the congregation was rapidly growing. Many of us were regularly present in these efforts. One evening at the close of the service, a young married lady of the church went to the altar at the invitation. She "prayed through" and testified that she had suddenly awakened to the fact that God was gone from her life. That, within itself, was quite perplexing to me. I wondered if God was some kind of fly-by-night guest who would slip out while we were asleep. But what was really curious to my young mind was the fact that after she had reestablished her relation to God—got re-saved—she announced that she wanted to remain at the altar before leaving and get sanctified. She did and made the profession of two works of grace in a matter of a few moments. Even though I knew little, if anything, about holiness theology, I felt there was something really artificial about these goings-on. I still do.

Subsequent to writing this remembrance I was both surprised and chagrined to discover an identical experience, reported approvingly, in one of the numerous holiness manuals that were published during the first half of the 20th century. The context of this report decisively revealed the consequences for experience of an inadequate theological paradigm as does a dialog by correspondence with a seasoned holiness theologian. After I entered the pastorate I carried on a dialog with my former seminary professor by mail regarding several issues in holiness theology including the question of backsliding. The question was whether or not a person can backslide from sanctification without backsliding from conversion. He argued that "the majority of the holiness leaders have leaned toward the view that you can't backslide from one without backsliding from the other" and quoted a popular writer who had once said to him: "If a person falls out of the second story of a building, he doesn't stop at the first story." The key to that imagery is the assumption that "you can't backslide from sanctification without deliberate sin, and if [one] deliberately sins, he [or she] can't keep any relation to God at all.[367] I thought then, and with much greater theological sophistication (I hope) still think that this is a perspective that is based on a completely inadequate understanding of sanctification and the divine-human

---

[367]Private letter to the author.

relation. It presupposes that Christian experience is a series of stages, like plateaus, each of which is somewhat discontinuous with the previous one and constitutes a "state" of being rather than a "degree" of relationship that may fluctuate from time to time as influenced by a number of factors.

I am suggesting that one way forward in seeking to preserve the authentic holiness message is to take a careful look at the nature of experience, especially as it relates to theological formulations. Al Truesdale has rightly called attention to the importance of this task, as well as the general neglect of it:

> In light of the importance of experience in the holiness movement, one might expect that the existential diversity of human and religious life—the real and complex contexts of experience—would have received careful and sustained attention. One would think that the proclamation of entire sanctification would be accompanied by sustained sensitivity to the psychical, social, religious, and domestic histories of those to whom the promise was addressed. The religious substance of the grace of entire sanctification, not the accidental existential forms of experience, should have provided the movement's determinative center.[368]

We have earlier noted that John Wesley, acknowledged as the fountain-head of the modern holiness movement, made a distinction between the "substance" or content of sanctification and the "circumstance" or "structure" of it. In his *Minutes of Several Conversations*, printed for the first time in 1789, he declared that the *substance* is settled, meaning that "all . . . agree to . . . salvation from all sin, by the love of God and man filling our heart . . . and that it may be attained before we die." He continued, "But, as to the *circumstance*, is the change gradual or instantaneous?" and answered, "it is both the one and the other,"[369] but affirms in his sermon "On Patience" that "the scriptures are silent on the subject" and from that concluded that "because the point is not determined, at least not in express terms, in any part of the oracles of God, Every man therefore may abound in his own sense, provided he will allow the same liberty to his neighbor,

---

[368]Truesdale, "Reification," 95-6.

[369] John Wesley, *Works*, 8:328-9.

provided he will not be angry at those who differ from his opinion, nor entertain hard thoughts concerning them."[370]

Thus he recognized the fluidity of experience and allowed for it. In a letter to Mary Cooke, Wesley counseled her concerning her apparent lack of certainty about her status before God to "hold fast what you have, and ask for what you want," on the principle that "There is an irreconcilable variability in the operations of the Holy Spirit on the souls of man, more especially as to the manner of justification."[371] But based on his experience, he concluded that entire sanctification is commonly, if not always an instantaneous work." However in the *Plain Account of Christian Perfection* he observed that we cannot tell how God must work, only how he normally works, and further admits the possibility that one might receive perfect love in the moment of justification.[372] This implies that for him the definitive source for understanding the pattern of religious experience was imprecise experience itself. This use of inductive reasoning about the structure of experience leaves the question open-ended as does all inductive logic. Therefore we may logically allow for considerable variability in the light of the diversity of persons in numerous ways, including types of personality.

Recognition of the influence of personality diversity has led some contemporary Wesleyan scholars to a re-evaluation of the life and work of Phoebe Palmer.[373] For many years, her so-called "altar

---

[370]*Works*, 6:490.

[371]*The Letters of the Rev. John Wesley, A.M.*, ed. John Telford (London: The Epworth Press, 1931), 7:298.

[372]*Plain Account of Christian Perfection* (K.C.: Beacon Hill Press of Kansas City, 1968), 31; cf. *Works*, 11:422-423..

[373]E.g. Elaine A. Heath, "Becoming a Bible Christian: Toward a New Reading of Phoebe Palmer's Sanctification Theology in Light of Roman Catholic Mystical Traditions," Ph.D. diss. Duquesne University, 2002; later published as *Naked Faith*; Palmer has also emerged in connection with feminist interests: Diane LeClerc, "Two Women Speaking 'Woman': The Strategic Essentialism of Luce Irigaray and Phoebe Palmer," *Wesleyan Theological Journal*, vol. 35, no. 1, Spring 2000.

theology," has been considered a deviation from the authentic Wesleyan perspective, leading to presumption and an intellectual faith that is not necessarily ethically transforming. Such criticisms have a large measure of validity. But when her own experience is viewed in the light of her personality in connection with the prevailing ethos of Methodist piety of the time, we can recognize the importance of recognizing the weakness of insisting on a particular form of experience as evidence of the reality of sanctifying grace.

With the adoption by Methodists at the grass roots of the methods of revivalism to promote the message of "full salvation," not only conversion but also sanctification came to be understood and articulated largely in terms of emotional states and processes. In this setting the emotions became a key element in the path to Christian perfection. Phoebe Palmer found herself constitutionally unable to experience this kind of "spiritual" phenomenon and thus turned to a less dramatic "shorter way," based on "naked faith" in the word of God.

At least one point at issue in this matter is Wesley's emphasis on "the witness of the Spirit," or the "assurance of faith." This is an issue with which he struggled both personally and theologically. Randy Maddox demonstrates that Wesley's "views on the importance of assurance and the ground of that assurance underwent several transitions over the course of his life and ministry."[374] Under the influence of the Moravians he thought at first that his Aldersgate experience of justifying faith would bring full and complete deliverance from all sin, all fear and all doubt. His experience did not demonstrate this completeness and he eventually came to recognize that there were both practical and theological problems with this conclusion. "By July 1747 he admitted to Charles that he had rethought the entire issue of whether justifying faith must always be accompanied by a distinct, conscious assurance of pardon," whereas earlier he had joined the two in absolute terms.[375] In a letter to Joseph Benson, May 21, 1781, he declared, "A consciousness of pardon cannot be the condition of pardon."[376]

---

[374]Maddox, *Responsible Grace*, 124f.

[375]Ibid. 126.

[376]On more than one occasion, I have heard evangelists say, "if you don't

It is clear that Wesley's experience and theological understanding had a reciprocal relation. The experiential influence enabled him to more adequately formulate his theological understanding which then in turn influenced his experience and teaching. I have occasionally said to my students that a person may be saved for some time (even many years or a lifetime) without ever being "justified by faith." It almost seems blasphemous to say such a thing but when you realize that the *awareness* of the basis of our acceptance by God is formed by our understanding, and consider how few people could actually articulate the doctrine of justification until they have developed a measure of theological sophistication, it makes perfect sense.[377] I would consider my own experience to be an example of this observation. My experience may not be typical but I suspect that many persons who have been converted from a similar background may have had much the same experience. As a teen-ager, I had little or no background in the Christian faith and for all practical purposes had no concept of what it meant to be a Christian. Under deep conviction (of course I did not know then what to call it, I only knew I was miserable for some unexplained reason) I went to the altar in a Sunday evening service to which I had reluctantly (dare I say "unwillingly") gone at the insistence of my parents who had recently been converted. I didn't know theology from breakfast food and when asked what I wanted God to do for me, all I knew to say was "I want to be clean." "Justification," "sanctification," "regeneration," and other such salvation terms would have been gobbledy-gook to me.

When did I come to the awareness that I was "justified by grace through faith?" I have no recollection. It may have been in the context of a college theology class, or a seminary course in systematic theology, or after further graduate study. It obviously came as a gradual dawning of understanding. But one thing is sure, I am now

---

know you are saved (or sanctified) I know you aren't." Certainly a well designed device to create doubt and response to the "altar call."

[377]N.T. Wright makes substantially the same judgment in a lecture on Romans to the Calvin Institute, except he said "never knew they were justified by faith," only that they had "faith in Jesus."

completely aware of the basis on which God accepts me "just as I am." Most people who describe their conversion in later years do so, I suspect, in terms of a developed understanding of theological matters that they did not have at the time.[378]

In exploring this issue, John L. Peters concludes that

> While Wesley was insistent on the pursuit of a definite goal— "holiness of heart and life"—he held no brief for orthodoxy of method. He found that the great majority of those claiming perfect love reported its reception as an instantaneous event. And so he preached it after that fashion. But if it could be realized in some alternate way, he had no intention of discounting it. As early as 1745, he had said: "I believe this love is given in a moment. But about this I contend not. Have this love, and it is enough."[379]

At least some of the academic theologians of the American Holiness movement recognized the legitimate flexibility of experience as dependent on many factors. Daniel Steele, Boston University professor and holiness advocate, advised his ministerial students:

> We learn from books and from the lectures of some theological professors that both regeneration and entire sanctification are states of grace sharply defined, entered upon instantaneously after certain definite steps, and followed by certain very marked results. But the young preacher soon learns that there are eminently spiritual members of his church whose experiences have not been in accordance with this regulation manner. They have passed through no marked and memorable crises. Hence they have no spiritual anniversaries. The young pastor is puzzled by these anomalies. At last, if he is wise he will conclude that the books describe normal experiences to which the Holy Spirit does not limit itself, and that an abnormal method of gaining a spiritual change or elevation is by no means to be discounted.[380]

---

[378]See, for example, *The Confessions of St. Augustine.*

[379]Peters, *Christian Perfection and American Methodism*, 56.

[380]Daniel Steele, *Steele's Answers* (Chicago: Christian Witness Co., 1912), 128.

One of the deeply dedicated ladies in the Sunday school class I sometimes teach gave a testimony that perfectly replicates Steele's analysis. She was reared in a non-holiness denomination that expected a clear-cut testimony of conversion, especially identifying when this took place. Sensing a call to foreign missions, she presented herself to the board of the denomination of which she was then a part. She tried to explain to them that she did not remember being born again with the rationale, "I don't remember being born, but the fact that I'm here proves it happened." She argued that her relationship to God began at such an early age that she needed to adjust language to fit the church's doctrine. In similar fashion her response to invitations to completely surrender to Christ and totally dedicate herself to the Lord led her to what she later learned to describe in Nazarene terminology as being sanctifying grace. As she put it, "If I had grown up hearing it worded differently and expecting it to be a defining moment, I might have remembered it as a life-changing moment. I remember it as a process that took longer than fits comfortably into [typical holiness] language." She and her family found a church whose doctrine most nearly approximated her experience. As I write this, she and her husband are just beginning a six months term of voluntary missionary service overseas.

E. P. Ellyson, one of the early General Superintendents in the Church of the Nazarene with a particular interest in Christian education and nurture, described as "normative" the possibility of a variability of experience:

> There are those, how many we cannot tell, who, as they thus walk in their full light, will be led by the Holy Spirit into this experience when they have no doctrinal knowledge or understanding as to what they have received. They have come to a clear consciousness of need and a deep hunger for a deliverance and blessing which they do not understand. . . . At some time later this person may hear the clear teaching . . . and . . . be shown by the Holy Spirit that this is the experience [s]he received as the great blessing.[381]

---

[381]E. P. Ellyson, *Bible Holiness* (K.C.: Nazarene Publishing House, 1938), 83-4.

While a college student, I had the wonderful opportunity to hear the great Methodist preacher, Clovis Chappell. The one thing I remember from his sermon was an illustration about the nature of conversion. Dr. Chappell had been a cowboy and spoke from his experience about breaking horses to ride. Some horses, he said, are broken by being restrained, saddled and ridden into submission. "Bronk-busting" they call it. Such horses know when they are domesticated. Others, he said, are treated differently. Someone simply gets close to them, feeds them sugar lumps, touches and speak to them, leans on them, allows them to smell the leather of the harness and eventually throws on a saddle, gets on and rides off. That horse never knows when it was broken. At that stage of my development, I reacted somewhat negatively to that illustration. I had seen too many traumatic struggles at an altar of prayer in the context with which I was familiar to accept the second form of "conversion." Maturity and experience has given me a somewhat different perspective.

N.T. Wright described conversion using the imagery of waking up, one used often in the New Testament. Some people wake up suddenly and sharply with the sound of an alarm clock. It is usually a rude and shocking experience to be thus shocked into consciousness. Paul, on the Damascus Road, experienced this kind of awakening and many other people have had a similar encounter. "For others, it's a quiet, slow process. They can be half-asleep and half-awake, not even sure which is which, until gradually, eventually, without any shock or resentment, they are happy to know that another day has begun." I really think John Wesley's Aldersgate experience was more like this. But Wright, sounding a lot like John Wesley's description of how Christian Perfection becomes an experiential reality, says: "But the point is that there's such a thing as being asleep and there's such a thing as being awake. And it's important to tell the difference, and to be sure you're awake by the time you have to be up and ready for action, whatever that action may be."[382]

Actually the same point may be poignantly illustrated by the phenomenon of falling in love. While there may be the rare occurrence of "love at first sight," I suspect it is rare and often ephemeral. Normally it seems to be the case that a casual relationship that

---

[382]N. T. Wright, *Simply Christian* (N.Y.: Harper Collins, 2006), 204-5; cf. Wesley, *Works*, 11:402, 442.

develops into a friendship issues in an awareness, without knowing precisely when it happens, that one is "in love" with the other person. There is an epistemological principle here that deserves further meditation and consideration as it involves a type of knowledge that transcends empirical knowledge.

One of my colleagues in the academy tells me that his wife, an exemplary Christian, has no memory either of "being saved," or of "being sanctified," but she knows she is. As he put it, by "industry standards," she is not saved. But living with her he knows better.

This discussion allows us to better understand the traditional concept of the holiness movement that "entire sanctification" is a "crisis experience." The term "crisis" actually means a turning point. The consecration that we have suggested as being the essence of "entire sanctification" is always a turning point and thus a "crisis." However, although always objectively a crisis, it need not necessarily be a subjective one marked by traumatic struggle. The latter form of experience tended to become normative under the influence of frontier revivalism which flourished during the 19th century.[383] The American holiness movement came to adopt the methods of revivalism to advance its message.

Many factors shape one's religious experience (including one's cultural experience) and it seems prudent to recognize that however variant it may be from ours, it might represent a real relationship with God that in love we should recognize and accept even though we may have serious questions about its nature. One of my earliest recollections of a religious phenomenon occurred while I was approximately 9 or 10 years of age. Each summer, I had the opportunity of spending two or three weeks (or until I got homesick) with my maternal grandparents in the country. Their situation was rather primitive with no electricity, running water, indoor plumbing or automobile but marked by loving relationships. On the occasion I remember, there was a brush arbor revival meeting in the community. The boys harnessed the mules to the log wagon and we rode some

---

[383]Cf. William Warren Sweet, *Revivalism in America* (N.Y.: Abingdon Press, 1944). I have suggested to Keith Drury that his celebrated announcement of the death of the holiness movement was really the death of this historically conditioned form of experience. He did not disagree.

distance to the site where crude benches were located on a dirt floor with a make-shift pulpit and altar at the front surrounded by straw.

I don't have a clue what was preached, don't even remember that part of the meeting. The one thing I remember was the invitation. My grandparents nearest neighbor, Nancy Phillips, went to the "mourner's bench" and for some time I was spell-bound as she wallowed around in the straw and finally "prayed through." My grandmother explained to me what happened. Nancy got the Holy Ghost (you have to pronounce it correctly). That was my first and only direct experience with "holy-rollers." As I think back on that, in the light of what I have been suggesting, I am inclined to believe that odd as it was (at least to me both then and now) Nancy had experienced a genuine encounter with God.

The natural response to this discussion is obvious. What, then, is the point of all this theologizing about the content of Christian experience? And the answer is just as obvious. A theology of Christian experience, shaped by the teaching of scripture, is important to give distinctive content to our experience of the divine and to give guidance to how it should daily be lived out. Apart from this, religion can become mere blind emotionalism or arid rationalism, or rampant superstition. The Roman Catholic, sincerely participating in the Mass or the Eastern Orthodox believer engaged in meditation before an icon may have a legitimate relation to God or, without sound guidance, may simply be the victim of superstition.

Paul's attempted guidance of the Corinthian church reflects the importance of sound doctrine for normative Christian experience. He did not invalidate their "charismatic" experiences, especially tongues-speaking, but proposed to them "a more excellent way" (1Cor. 12:31). This letter reflects a "confrontation" between two views of "spirituality." Paul is attempting to show them that their version is subnormal whereas the "way" to which he is calling them is authentically Christian, although it goes counter to the "spirit of the age" that had so deeply infected their view and practice regarding power and authority. His boasting, in contrast to theirs, is in his weakness, not in his charismatic gifts (2 Cor. 12:5b, 9, 10b). In Michael J. Gorman's summary statement, "The distinctive feature of Paul's experience of the Spirit, and his resulting understanding of the essence of this Spirit, is the paradoxical symbiosis (union) of power and weakness, of power and cruciformity. The charismatic Spirit is also the cruciform spirit."[384]

Wesley's sermon on "Catholic Spirit," sheds considerable light on this matter. In a generous spirit, he recognizes that the unity of believers has nothing essentially to do with their holding identical opinions or participating in the same "modes of worship," but rather entails their loving God with their whole being and their neighbor as themselves and the manifestation of this love in relations as described in 1 Corinthians 13. It is on this basis that he declares to all and sundry, "if your heart is right as my heart is right, give me your hand." Or as he summarizes his point, "Catholic love is a catholic spirit."[385] It should be immediately recognized that what he here described is his definition of what constitutes Christian perfection. The implications of this are wide-ranging, in part suggesting that the essence of holiness must not be restricted to a traditional formulation or prescribed set of terms or a special liturgy or even by a specified pattern of experience.

Understanding experience in this way enables us to recognize the authentic message of holiness in the wider Christian world. I have discovered in attempting to read rather extensively, that the biblical perspective of sanctification is not dead, but rather it is alive and well. The essence of *biblical* sanctification is being proclaimed and written about all over the place. The language is quite different from the clichés and formulas of the 19th century American Holiness Movement, but the essence of the biblical understanding is being clearly taught and supported. And for that we should give praise to the holy God who, in his covenant faithfulness, will not allow his project of restoring humanity to the lost image, in which they were created, to die.

---

[384]Michael J. Gorman, *Cruciformity, Paul's Narrative Spirituality of the Cross* (Grand Rapids: Wm. B. Eerdmans Pub. Co., 2001), 52.

[385] *Works*, 5:503.

Chapter 10
The Dynamic of Sanctification

Thesis: Consistent with the thoroughgoing eschatological orientation of New Testament theology, the dynamic of sanctification is not an experiential event in the past but the goal of the new creation inaugurated by the death and resurrection of Jesus Christ.

We have proposed, based on biblical exegesis (chapter 6), that "entire sanctification" can be best defined biblically as a whole-person consecration of a "cleansed" self to the worship and service of God. The intent of this presentation of the whole person is toward an ongoing transformation involving increasing conformity to the image of God as divinely intended in the creation and embodied in the person of Jesus Christ (Romans 12:1-2; 6:22, etc.). This interpretation gives a particular shape to the ethical dimension of the sanctified life.

According to Daniel Harrington's analysis, the history of Christian ethical thinking has passed through 7 periods.

> Each era has been distinguished by a primary emphasis either on avoiding evil or sin, or on becoming a disciple of Christ. When the latter emphasis prevailed, moral theologians relied on Scripture as their primary text, developed an integrated anthropological profile for the Christian, and pursued a much more positive agenda that accommodated the interests often relegated to ascetical theology (the branch of theology that trains one in holiness).[386]

The Patristic period was primarily dominated by the debates about Christology and Trinitarian theology but even these had implications for the shaping of Christian morality and their language and conceptuality were heavily biblical. This is significant for our purposes since John Wesley was profoundly influenced by the eastern fathers of this period. Beginning in the sixth century, referred to as the penitential period, the practice of confessing one's sins with some regularity began. Emphasis was placed on the seven deadly sins: pride, envy, anger, sloth, avarice, gluttony, and lust. ". . . moral theology was

---

[386]Daniel J. Harrington & James F. Keenan, *Jesus and Virtue Ethics* (N.Y.: Rowman and Littlefield, 2002), 1.

shaped predominantly by a concern about the sins one should avoid, and not about the good to be pursued." The result was a moral [spiritual] narcissism. The penitents became anxious about their individual souls, not the needs of the kingdom.[387] In summary, the one approach placed primary emphasis on the problem of sin, its removal and subsequent avoidance, while the other stressed an ethical goal to be achieved, usually identified as the restoration of the image of God lost in the Fall.

These approaches have "see-sawed" back and forth through history the one emphasizing obedience to rules or duty (in ethics referred to as deontological) and the other focusing on achieving the highest good, thus being teleological in nature. The latter, when emphasizing the development of character, is referred to as "virtue ethics." Recent ethical emphasis has manifested a significant return to an appreciation for virtue ethics in contrast to various forms of ethics that focused on defining right and wrong acts instead of the formation of character.[388]

The structure of virtue ethics derives from the early Greek philosopher, Aristotle. His classic statement is found in his *Nicomachian Ethics*. The theological version of this approach was classically developed by St. Thomas Aquinas in the Middle Ages. It is of significant interest that as a student at Oxford University, John Wesley studied Aristotle's ethics, which was the standard ethics text at the University, and both used in his teaching and recommended to his preachers a commentary on Aristotle's ethics.

When viewed from the perspective of the various understandings of the Christian life briefly described above, the 19th and early 20th century American holiness movement demonstrated characteristics of the "deontological" approach to ethics,[389] and when applied to its understanding of sanctification, which was unavoidable,

---

[387]Ibid. 2-3.

[388]William C. Spohn, "The Return of Virtue," *Theological Studies* 53 (1992), 60-75. Alasdair MacIntyre, *After Virtue* (Notre Dame, IN: University Press, 1981).

[389]Dunning, "Nazarene Ethics."

led to some of the problems identified by Mark Quanstrom's study of holiness theology in the 20th century.

The dominant concern of most of the holiness literature, especially the so-called "holiness classics" was with the problem of sin and its "removal."[390] While this is clearly a legitimate issue, near exclusive preoccupation with it tended to result in a failure to adequately take into account the challenge of the New Testament to "go on to maturity" in the Christian life (Hebrew 6:1-3). Thus the experience of "entire sanctification" came to be sensed by the popular mind as the "end" (telos) of the Christian life, which created a stultifying mentality (see discussion in Introduction). The focus of Christian experience was on a past event as a moment in which one is "delivered from all sin" (including original sin) rather than a future goal to be pursued.

There is considerable evidence that this preoccupation had negative spiritual consequences. In an analysis of the characteristics of the Keswick view of sanctification vis-à-vis the Wesleyan, Everett L. Cattell demonstrates that there is more commonality than difference between the two positions and concludes with a significant observation: "As I have moved for years among both camps, I have often felt among Keswick people a more earnest striving after holiness than among our own, while at the same time sensing a real lack in the area of arriving.."[391] J. O. McClurkan, whose theology of the Christian life mediated between the Keswick teaching and that of the holiness movement of his day, noted that the "narrow emphasis on a second work of grace" has resulted in an "instability and dryness, which he found to be widespread in the holiness movement."[392] Most of us, I think, would concur with N.T. Wright who observed that "We would all prefer to live with people who knew perfectly well that they weren't good enough for God, but were humbly grateful that God

---

[390]Cf. Jesse T. Peck, *The Central Idea of Christianity*, 5-6; Richard S. Taylor, *A Right Conception of Sin*, 9-11; *Exploring Christian Holiness, The Theological Formulation*, 47-101; J.B. Chapman, *The Terminology of Holiness*, 24-40;Thomas Cook, *New Testament Holiness*, 7-8;.

[391]"Appraisal of the Keswick and Wesleyan Contemporary Positions," *Insights into Holiness*, ed. Kenneth E. Geiger (K.C.: Beacon Hill Press, 1962), 17.

[392]Strickland and Dunning, *J.O. McClurkan*, 91.

loved them anyway, than with people who were convinced that they had made it to God's standard and could look down on the rest of us from a lofty moral mountaintop."[393]

An analysis of the ethical understanding of John Wesley reveals that his ethical guidance was primarily teleological in nature.[394] Virtually all recent studies in Wesley's theology conclude that his entire soteriological perspective was teleological, i.e. goal oriented.[395] It is an order of salvation that is aimed at the perfection of human persons. So it may be concluded, in Lindstrom's words, that in "the process of salvation this idea of gradual development is combined with an instantaneous element . . . . With this teleological aim his conception of salvation must obviously be determined principally by the idea of sanctification."[396]

And even with his insistence on the instantaneous aspect, as Robert Fraser has argued, growth toward maturity was his primary interest rather than the instantaneous. Fraser illustrates this with a letter John wrote to Charles in 1767 in which he said, "Go on, in your own way, with what God has peculiarly called you to. Press the instantaneous blessing: then I shall have more time for my peculiar calling, enforcing the gradual work."[397] The broader *telos* to which that process is directed is the consummation of the Kingdom as reflected in the petition of the Lord's prayer, "thy kingdom come on earth as it is in heaven." In the full answer to this prayer,

all the inhabitants of the earth, even the whole race of mankind, may do the will of their Father which is in heaven as *willingly* as the holy angels; that these may do it *continually*, even as [the angels], without

---

[393]*After You Believe*, 61.

[394]Dunning, "Nazarene Ethics;" *The Quest for Happiness* (Nashville: Southwood Press, 2016).

[395]Cf. Clarence Bence, "John Wesley's Teleological Hermeneutic," Ph.D. Diss., Emery University, 1981.

[396] Lindström, *Wesley and Sanctification*, 120-122.

[397]Fraser, "Tensions in Perfectionism," 19.

any interruption of their willing service. Yea, and that they may do it *perfectly*; that "the God of peace . . . may make them perfect in every good work to do his will, and work in them all which is well-pleasing in his sight.[398]

This teleological emphasis can be viewed as an implication of Wesley's Arminian theological position. Henry Knight points out the contrast of this perspective with Calvinism "which sees all history being determined before creation," whereas for Wesley, "new possibilities are continually opened through the creative power of the Holy Spirit."[399]

As noted, in the 19th century holiness paradigm attention was focused almost exclusively on a past event. As a result there were two related issues that have plagued the modern holiness movement from the post-Civil War period until the present. During that period the movement generally divided over the question of process versus crisis. John Wesley himself, who was considered the "father" of the movement, had continually insisted on both although his emphasis shifted during his long lifetime and left a legacy of ambiguity since he did not fully explain how they two can coexist. His successors in this country, for various reasons, seemed unable to maintain the balance that Wesley sought. The majority of teachers in the Methodist church came to largely emphasis the idea that holiness was exclusively a gradual process whereas, chiefly in reaction to this tendency, the supporters of the "second blessing" teaching came to almost exclusively emphasize the instantaneous character of entire sanctification.[400] This gave rise to the second issue. There was increasing difficulty in describing precisely what occurred in the moment of entire sanctification, with the result that some claimed too

---

[398]*Works*, 5:337.

[399]Henry H. Knight III, *The Presence of God in the Christian Life: John Wesley and the Means of Grace* (Metuchen, N.J.: Scarecrow Press, 1992), 73.

[400]Cf. J. Kenneth Grider, "Entire Sanctification: Instantaneous—Yes; Gradual—No," *The Preacher's Magazine*, March-April, 1971, 43, 47. He says "Within the holiness movement, all the theologians and exegetes have taught that entire sanctification is received instantaneously. If anyone were to deny this, he would not be part of the holiness movement."

much thereby creating numerous practical problems. Mr. Wesley, himself, had faced this issue with some of his followers and strenuously opposed what he referred to as "enthusiasm" and warned against setting the standard too high as well as too low.

Most of the teachers and many of the preachers in the American Holiness movement, however, spent a lot of effort in carefully defining what sanctification was not. As a convert to Christ in a holiness church during the 1940's many of the sermons I heard began in this way. The result was that holiness theology seemed to have its greatest precision in this negative mode. The positive claims generally affirmed that entire sanctification "eradicated" original sin or inbred sin. The problems arose in attempting to define original sin in such a way as to assure the validity of the claim. In a scholarly article noted earlier describing how the late 19th century holiness movement defined original sin, Paul M. Bassett demonstrated that during those years there was a constantly shifting understanding of its nature with a correlative understanding of the results of entire sanctification. One of his summary paragraphs described this situation:

> Holiness people believe that the gift of entire sanctification completely resolves the problem of original sin/inherited depravity in the already-justified believer. In the period covered by this paper [1867-1920], this resolution was usually referred to as a cleansing or, with some debate about the term, as an eradication. [On the other hand] holiness people have continually insisted that this religious experience does not entail intellectual, physical, moral or ethical perfection.[401]

Simple logic tells us that these two claims are in significant tension with each other. If the former claim is allowed, the result would be a state of perfection equivalent to that of the first pair as created by God, in a word, "Adamic-perfection," and this would eliminate the second claim. If the latter claim is allowed, it calls into

---

[401]Paul Merritt Bassett. "Culture and Concupiscence: The Changing Definitions of Sanctity in the Wesleyan Holiness Movement, 1867-1920," *Wesleyan Theological Journal*, vol. 28, Numbers 1 and 2, Spring-Fall, 1993, 59-127.

question the validity of the former and raises the question of precisely what occurs in the moment of "entire sanctification."

Richard S. Taylor makes an interesting observation that addresses this issue while discussing "Holiness and the Meaning of Maturity:" "Problems arise when we are reminded that John Wesley often ascribed maturity to entirely sanctified people; in fact, he wrote as if the second blessing brought one at once into spiritual maturity."[402] There is in fact considerable ambiguity in Wesley's discussions of Christian perfection.

Mark Quanstrom's study of the history of holiness theology in the 20th century has demonstrated that under the influence of a more adequate understanding of human nature and the experience of the people of God, teachers of sanctification have been progressively reducing the expansive claims of many early teachers about what is "eradicated" in the second blessing and correlatively increasing the area referred to as the human, thus leaving more and more room for explaining the remaining imperfections of the "sanctified life."[403] The tensions reflected in the logically conflicting claims concerning the result of entire sanctification eventually resulted in what Mildred Bangs Wynkoop referred to as a "credibility gap" and points to the necessity of a "paradigm shift" in holiness theology.

The 1985 a motion was proposed to the general assembly of one of the largest holiness denominations to remove the term "eradication" from the creedal statement on sanctification along with the elimination of the statement that the effective agency of this action was by the "baptism with the Holy Spirit." The motion failed and those who supported the motion claimed that this failure was continuing an understanding of the experience that would guarantee its "permanent irrelevancy."[404] Of course, there are other ways of coming to terms with the prevailing problems other than doing the sweaty and often times dangerous work of attempting to formulate a more adequate paradigm to explain the sanctifying work of the Spirit in

---

[402]Richard S. Taylor, "Holiness and the Meaning of Maturity," *The Preacher's Magazine*, September/October/November, 1994, 4-6.

[403]Mark R. Quanstrom, *A Century of Holiness Theology.*

[404]Ibid. 141. The term "eradication" was later removed in 1997 and the phrase, "baptism with the Holy Spirit" was modified in 2009.

human life. One can take the approach of continuing to affirm the claim for the "eradication" of the carnal nature (carnality is a misleading word, being used as a noun whereas the scripture always uses carnal [fleshly] in an adjectival way) and insisting that the problem is the resistance of believers to "paying the price" of a total "dying out" to self.[405]

By implication, this was apparently the existential approach I observed during my teen age years. Many of my peers responded to the Sunday evening altar call every week. They had been a week before and "prayed through" to an experience of entire sanctification but returned the following week to do it again. In a number of cases this scenario was repeated week after week. N. T. Wright uses an analogy from his marriage counseling that throws considerable light on this phenomenon.

> I've constantly had to say to puzzled young people exploring love, sex, and marriage, the excitement of romance is like the excitement of striking a match. It's sudden, sparky, and dramatic—and it doesn't last long. The question is, What are you going to do with the match once you've struck it?
> The answer . . . is that you will use the match to light a candle.[406]

What my fellow teens were doing with their repeated visits to the altar was continually striking matches, whereas if they had understood sanctification according to the paradigm we are suggesting, they would have lit a candle and proceeded to implement the flame. What appeared to them as a failure of their altar experience to take would have been seen as an occasion for disciplined growth in grace.

The repeated emphasis of holiness teachers that the full perfection of human nature awaits the consummation is within itself an implicit claim that there is a partial nature to any experience of grace within the conditions of existence. And the sub-structure of New Testament theology explicitly supports this understanding. Utilizing

---

[405]Richard S. Taylor, "Why the Holiness Movement Died," 7-27.

[406]N. T. Wright, *After you Believe* (N.Y.: Harper Collins, 2010), 221.

the "eschatological dualism" of much rabbinic theology of the Second Temple period, the New Testament affirms that the new age of the Spirit has broken into history with the Resurrection of the Messiah Jesus but while the rule [kingdom] of God has thereby been inaugurated, its full consummation awaits the second advent. Thus we are living in the "last days," that period between the first and second comings marked by a provision for a radical transformation of human life that is lived in anticipation of the full, universal redemption of all things [see Romans 8].

Thus what I am proposing is a paradigm that would both affirm the reality of an experience of a deeper relationship of grace and at the same time, both allow and make necessary, an ongoing life of sanctification. What we have learned during the last 100 years is that there is no "quick-fix" for the fallenness of humanity. The holy character that the ethical injunctions of the scripture call for are always in process as we self-consciously choose to practice them until they approach the character of "second-nature." This involves both unlearning and ceasing to practice old ways and learning to practice the Christlike ways that Paul refers to as "putting off the old man" and "putting on the new man" (cf. Rom. 6:6; Eph. 4:19-25; Col. 3:9).

In a remarkably helpful discussion of the third Beatitude ("Blessed are the meek") Wesley argues that grace does not extinguish the passions but enables us to "regulate" them. "It does not destroy but balance[s] the affections, which the God of nature never designed should be rooted out by grace, but only brought and kept under due regulations." The meek "do not desire to extinguish any of the passions which God has for wise ends implanted in their nature; but they have the mastery of all: They hold them all in subjection, and employ them only in subservience to those ends."[407]

Albert Outler finds here a reflection of the influence of St. Thomas Aquinas but the way Wesley elaborates this principle of regulating the affections is very similar to the way Aristotle explains a moral virtue. But then, Thomas' ethics was built on Aristotle. Aristotle defined a moral virtue as a mean between the extremes of excess and defect, between too much and too little (moderation). This was not a mathematical mean since persons differ so much, it was a "mean

---

[407]*Works,* 5:263.

relative to me." Using this principle he explored an extensive variety of virtues.

Wesley describes "meekness" in a similar fashion: "It poises the mind aright. It holds an even scale, with regard to anger, and sorrow, and fear; preserving the *mean* in every circumstance of life, and not declining either to the right hand or the left."[408]

Whereas Aristotle developed the "Golden Mean" in a quantitative way, Wesley taught that the affections should be regulated in a qualitative way. For instance, for Aristotle, the mean of courage was a mid-point between cowardice (defect) and foolhardiness (excess). Wesley, on the other hand, acknowledged that emotions like anger were not to be eliminated but controlled by Christlike criteria. After all, Jesus manifested anger in driving the moneychangers out of the Temple, hence "all anger is not evil."[409] He explains: "And thus even the harsher and more unpleasing passions are applicable to the noblest purposes; even hatred, and anger, and fear, when engaged against sin, and regulated by faith and love, are as walls and bulwarks to the soul, so that the wicked one cannot approach to hurt it."[410]

One might even detect this principle at work in his advice about the use of money, very much like Aristotle's description of generosity as a mean between extravagance and stinginess. The three rules Wesley advocated are quite familiar: make all you can, save all you can and give all you can. But all three have qualifications. The third rule is not interpreted to recommend poverty but a regulated use of wealth that involves a judicious distribution of surplus possessions to oneself, family and the community of faith and then beyond if there is sufficient. He virtually advocates the principle that "charity begins at home," rather than reducing oneself to poverty by indiscriminately giving everything away.

We have sought to demonstrate that Wesley's ethic is "teleological" in nature, that is, it is goal oriented with the goal being

---

[408]Ibid. Emphasis added.

[409]"Christian Perfection," *Works*, 6:17.

[410]*Works*, 5:263.

holiness of heart and life centrally defined as "having the mind that was in Christ." This approach to ethics has a means-end structure. The practices of the Christian life are ordered with the purpose of enabling the believer to achieve the goal. This reflects the structure of a virtue ethic, which N.T. Wright correctly defines as a quality that doesn't come naturally. It's something you have to work at in the power of the Spirit. But he correctly notes that "the Christian believes that virtue is itself a work of grace, it is not a work which happens automatically, easily, or without the Christian equivalent of the hard moral effort of which the pagan theorist had spoken."[411] Existential problems arise when it is believed that there is some more-or-less magical "zapping" that creates the virtues of the Christian life without engaging in the disciplines or means necessary to develop them. In a word, there are "means of actualizing the sanctified life," commonly referred to as "means of grace." From an Orthodox perspective, Dylan Pahman said "Spiritual disciplines are tools to be used for a goal. They must not be pursued as an end in themselves, or to gain the notice and admiration of others," and quotes an Egyptian desert father, St. Moses the Ethiopian, who describes them as "rungs of a ladder up which [the heart] may climb to perfect charity."[412]

The popular way of using the term "means of grace" tends to restrict its application to two rituals or ordinances (for Protestants), baptism and eucharist. Wesley broadens the concept considerably and interprets it to mean "outward signs, words, or actions ordained of God, and appointed for this end—-to be the *ordinary* channels whereby [God] might convey to men preventing, justifying, or sanctifying grace." These include prayer, "searching the Scriptures," (whether reading, hearing [preaching] or meditating thereon) as well as the two regular sacraments.[413] While the means may become ends in themselves, this is a distortion. As long as one keeps her eye on the goal, they ideally function to create an ever more intimate conformity to the perfection of love.

---

[411]Lecture given to the Christian Aid Act Justly Conference, March, 2007. Taken from www.ntwrightpage.com; *After You Believe*, 125.

[412]"The Yeast We Can Do," in *Touchstone* March/April 2013, 24.

[413]"The Means of Grace," *Works*, 5:187.

I have come to believe that the clue to an experientially sound paradigm for the New Testament view of the Christian life is found in Paul's words in Phil. 3:12-16: "Not that I have already obtained this or am already perfect; but I press on to make it my own, because Christ Jesus has made me his own. Brethren, I do not consider that I have made it my own but one thing I do, forgetting what lies behind and straining forward to what lies ahead, I press on toward the goal for the prize of the upward call of God in Christ Jesus. Let those of us who are mature [perfect (KJV)] be thus minded; and if in anything you are otherwise minded, God will reveal that also to you. Only let us hold true to what we have attained."[414] (RSV)

In the space of a few verses, the Apostle both denies and claims perfection. The only logical conclusion that can be drawn from this passage is that *the perfection he claims (v. 15) is characterized by the unswerving pursuit of the perfection he denies (v. 12).* This implies that "entire sanctification" is appropriately understood as a total commitment to an ethical lifestyle lived out in terms of a focused pursuit of the goal of God's creative intention for the human race. And note the powerful emphasis in this passage on the human contribution to this pursuit reflected in phrases like "I press on," and "straining forward."

Ultimately that appears to be what John Wesley is really attempting to say, oftentimes ambiguously, about "entire sanctification." His repeated emphasis on the scriptural phrase, "the single eye," a phrase taken from the Sermon on the Mount and the title of one of his sermons, clearly points in this direction. A "single eye" includes both simplicity and purity, the former being the intention and the latter referring to the affections.[415] This means that it is the

---

[414]See Wesley D. Tracy, et. al., *The Upward Call* (K.C.: Beacon Hill Press of Kansas City, 1994) for a guide book to implementing this passage. N.T. Wright points out that Romans 5:1-2 is one of "the passages where it is most clear that Paul is thinking of the future goal as the thing which forms character in the present." *After You Believe,* 90.

[415]In commenting on these two virtues he says: "By that simplicity you always see God, and by purity you love him." "On Dissipation," *Works,* 7:449. When both intention and focused affections are present they direct the "understanding, passions, affections and tempers," as a result of which the soul

believer's "intention in all things, small and great, in all thy conversation [manner of life], to please God, to do, not thy own will, but the will of Him that sent thee into the world." When referred to the affections it clearly means loving God with *all* one's being. This emphasis is further seen in his repeated stress on "purity of intention" and focused love as embodied in the two summary commandments as identified by both the Old Testament and Jesus. Wesley professed to have first discovered this paradigm in reading four works early in his Christian pilgrimage: Jeremy Taylor's *Rule and Exercises of Holy Living and Dying,* Thomas a'Kempis' *Imitation of Christ,* and William Law's *Christian Perfection* and *Serious Call to a Devout and Holy Life.* From the first two in particular he came to see the importance of "simplicity of intention and purity of affection." On this basis he shifted the emphasis on sanctification from law-keeping to intentionality and this came to focus in terms of "love." Thus he came to uniformly define "entire sanctification" or "Christian Perfection" as "loving God with all your heart, soul, mind, and strength, and your neighbor as yourself." "Such a love as this engrosses the whole heart, . . . Takes up all the affections, . . . fills the entire capacity of the soul and employs the utmost extent of all its faculties."[416] This reflects what we have previously referred to as "focused love."

His interpretation of "Dissipation" carries the same accent. The common understanding of that term refers it to those "who are violently attached to women, gaming, drinking; to dancing, balls, races, or the poor childish diversion of 'running foxes and hares out of breath.'" But Wesley defines it as "the uncentring the soul from God." Here he admits that this "uncentering" may be present in the believer

---

"shall be filled with holiness and happiness." "On a Single Eye," *Works,* 7:297-299. Somewhat oddly Wesley makes an "all or none" judgment about the "single eye": "It is certain there can be no medium between a single eye and an evil eye; for whenever we are not aiming at God, we are seeking happiness in some creature," which is idolatry. This is reflective of the Stoic philosophy who took the same exclusivistic view of virtue. It seems to leave no room for growth, which is clearly contrary to Wesley's oft repeated emphasis along with his denial that there is any "perfection of degrees" that does not admit of continual increase. The answer may lie in the dynamic involved in the concept of "habituated affections" similar to Thomas Aquinas, which seems to be Wesley's understanding of development in holiness.

[416]"The Almost Christian," *Works,* 5:21.

in whom there remains the "carnal mind" and declares that "The radical cure of all dissipation is, the 'faith that worketh by love'."[417]

We have suggested that the ethical philosophy of Aristotle provides the structural paradigm for Wesley's understanding of the Christian life where a "final form" [perfect Christlikeness for St. Paul and Wesley] is the dynamic element that exerts an attractive influence drawing one toward its actualization. If we can recognize the difference between normal human growth and development and spiritual growth, Wesley's analogy of the relation between regeneration (the beginning point of the Christian life) and sanctification is a good example of this perspective: "A child is born of God in a short time, if not in a moment. But it is by slow degrees that he afterward grows up to the measure of the full stature of Christ. The same relation, therefore, which there is between our new birth and our sanctification."[418]

Of greater importance is the fact that the biblical perspective is also teleological. Alasdair MacIntyre, in an analysis of Aristotle's ethics notes that "The New Testament's account of the virtues, even if it differs as much as it does in content from Aristotle's . . . does have the same logical and conceptual structure as Aristotle's account. A virtue is, as with Aristotle, a quality the exercise of which leads to the achievement of the human *telos.*"[419]

In practical terms, this implies that the Christian life is a lifetime of utilizing all relevant means to cultivate those qualities that reflect the mind of Christ in attitude, disposition, motive and behavior, energized by a moment that could occur experientially at any point in the believer's experience that is an infilling of a love that expels whatever is contrary to exclusive love for God and neighbor and focuses ones energies and goals toward pursuing the "upward call."

---

[417]*Works,* 7:449.

[418]*Standard Sermons*, 2:240. It is interesting that Oswald Chambers equates regeneration with entire sanctification, and refers to it as "but the beginning of the purpose of the Christian life, *The Psychology of Redemption* (London: Marshall, Morgan & Scott, 1955), 31.

[419]Alasdair MacIntyre, *After Virtue* 184.

This interpretation can easily be misunderstood. To avoid that misunderstanding, we must say "it is simply not the case that God does some of the work of our salvation and we have to do the rest. It is not the case that we begin by being justified by grace through faith and then have to go to work all by ourselves to complete the job by struggling, unaided, to live a holy life."[420] While there are numerous issues that may need to be addressed, this proposal simply means that *the dynamic of the holy life is the future and not the past*. Virtually all of the struggles of the holiness movement to explain what happens in entire sanctification are thereby obviated and all energies can then be directed toward implementing the actualization of that goal. This paradigm is beautifully expressed in 2 Corinthians 3:18—"And we all, with unveiled face, beholding the glory of the Lord [Jesus], are being changed into his likeness from one degree of glory to another; for this comes from the Lord who is the Spirit."

---

[420]N. T. Wright, *After You Believe*, 60.

Chapter 11
"Love God and do as you please"[421]

Thesis: The tension between legalism and spontaneity is properly addressed by a true understanding of the nature of rules, which function as means to growth in holiness.

Rules are important. If there were no "rules of the road," such as driving on the designated side of the road, the result of each individual "doing his own thing" would likely be disaster. Peace and safety in any society is dependent on certain rules having to do with how persons relate to each other, their persons and their property. While there are those who resist having rules imposed upon them in their religious life, usually appealing to the guidance of the Holy Spirit, the dangers of unguided subjectivity have often become obvious.

Early holiness theologian Daniel Steele suggests this point using a similar illustration:

> The iron rails can communicate no power to impel the train; but they are indispensable to direct whatever force may be applied, whether gravity, steam, or electricity. The absence of the rails at any given point of the track is ruin. Thus it is with the law of God. It has no power to impel or to attract the soul Godward: but its perpetual office is to guide the chariot wheels of the divine love, impelling souls upward along the heavenly way.[422]

---

[421]One of the most familiar pieces of advice given by St. Augustine of Hippo (354-430) found in his Seventh Homily on 1 John. It has sometimes been mistakenly interpreted as granting unlimited freedom in ethical behavior. Conversely, it suggests the most demanding criteria for the ethical dimension of the Christian life. The full version goes a little like this: "Love God and do whatever you please: for the soul trained in love to God will do nothing to offend the One who is Beloved." Since Christian perfection is classically defined as loving God with one's whole being, it nicely exemplifies the essence of the ethical dimension of the sanctified life. Rather than eliminating the need or importance of rules, it implies their necessity if they are interpreted in a particular way. This is what we are exploring in this chapter.

Historically, the importance of rules (or law) in providing guidance in the Christian life is illustrated by the contrasting understanding of the two major Protestant Reformers, Martin Luther and John Calvin. In reaction to the Catholic teaching of works-righteousness, Luther took a negative view of the law so far as its having a role in the Christian life. Luther and his Wittenberg associate Philip Melanchthon generally identified two uses of the Law: it keeps sin in check, even among unbelievers; and it works penitence in sinners' hearts, in preparation for the Gospel.[423] Paul Tillich describes in his own unique terminology the results of Luther's insistence on the more or less limitation of ethical guidance to the work of the Spirit:

> In Lutheranism the emphasis on the paradoxical element in the experience of the New Being was so predominant that sanctification could not be interpreted in terms of a line moving upward toward perfection. It was seen instead as an up-and-down of ecstasy and anxiety, of being grasped by *agape* and being thrown back into estrangement and ambiguity. . . . The consequence of the absence in Lutheranism of the Calvinistic and Evangelistic valuation of discipline was that the ideal of progressive sanctification was taken less seriously and replaced by a great emphasis on the paradoxical character of the Christian life.[424]

John Calvin, on the other hand, emphasized the importance of what is commonly referred to as the "third use of the law."[425] He described it in the *Institutes* in graphic language:

---

[422]*Milestone Papers* (Holiness Data Ministries, NNU website), 8.

[423]Ryan C. MacPherson, "A Lutheran View of the Third Use of the Law," Ryan C. MacPherson web site. MacPherson argues that Luther implicitly recognized a "third use of the Law" but the majority of Reformation scholars differ.

[424]Paul Tillich, *Systematic Theology*, 3 vol. in 1 (Chicago: University Press, 1967), 230-31.

[425]Luther's view of the law has impacted the interpretation of the Pauline writings, especially Romans, which until the work of E. P. Sanders, *Paul and Palestianian Judaism* (1977) read Paul as having a negative view of the law. The "new perspective on Paul," arose out of the recognition, stimulated by Sanders, that Second Temple Judaism did not see law-keeping as a means of gaining the favor of

The third use of the Law . . . has respect to believers in whose hearts the Spirit of God already flourishes and reigns. . . . it is the best instrument for enabling them daily to learn with greater truth and certainty what that will of the Lord is which they aspire to follow. . . . In this way the saints must press on; for, however eagerly they may in accordance with the Spirit strive toward God's righteousness, the listless flesh always so burdens them that they do not proceed with due readiness. The Law is to the flesh like a whip to an idle and balky ass, to arouse it to work."[426]

With this emphasis, Calvin developed an understanding of sanctification that was very similar to John Wesley, in fact, up to a point it was virtually identical. In one such passage he says:

We confess that while through the intercession of Christ's righteousness God reconciles us to himself, and by free remission of sins accounts us righteous, his beneficence is at the same time joined with such a mercy that through his Holy Spirit he dwells in us and by his power the lusts of our flesh are each day more and more mortified; we are indeed sanctified, that is, consecrated to the Lord in true purity of life, with our hearts formed to obedience to the law.[427]

But he is always careful to qualify these descriptions with the disclaimer that one can ever be fully sanctified short of death. Only at that point will the falling short of the perfect law of God be put to an end. Of course, in the context of the perfect law, Wesley affirms the same.

From the Wesleyan perspective, the question is not whether or not there should be "rules" but how they function. Herein lies a significant difference between the dominant perspective of the 19th century holiness movement and that of Wesley himself. The tendency

---

God but in a more positive way. That is why N.T. Wright noted that "had the dominant view of Paul prior to Sanders been Reformed [Calvinist] rather than Lutheran, the New Perspective might never have been necessary." "Redemption from the New Perspective," 71.

[426]Calvin, *Institutes of the Christian Religion*, 2.7.12.

[427]Ibid. III, xiv, 9.

of the former is to speak of rules as "evidence" that one either *is* or is *seeking to be* "cleansed from all indwelling sin.," thus focusing on a "completed event" in the past. Since, as we have observed, their primary emphasis is on an instantaneous work of grace, monergistic in nature, it would be contradictory to speak of "means" of grace to achieve the *telos* of entire sanctification. Furthermore the goal of sanctification is generally interpreted as deliverance from inward sin rather than the restoration of the image of God. While informed teachers did not explicitly teach that entire sanctification was the terminus of the Christian life, in the popular mind of many, there was little practical room for growth following the actualization of the state of grace called entire sanctification. The question must then be raised as to the function of the rules in the life of one who has attained this "state of grace." One must conclude that they serve as criteria for determining that one has arrived at the point of full cleansing from indwelling sin.

Historically there was little difference between Wesley's rules for his Methodist people and the general rules in holiness manuals. Thus the question is, what was the purpose for Wesley's imposition of a disciplined life upon both himself and his followers? The answer may be learned by looking at Wesley's definition of religion as a "constant ruling habit of soul, a renewal of our minds in the image of God, a recovery of the divine likeness, a still increasing conformity of heart to the pattern of our most holy Redeemer."[428]

Here is expressed the ideal of maturity that gave vitality to the gradual element in Christian perfection. It recognizes a "perfection" that admits of continual increase.[429] It is this ideal that is, as Peters puts it, "the result of a discipline of life, energized initially by the grace of God and utilizing the instantaneous enduement in a more expeditious growth toward spiritual maturity."[430]

---

[428]John Telford, ed., *The Letters of John Wesley,* 8 vols. (London: Epworth Press, 1931), 1:152.

[429]Wesley insisted that there was no such thing as a "perfection of degrees as it is termed, none which does not admit of continual increase." Outler, *Standard Sermons*, 2:156.

[430]Peters, *Christian Perfection*, 65.

Thus it was that the rules and methods were prudential means that were ordained toward achieving this "ruling habit of mind," this complete "recovery of the divine likeness." It has already been observed that Wesley could speak meaningfully of means to holiness; therefore this is perfectly in accord with his theological understanding.

This is consistent with N.T. Wright's description of the nature of rules: "The rules are to be understood, not as arbitrary laws thought up by a distant God to stop us from having fun (or to set up some ethical hoops to jump through as a kind of moral examination), but as the signposts to a way of life in which heaven and earth overlap, in which God's future breaks into the present, in which we discover what genuine humanness looks and feels like in practice."[431]

As a young pastor in the context of that wing of the holiness movement that was deeply committed to what has been called "a puritan ethic," I constantly found myself attempting to justify the rules prohibiting certain forms of amusement, especially to the young people. They were not really rebellious but sincerely seeking to understand why these matters that were prohibited were "wrong." That experience was the catalyst that has led me to a career long interest in ethics. As I struggled with these issues, I finally came to a position that became the basis for my first published book.[432] Without, at that time, an intimate knowledge of Wesley's theology, I arrived at a teleological response to the issues in question. This perspective has informed my preaching and teaching throughout the succeeding years. This explanation did not fully satisfy all of my inquiring young parishioners but it did help them to see that they were asking the wrong question. They should not have been asking about the "wrongness" of the prohibited matters but rather whether or not they were helpful toward fostering Christian maturity. Unfortunately, I had not been taught by my early theological education that sanctification should be interpreted biblically as "renewal in the image of God."

If the purpose of the election of Israel was to a vocation to be God's paradigm for the Creator's intention for the human race, and that purpose was to be manifested by their holiness, and that holiness

---

[431]N. T. Wright, *Simply Christian*, 225

[432]*Our Standard of Conduct* (K.C.: Beacon Hill Press, n.d.)

was defined by the law, then the purpose of "discipline" is illuminated by the purpose of the law. We may gain much insight from Moses' "farewell address" to Israel on the plains of Moab prior to their entrance into the Promised Land as recorded in Deuteronomy.[433] Against the background of the situation (on the threshold of entering the Promised Land) these speeches imply the nature and purpose of the law. An analysis of the re-presentation of the law in light of the upcoming new form of life to be entered into and the nature of the culture they would encounter suggests that the purpose of this edition of the law was to provide barriers against the encroachments of "pagan" culture.

The Canaanite culture was dominated religiously by Baal worship and its whole way of life was structured around this religion. Baal was a fertility deity who had a wife named Ashtoreth and as with fertility cults, worship revolved around sexual activity. This was designed to make the soil productive and since Canaan was "a land flowing with milk and honey," with luxuriant growth of fruit (see Numbers 13:23) it appeared to be successful. In addition, there were numerous shrines where a Baal was worshiped so that there were numerous Baalim, each named for the location of his shrine, e.g. Baalpeor, the Baal worshipped at Peor.

Moses knew that this situation would present a temptation to conform to the cult of success, resulting in a compromise of the moral standards Yahweh required of his people. And the many Baalim could result in a compromise of the unity of Yahweh. This is at least the perversion of the nature of God and the resultant requirement of his people that is reflected in the Shema of Deuteronomy 6:4-5: "Hear O Israel: The Lord our God is one Lord; and you shall love the Lord your God with all your heart, and with all your soul, and with all your might."

A description of the tragic results of failing to follow this rule is found in Numbers 25:1-9 when the men were seduced in the context of the worship of the Baal of Peor to engage in blatant immorality. Ultimately the failure to take this "rule" seriously is dramatically

---

[433]It is irrelevant to this analysis whether the biblical description of this event is to be taken literally or as the work of a later scribe as suggested by much liberal Old Testament scholarship.

described in the book of Hosea with the result that Israel eventually lost the land.

Such events as the Baalpeor incident would possibly suggest that we are dealing with a legalistic legislation that simply emphasizes negatives. But the contrast to the judgment on the violators there as expressed by Moses in Deuteronomy 4:4 suggests that the more important purpose was to enable Israel to maintain a right relation to Yahweh: ". . . but all of you who *held fast* to the Lord your God are still alive today." This same phrase is repeated in 10:20 with the note in the NIV defining the meaning in highly personal terms: "As a man is 'united' to his wife, and as Ruth 'clung' to Naomi."

The context of the instructions given in Deuteronomy is the covenant. This last point highlights the fact, seldom recognized, that there is a significant difference between a covenant and a contract. Elmer Martens offers a helpful distinction between the two:

The contract is characteristically *thing*-oriented. The covenant is *person*-oriented and, theologically speaking, arises, not with benefits as the chief barter item, but out of a desire for a measure of intimacy. . . . The conditions set out in a contract require fulfillment of terms; the obligation of covenant is one of loyalty. . . . A ticking off of terms in check-list fashion can reveal a broken contract, and the point of brokenness can be clearly identified. A covenant, too, can be broken, but the point at which this transpires is less clear, because here the focus is not on stipulations, one, two, three, but on a quality of intimacy.[434]

The law also has the purpose of embodying God's provision for the well-being of society. Apart from exploring the particular provisions, it can be generally said that the law gives direction for the political and social life of the community that gives all persons access to impartial justice. In one sense, its economic provisions give instructions that would prevent a caste society from permanently developing between rich and poor. They call for honesty and fair

---

[434]*God's Design*, 73. This distinction addresses the question of "backsliding" discussed in a previous chapter.

dealing in business relations and full respect for persons as of inherent worth.

All the laws give guidance for both individual and corporate life that, if followed, would enable their mission as a witness to the nations. Moses states this purpose in Deuteronomy 4:5-8: "See, just as the Lord my God charged me, I now teach you statutes and ordinances for you to observe in the land that you are about to enter and occupy. You must observe them diligently, for this will show your wisdom and discernment to the peoples who, when they hear all these statutes will say, 'Surely this great nation is a wise and discerning people!' For what other great nation has a god so near to it as the Lord our God is whenever we call on him? And what other great nation has statutes and ordinances as just as this entire law that I am setting before you today?"

The next legitimate question concerns the source of the "rules" that should function in this teleological fashion. Other than the scripture, which is a given, I would suggest that the interpretation of the image of God can provide a sound guide to this question. Since the image is the *telos* toward which the entire process of sanctification is tending, guidance in the implementing of each of these aspects would be relevant as "rules." In this way they would transcend the basic issue of "right and wrong" and focus more on the prudential purpose of actualizing the "mind of Christ."

One of the fundamental elements in this perspective is the recognition that it is the image of God in mankind that identifies the nature of true humanness. Thus whatever dehumanizes is to be avoided and what enhances authentic humanness is to be enjoined. While this provides a principle of discrimination, the fact is that the application of a principle is more difficult. John Wesley recognized this in a letter to one of his Society members: "General rules are easily laid down, but it is not possible to apply them accurately in particular cases, without the anointing of the Holy One." Since it is impossible to provide an exhaustive directory of rules, the essential element in correctly making use of general precepts or principles in particular circumstances is a spiritual one. This Wesley calls "the anointing," which reflects his acquaintance with 1 John 2:27 and stresses the fact that divine aid is indispensable in ethical behavior consonant with Christian perfection.

One further aspect of the question of rules needs consideration. The corporate nature of the Christian faith suggests that the body of Christ has a significant role in identifying the pattern of life that most effectively reflects the believer's pursuit of the "upward call." Apart from support and sustenance by the body, individual believers are susceptible to being lured aside from the "high road" by various factors that assert an insidious influence on their perceptions. Thus the importance of what can legitimately be referred to as "the conscience of the church." Rightly understood, this does not mean that others, not even a hierarchical figure, should impose rules upon the individual arbitrarily. It means that in the experience of the body, there is the greater likelihood that both hindrances to spiritual growth and matters that enhance it can be identified. In a sense, the church could provide a system of checks and balances. While there are numerous questions raised by this observation, such as the question of the parameters of the "church" in question, the principle is sound.

184

Chapter 12
Decision and Consequence

Thesis: The actualization of the virtues that constitute the ideal of Christlikeness are the result of deliberation and decision to manifest them in the various contexts in which they are appropriate with the consequence that their expression moves their practice toward "second nature," or habituated virtue similar to Aristotle's (or Thomas Aquinas) ethics, which provided the structural paradigm for John Wesley's ethics.

During my sophomore year in college I enrolled in a course in psychology. As I remember, I received an A in the course, which is better than many of my other ones. But I only remember 2 or 3 things from the course, neither of which had anything to do with psychology as I now understand it. The professor was a unique individual who marched, academically, to his own drumbeat. He attempted to teach us a method by which we could remember numerous names; demonstrated his own remarkable memory, which he credited to a method he called "muscularization," by reciting the poem Kubla Khan while working a long division arithmetic problem on the chalk board. To make another point, he told us a story that came to mind as I was thinking about the thesis of this chapter.

The story was about an engineer of a train who spent a lot of time thinking about what he would do if an object suddenly appeared on the track in front of his speeding engine. What would he do if there was not time and space enough to get the train stopped? It was his judgment that a speeding locomotive would have a much better chance of staying on the track and upright if it ran full force into a stationary object (I can't vouch for the validity of his conclusion). As he mulled it over and over in his mind, he imagined the situation and how he would react.

Suddenly one day it happened. He rounded a bend in the road and there in front of him was a stalled truck. Without thinking, as if by second nature, he automatically shoved the throttle forward giving the engine all the power available and lo and behold the cowcatcher knocked the truck off the track and his engine remained firmly on it. It worked! But the point of the story is not some principle of physics but the principle that certain forms of behavior can become so ingrained in ones thinking and responses that appropriate reactions take place without premeditation, "second nature."

The point of the story has tremendous implications for the development of character which is the personal aspect of the *telos* of the life of holiness. This is a sound application of a genuine psychological principle. Psychologist Gordon Allport, in describing human moral development makes the point that sincere persons generally respond to certain stimuli in accord with the concept of the person they either think they are or desire to be. The result of such volitional response actually moves that person toward that ideal so that repeated reactions condition such responses until they may become more like "second nature."[435]

In one of his books, Oswald Chambers developed the thesis that the psychology of the sanctified life is perfectly illustrated in our Lord's life as set forth in the gospels. The essential message of the book was expressed in an earlier lecture like this: "In the Life of our Lord, as Son of Man, when He transformed innocence into holiness by a series of moral choices, He gave the pattern forever of how a holy character was to be developed."[436]

What we are talking about here is in accord with our discussion in chapter 10 where we argued that the dynamic of sanctification is the goal of new creation embodied in the concept of the image of God, which takes the structural pattern of a virtue ethic. "Virtue, in this strict sense," says N.T. Wright, "is what happens when someone has made a thousand small choices, requiring effort and concentration, to do something which is good and right but which doesn't 'come naturally'—and then, on the thousand and first time, when it really matters they find that they do what's required 'automatically,' as we say."[437]

---

[435]*Becoming* (New Haven: Yale University Press, 1955), 65-77. He says, "Striving, it is apparent, always has a future reference," 51.

[436]David Lambert, "Foreword" to Oswald Chambers, *The Psychology of Redemption* (London: Marshall, Morgan & Scott, 1955), 5.

[437]N. T. Wright, *After Your Believe*, 20.

I developed in another project a simple outline of spiritual growth that implements this perspective along with the other necessary elements involved in an increasing conformity to the image of God. It involves three elements: (1) intention, (2) goal, and (3) occasion.[438] We have repeatedly insisted that biblically, as well as central to Wesleyan theology, the goal is the restoration of the image of God. This *telos* as a multi-faceted goal is explored in chapters 4 and 5.

We can also speak of the goal in terms of Christlikeness since Jesus is the perfect embodiment of the image of God under the conditions of existence. Without a known destination, we would find ourselves in a situation like the late Albert Einstein. According to the story, which may be apocryphal, Einstein was once traveling from Princeton on a train when the conductor came down the aisle, punching the tickets of every passenger. When he came to Einstein, Einstein reached in his vest pocket. He couldn't find his ticket, so he reached in his trouser pockets. It wasn't there, so he looked in his briefcase but couldn't find it. Then he looked in the seat beside him. He still couldn't find it.

The conductor said, "Dr. Einstein, I know who you are. We all know who you are. I'm sure you bought a ticket. Don't worry about it." Einstein nodded appreciatively. The conductor continued down the aisle punching tickets. As he was ready to move to the next car, he turned around and saw the great physicist down on his hands and knees looking under his seat for his ticket. The conductor rushed back and said, "Dr. Einstein, Dr. Einstein, don't worry, I know who you are. No problem. You don't need a ticket. I'm sure you bought one." Einstein looked at him and said, "Young man, I too, know who I am. What I don't know is where I'm going."[439]

Here is where the role of conscience enters the picture. As we saw in chapter 6, conscience cannot be biblically considered as a

---

[438]H. Ray Dunning, *Grace, Faith and Holiness* (K.C.: Beacon Hill Press of Kansas City, 1988), 472. N.T. Wright points out that Aristotle, whose ethics is the paradigm for virtue ethics, developed a similar threefold pattern of character transformation: "there is first the 'goal,' the *telos*, the ultimate thing we're aiming at; there are then the steps you take toward that goal, the 'strengths' of character which will enable you to arrive at that goal; and there is the process of moral training by which these 'strengths' turn into habits, become second nature." *After You Believe*, 33.

[439]Told in a Yokefellows newsletter some years ago.

separate "faculty" but the function of the whole person that "continually assesses our tempers, thoughts, words, and actions by the moral standard by which we are supposed to live."[440] However, conscience is a subjective response to an external stimuli, i.e. the content of conscience is learned. This is why it is so important in spiritual growth to give careful attention to God's revealed ideal for humanity, which is their restoration in the image of God.

Flowers and vegetables also have a *telos* but there is a significant difference. A flower's telos is a bloom, vegetables are intended to produce an edible product but achieving their *teloi* is completely dependent on external stimuli. The environment must be congenial, the appropriate proportion of rain and sunshine along with suitable temperatures in addition to being planted in soil with nutrients. Neither of the natural plants ever make a decision to grow, it just comes naturally. This is not so with human beings who would achieve the *telos* of their true personhood. There must be a definite intention to approximate the ideal embodied in the goal.

This point is similar to Mildred Wynkoop's criticism of the theology of the 19th century paradigm, describing it as involving a magical concept. She says "any concept of acquiring what we want without recourse to appropriate means is belief in magic. . . . [Since] Man's problem is not a substructure of some alien substance clinging to his soul but his own alienation from God."[441]

It is at that point that the understanding of entire sanctification as a consecration to a "single minded" pursuit of the image of God becomes significant. This event can be defined as a reorientation of ones life focus. Psychologist Gordon Allport describes such an event: "It sometimes happens that the very center of organization of a personality shifts suddenly and apparently without warning. Some impetus, coming perhaps from a bereavement, an illness, or a religious conversion, even from a teacher or book, may lead to a reorientation."[442]

---

[440]Maddox, *Responsible Grace*, 70 in describing John Wesley's view of conscience.

[441]*Theology of Love*, 164.

188

Allport further gives an illuminating analysis of the result of such a reorientation in the religious life: "To say that a person performs certain acts and abstains from others because he fears God's punishment would be to travesty the experience of most religious people, whose consciences have more to do with love than with fear. An inclusive path of life is adopted that requires discipline, charity, reverence, all experienced as lively obligations by a religious person."[443]

It is important to emphasize at this point that we are not talking about simply another program of self-help advice. Just as we emphasized earlier that the act of complete consecration needs the enablement of the Holy Spirit as much as does the confession that "Jesus is Lord," likewise the pursuit of the *telos* of the image of God according to the pattern of virtue ethics is not an unaided human capability. The vision of the goal apart from divine intervention can become an elusive ideal as St. Augustine described in his *Confessions*. After pursuing the "truth" through various philosophies, he finally discovered the writings of the "Platonists," (neo-Platonism) and felt that he had "found the unchangeable and true eternity of Truth, above my changeable mind." But, plaintively, he declared, "I was not able to fix my gaze thereon; and my infirmity being beaten back, I was thrown again on my accustomed habits, carrying along with me naught but a loving memory thereof, and an appetite for which I had, as it were, smelt the odor of, but was not yet able to eat." He described his experience in picturesque language: "It is one thing, from the mountain's wooded summit to see the land of peace, and not to find the way thither . . ; and another to keep to the way that leads thither." He found the answer in "that Mediator between God and man, the man Christ Jesus."[444]

Paul's words in 2 Corinthians 3:18 emphasize the same truth: "And we all, with unveiled face, beholding the glory of the Lord, are being changed into his likeness from one degree of glory to another; *for this comes from the Lord who is the Spirit.*" (Emphasis added)

The fallen state of humanity is reflected in the fact that the list of unclean or evil matters to which Jesus referred as coming from the

---

[442]*Becoming*, 87.

[443]Ibid. 72-3.

[444]*The Confessions*, Book VII, cc. XVII-XXI.

heart in Mark 7:14 -22 (sexual immorality, theft, murder, adultery, greed, wickedness, treachery, debauchery, envy, slander, pride, stupidity) are not behaviors and "affections" that have to be learned. As N.T. Wright notes, "These are things, sadly, that you don't have to work at. You don't have to think through the challenge of how to perform them, and practice hard because they are so difficult and demanding. No: they bubble up, unbidden and unhindered, from within, even from within those of us nursed and schooled in traditions of piety, devotion, worship, study, and self-denial."[445] By contrast, the virtues of the sanctified life have to be worked at in cooperation with the work of the Spirit. While this pattern is similar to Aristotle, as modern Christian ethicists are recognizing (and Wesley embodied), it is here that the difference lies. But even after the gift of the Holy Spirit at Pentecost, the early Christians still had to struggle to implement the ideals of Jesus' pictures of the kingdom of God, implying that there is no "magical" cure to the human condition apart from human cooperation with divine grace. N.T. Wright's summary is right on target: "the Christian believes that virtue is itself a work of grace, it is not a work which happens automatically, easily, or without the Christian equivalent of the hard moral effort of which the pagan theorists [Aristotle, et. al.] had spoken."

But progress in the sanctified life does not occur in a vacuum. It takes place only in the context of situations that require response in the light of the ideal. That is what is meant by "occasion" as an essential element of growth. How we choose to respond to actual difficulties, opposition or reverses creates character, whether good or bad.

Patrick Eby belabors the point that Charles Wesley emphasized the significance of persecution as a necessary prerequisite for more perfectly reflecting the image of God. He notes that "Although Charles Wesley's theology of suffering was based on his reading of the Scriptures, it was strengthened by the witness of those in the [Methodist] movement who were coming to the same conclusion," since the movement was flourishing under persecution. In a word, "suffering was part of what was required for one to become perfect—

---

[445]*After You Believe*, 110.

another word Charles used to describe being restored in the image of God."[446]

That Charles sought to be in situations where he was opposed and persecuted (as when he and John were in Georgia) sounds a bit morbid to us moderns, but the principle at work is a sound one. From Paul's initial vision on the Damascus Road, as well as possibly subsequent visions (2 Cor. 4:3-4), he had come to see that the way to the glory of God was through suffering. The vocation of Christ had led through suffering (crucifixion) to exaltation (resurrection). This is why he could come to summarize the gospel as "the gospel of the glory of Christ, who is the likeness of God." Since his goal was to reflect the glory (image) of God (2 Cor. 3:18), it involved the replication of the sufferings of Christ as the means to that *telos*. This is no doubt the significance of his comment in Galatians 6:17: "From now on, let no one make trouble for me; for I carry the marks (Greek *stigmata*) of Jesus branded on my body."

Paul connects the revelation of the glory (image) of God with the "new creation" inaugurated by the death and resurrection of Christ by drawing on the paradigm of the original creation of light out of darkness (2 Cor. 4:6). The light of the new creation "has shone in our hearts to give the light of the knowledge of the glory of God in the face of Jesus Christ." In his discussion of his ministry of the new covenant in contrast to Moses' ministry of the old covenant (2 Cor. 3-4) Paul makes it clear that the ongoing transformation of the participant in the new age of salvation is not the result of unaided human initiative, it is through the agency of the Holy Spirit, who he identifies with the Lord (Jesus). His imagery of human inability to this end is beautifully depicted in 4:7—"But we have this treasure in clay jars, so that it may be made clear that this extraordinary power belongs to God and does not come from us."

Properly interpreted the familiar Romans 8:28 (which should never be interpreted alone but with verse 29) is making the same point being emphasized here: "We know that in everything God works for good with those who love him, who are called according to his purpose. For those whom he foreknew he also predestined to be conformed to the image of his Son. ." "Good" is a purpose word, not a

---

[446]"The One Thing Needful," 133, 135. One wonders what John would have said about the sufferings he endured at the hands of his wife.

pointer to a hedonistic outcome. And the purpose (good) God intends to be the outcome of everything that comes to us is clearly stated. The secret to this "promise" being fulfilled is not some "magical" action on God's part exclusively but a response-decision on our part to choose the reaction that is in conformity to the character of Christ, "the mind of Christ."

It is here that the Wesleyan emphasis on "the single eye" as a virtual synonym for "entire sanctification" is seen to be important as reflected in Eby's report of a sermon by Charles: "On March 14, 1736, Charles addressed his small congregation about the adventure they were beginning in Frederica. As he spoke to them, he turned to a theme that would continue to be a major focus of his theology; he challenged them to have a 'single eye', which was focused on the 'one thing needful, namely the recovery of the image of God'."[447] Early on, the Oxford Methodists interpreted "the single eye" in what we might think an extreme ascetic way, namely remaining single. Charles modified his understanding both as a result of his marriage and in relation to his musical sons.[448]

Practicing activities until they become "second nature" is or can be something like stimulus/response. The saying that "practice makes perfect" is appropriate here. As professional golfer Gary Player said when told that he was lucky, "Yes, and I've noticed that the harder I practice, the luckier I get." Participants in sports go through repeated situations in practice so that when that situation occurs in a live contest they will immediately respond without having to "free lance." I have always been in awe of a pianist who could play a difficult tune without looking at the keyboard while talking to someone about something else. No doubt the result of hours and hours of practice.

But what Wesleyan theology and biblical ethics enjoin as Christlike disciples goes beyond overt behavior and includes what Wesley called "affections." Affections "are not simply passive

---

[447]Eby, "One Thing Needful," 1. See John's sermon on "On a Single Eye," *Works*, 8:297-305.

[448]Ibid. 23.

'feelings' for Wesley, they are motivating dispositions of the person. In their ideal expression, they integrate the rational and emotional dimensions of human life into a holistic inclination toward particular choices or actions. Thus, the primal example of an affection for Wesley is love of God and neighbor."[449]

In a letter to one of his correspondents, he declared: "To love God I must be like him, holy as he is holy; which implies both the being pure from vicious and foolish passions and the being confirmed in those virtues and rational affections which God comprises in the word 'charity.' In order to root those out of my soul and plant these in their stead I must use *(1) such means as are ordered by God, (2) such as are recommended by experience and reason.*"[450] (emphasis added). In a letter to one of his preachers who had created problems for the movement by claiming "sinless perfection," John Wesley decried his teaching as "enthusiasm" (fanaticism) for, among other things, "expecting the end without the means."[451]

Thus Wesley explicitly recognizes the role of means in developing the inward virtues which may be roughly equated with the "fruit of the Spirit" listed by Paul in Galatians 5:22-23. In his *Explanatory Notes upon the New Testament* he explained both that the reference is singular (not fruits) and that all are expressions of love.[452]

Randy Maddox, in a significant essay,[453] demonstrates that "Wesley's model of holiness of heart and life was consciously framed within a very specific moral psychology [and] that Wesley's immediate heirs decisively (though without realizing it!) rejected his moral psychology, opting for an alternative psychology within which his distinctive emphases regarding Christian Perfection made little sense." Maddox' thesis is that this shift in "moral psychology" is the major factor in "the present malaise" of the holiness movement and

---

[449]Randy Maddox, *Responsible Grace*, 46.

[450]From a letter to "Aspasia" of July 19, 1731.

[451]Quoted in Eby, "One Thing Needful," 198.

[452]John Wesley, *Explanatory Notes upon the New Testament* (London: The Epworth Press, 1954).

[453]"Reconnecting the Means to the End."

returning to Wesley's model is the "most promising agenda . . . for recovering" its relevance in the modern world. It is precisely this approach that I have been seeking to explore in this project.

While doubtless few of the popular teachers of holiness were aware of it, one major reason for the abandonment of Wesley's "affectional psychology" was a major transition in the dominant philosophical tradition in the United States. The empiricism of John Locke, which had influenced Wesley as well as the American constitution, was gradually replaced by the philosophy of Scottish Realism or Common Sense philosophy, developed by Thomas Reid in reaction to the extreme skeptical empiricism of David Hume.[454] In Wesley's anthropology, the term "will" was the term he used for the affections rather than the power of contrary choice as in contemporary usage. "Liberty," was the term he used for the function of the person in this sense. Hence the motivating aspect of the human person was the affections and it was Wesley's teaching that these "affections" could be cultivated by the means of grace until they would not be simply transitory but so focused that they became enduring "tempers." He identified the essence of true religion as nothing short of holy tempers.[455] But these were not experienced instantaneously. "Rather," as Maddox explains, "God's regenerating grace awakens in believers the 'seeds' of such virtues. These seeds then strengthen and take shape as we 'grow in grace.' Given liberty, this growth involves responsible cooperation, for we could instead neglect or stifle God's gracious empowerment."[456]

Consistent with Common Sense philosophy, which rejected the identification of the will with the affections and insisted instead that the will manifested rational control of decisions, the affectional psychology of Wesley was abandoned. The result of Common Sense philosophy was that "only intentional acts have moral status," and

---

[454]George M. Marsden, *Fundamentalism and American Culture* (N.Y.: Oxford University Press, 1980), 14ff. This philosophy became the basis of fundamentalist thought.

[455]*Works,* 7:56.

[456]"Reconnecting the Means to the End," 41.

"habituated tempers were *amoral*, if not indeed subversive of truly moral choice, since they operate with minimal conscious intentionality."[457] This perspective is clearly reflected in a discussion of "original sin" in the early 20th century: ". . . since none of these infirmities have a moral quality in them, they must not be considered as part of the Adamic depraved moral nature, or original sin."[458]

This was a significant transformation of Wesleyan thought since Wesley referred to the "unholy tempers" that remained in the regenerate as "inward sin," and occasionally referred to them as original sin. The "second blessing" teachers, as we have noted earlier, came to distinguish original sin from these "unholy tempers" and identified it as a principle that was "deeper down and farther back," with "distortions in our affections being among its secondary effects."[459] This became the basis for explaining the struggles of unsanctified believers. Unlike Wesley, who believed these could be addressed by the means of grace, "They argued that the true obstacle to holy living is not wrong inclinations, which might be defused or reshaped, but this deeper lying evil principle. . . . The only thing that will suffice is for this principle to be entirely removed from the believer's life," and this was interpreted as occurring in an instantaneous experience which came to be referred to as the baptism with the Holy Spirit. The result of this "eradication of original sin" accompanied by the Spirit's empowering presence [would be] *spontaneous rational control* over their affections [flowing freely]."[460]

One classic expression of this position is found in Daniel Steele's *Milestone Papers*: "The great work of the Holy Spirit in entire sanctification which is always instantaneous in fact, and usually instantaneous in the consciousness of the believer, is to rectify the will, poise the passions aright, hold in check all innocent, and eradicate all

---

[457]Ibid. 45.

[458]Richard S. Taylor, *A Right Conception of Sin*, 97.

[459]This interpretation is doubtless the basis of the pervasive "substantival" expressions of the 19th century holiness theology. Cf. Leroy E. Lindsey, Jr., "Radical Remedy." Lindsey suggests that the phrase, "deeper down and farther back" was introduced into holiness vocabulary by Methodist Bishop L.L. Hamline in 1869.

[460]Maddox, "Reconnecting," 49-50.

unholy appetites, and to enthrone the conscience over a realm in which no rebel lurks."[461]

This analysis demonstrates, among other things, why Wesley had suggested early in the revival that "entire sanctification" was a mature experience normally occurring only near the end of life following a long period of growth in habituating the affections. It also explains the widespread testimony of so many who grew up under the preaching informed by this Reidian "moral psychology" who became disillusioned with the ideal after repeated attempts to experience the "spontaneous rational control of their affections or passions." This would be especially true of adolescence which is by nature a period of "storm and stress," with "hormones hopping," and other tensions at full force both internally and externally.

Our proposal is, of course, different from Wesley in that I have suggested a different meaning of "entire sanctification," based on the exegesis of the most relevant passage. But if interpreters like John L. Peters and Mildred Wynkoop are correct, there is not really that much difference. If Christian perfection is viewed as the goal of the process of sanctification, entire sanctification can then be seen as the consecration of oneself to the focused pursuit of that goal rather than the achievement of the goal. And that fits comfortably with the central motif of the New Testament as expressed by the eschatology of both realized and anticipated kingdom of God.

A common claim among teachers of the 19th century holiness tradition is that growth in grace (progressive or gradual sanctification) occurs before the "moment" of entire sanctification but growth accelerates after that event.[462] The explanation is that the "eradication" of original sin removes a hindrance to growth thus facilitating its efficiency. We have demonstrated the theological and biblical inadequacy of such an explanation but offer an alternate and sounder

---

[461]Daniel Steele, *Milestone Papers*, Digital Edition, 07/14/95, Holiness Data Ministry, 65.

[462]In the *Plain Account of Christian Perfection*, Wesley stated that "One perfected in love may grow in grace far swifter than he did before." Quoted in Matthew R. Schlimm, "The Puzzle of Perfection: Growth in John Wesley's Doctrine of Perfection," *WTS Journal*, vol. 38, No. 2 (Fall, 2003), 126.

explanation for the phenomenon. If one is focused on actualizing the goal, which is what the concept of a "single eye" indicates, this provides the impetus for implementing the pattern of growth explored in this chapter.

This explanation highlights what the perceptive reader should already have detected. In terms of an analogy used early in this study, we have "kept the stars in their courses," while offering an exegetically derived theological interpretation of the Christian life. Nothing essential to the "higher life" has been invalidated or called into question, only an alternate paradigm of theological explanation has been proposed. Even the structure of experience has been supported without appealing to a "magical" action of God. This paradigm furthermore provides a reasonable explanation for several anomalies that the traditional theology has never been able to resolve.

APPENDIX A
The Pauline Dichotomies

It is the purpose of this appendix to suggest how the unique dichotomies of Paul have come to be interpreted in the light of the advances in exegetical methods resulting in a significant reinterpretation of Pauline theology. It becomes an important aspect of the alternate paradigm to the 19th century holiness theology I have been exploring since these dichotomies played a major role in the apologetics of the American holiness movement. This survey will entail pointing out some of the inadequacies of that perspective, which was apparently mediated to its proponents by the two-nature view of the Plymouth Brethren that led them to a misunderstanding of biblical anthropology and thus—in part--to the problems described by Mark Quanstrom cited in the Introduction to this project.

There have been several factors that contributed to the emergence of a new paradigm in Pauline theology, especially those aspects that impinge on the traditional holiness hermeneutic. My survey of these factors is largely dependent on secondary sources rather than primary research and they constitute a constellation. I present them in no particular order of significance, importance or chronological priority.

One influence was given classic expression in an essay by Krister Stendahl entitled "The Apostle Paul and the Introspective Conscience of the West."[463] His thesis was that Paul's original concerns had to do with Jew and Gentile relations in the light of the work of Christ but that by the second century these burning issues that occupied the early church had basically disappeared due to the fact that as a result of the two Jewish revolts against Rome (A.D. 66-74 and AD 135) there were very few Jewish believers in Jesus as the Messiah.[464] The result, in the interest of relevance, was a shift among

---

[463]Krister Stendahl, "The Apostle Paul and the Introspective Conscience of the West," *Harvard Theological Review* 56 (1963) 199-215; reprinted in *Paul Among Jews and Gentiles* (Philadelphia: Fortress, 1976), 78-96.

[464]This point was emphasized by Walter Russell, "Insights from Postmodernism's Emphasis on Interpretive Communities in the Interpretation of

Christian interpreters away from a perspective that was sensitive to Jewish-Gentile relations within the Church to a perspective that was essentially Gentile in its orientation. This posed different questions from the ones Paul was addressing.

Paul's problem came to be interpreted as a "human problem." Furthermore since "Paul meant relatively little for the thinking of the Church during the first 350 years of its history," it was St. Augustine who brought him into the mainstream of Christian theologizing and became the source of the "introspective conscience," which in turn fed into the medieval period with its emphasis on self-examination, penance and good works as preparatory for salvation. As Stendahl put it, "Where Paul was concerned about the possibility for Gentiles to be included in the messianic community, his statements are now read as answers to the quest for assurance about man's salvation out of a common human predicament."[465] This medieval ethos was the context for Martin Luther's existential anxiety and even though he found assurance in justification by faith, along with the other Reformers, especially John Calvin, he perpetuated this same perspective so that Paul's theology has been misunderstood in recent centuries because it has been read through the lens of Luther and the Reformation.

Walter Russell, among others, has demonstrated that "This understanding has been overturned within the last few years through better literary analysis of Galatians and through better sociological/anthropological analysis of first-century Mediterranean people like the Galatians."[466]

Another major factor in the paradigm shift was a dramatically different understanding of second Temple Judaism that can be traced to the work of E. P. Sanders.[467] Sanders challenged the traditional understanding that first century Judaism was a legalism, basing

---

Romans 7," *Journal of the Evangelical Theological Society*, (December 1994), 514.

[465]Stendahl, "Introspective Conscience," 206.

[466]Walter Russell, "Does the Christian have 'Flesh' in Gal. 5:13-26?", *Journal of the Evangelical Theological Society* 36/2 (June 1993), 182. Cf. also T.D.Gordon, "The Problem at Galatia, *Interpretation* 41 (1987) 32-43.

[467]E. P. Sanders, *Paul and Palestinian Judaism* (Philadelphia: Fortress, 1977); *Paul, the Law and the Jewish People* (Philadelphia: Fortress, 1983).

salvation on works-righteousness. He coined the phrase, *covenantal nomism* to describe how the law was understood to function. Earlier scholarship of Judaism had made the same point but the work of Sanders seemed to precipitate a significant change so that recent scholars have asserted that the Judaism of the first century was not a religion based on earning acceptance with God through the merit of righteousness based on the works of Law—obedience.

The corollary of these two factors has been a widespread return to the recognition that the dominant problem Paul was addressing in Romans and Galatians was the Jew-Gentile problem. This was directly related to another development in New Testament studies. One of the major Pauline scholars emphasizing this development was Hermann Ridderbos. In a programmatic statement he wrote:

> The governing motif of Paul's preaching is the saving activity of God in the advent and the work, particularly in the death and the resurrection, of Christ. This activity is on the one hand the fulfillment of the work of God in the history of the nation Israel, the fulfillment therefore also of the Scriptures; on the other hand it reaches out to the ultimate consummation of the parousia of Christ and the coming of the kingdom of God. It is this great redemptive-historical framework within which the whole of Paul's preaching must be understood and all of its subordinate parts receive their place and organically cohere.[468]

It is in the light of this "eschatological dualism"--to which Ridderbos referred as a "redemptive-historical framework--that the Pauline dichotomies are best interpreted. In addition, the corporate character of biblical though should be included as a formative factor in the interpretative task.

The major dichotomies with which we will concern ourselves are: Adam/Christ, Flesh/Spirit, "old man"/"new man". There are several more.[469] These are the ones that have been the focus of

---

[468]Hermann Ridderbos, "The Redemptive-Historical Character of Paul's Preaching," in his *When the Time Had Fully Come, Studies in New Testament Theology* (Grand Rapids: Eerdmans, 1957), 44-60.

[469]Greathouse lists 9, *Romans 1-8*, 176.

holiness theology. Each of these dichotomies were interpreted by earlier holiness apologists as abstract parts of the regenerate Christian rather than descriptions of the whole identity of persons and described them as depicting a battlefield of opposing forces. This interpretation can be traced back historically to the later view of St. Augustine but the early holiness writers derived their understanding from the two-nature theory of the Plymouth Brethren. Their distinctive emphasis came to be the claim that the "old nature" was eradicated resulting in profound problems (both theoretical and ethical) concerning the continuing presence of "sin" in the entirely sanctified, which John Wesley clearly recognized. While there may be an exegetically permissible application of these dichotomies to personal life, for Paul the basic sense is corporate in nature. The context in which they are used is the eschatological dualism that informs all Paul's theology. The "present age" has been invaded by the "age to come," inaugurated by the death and resurrection of the Messiah Jesus so that there is now an overlapping of the two aeons or ages. Each of these aeons has its own unique characteristics and those who "inhabit" them participate in those characteristics. The "old" characterized by "death," the "new" by "life." But even those who have, by faith and baptism, experienced the "powers of the age to come" (Heb. 6:5) are still subject to the curse of death that flows from the sin of Adam (Romans 5:12). This leads us to the first dichotomy.

Adam/Christ. The entire human race is divided into two categories described as either "in Adam" or "in Christ." These are not to be understood as mystical categories but rather as "spheres of existence," corresponding to "the present age" and "the age to come." As W.M. Greathouse says, "Adam and Christ are the heads of two humanities or aeons—two contrasting, overlapping ages, realms, or orders of human existence. The old—initiated by Adam's disobedience—is an order in which sin reigns in death. The new—initiated by Christ's obedience—is an order where grace reigns through righteousness to eternal life."[470]

Before the Christ-event everyone was "in Adam." In terms of Paul's central concerns in Romans and Galatians, the Jews who are living under the law are still "in Adam." Anyone, and this includes the Gentiles, who is not "in Christ," is "in Adam." This could possibly

---

[470]*Romans 1-8*, 172.

explain the obviously different way of describing the old order and those who are within it in Ephesians and Colossians, letters that are primarily addressed to Gentile churches.

By contrast the prevailing understanding in much post-Lutheran exegesis viewed these categories as referring to individual life seen as before conversion (baptism) and after. This perspective is embodied in the prayer of the baptismal ceremony of the Southern Methodist Episcopal Church: "O merciful God, grant that the Old Adam in these persons may be so buried that the new man may be raised up in them. Amen. Grant that all carnal affections may die in them, and that all things belonging to the Spirit may live in them. Amen."

The more exegetically adequate understanding of the corporate nature of these concepts is reflected in Greathouse's words:

> Our past may be defined by our solidarity with Adam and all of the rest of fallen humanity, And in a sense, because we are subject to bodily death, we continue to live in Adam. But since we have been justified by faith, our present is defined by our solidarity with Christ and his cross, and our future will be determined by his resurrection. . . . The new age has dawned in Christ Jesus our Lord, and all who are in him have been taken out of the old order of Adam, where sin reigns in death, and transferred to the new order of Christ, where grace reigns in righteousness to eternal life. . . some expositors speak of Adam and Christ as 'fields of force.' From each radiates forces that touch us profoundly."[471]

Flesh/Spirit. The term *flesh* (Gk. *sarx*) and its translation has been the subject of much scholarly research. One of the complicating factors has been the diversity of uses to which it has been put in the Pauline letters. George Eldon Ladd refers to its use as "the most difficult and complicated aspect of the Pauline psychology."[472] He identifies 5 different uses but the one that is appropriate for our survey here is what he calls the "ethical" meaning. In a detailed study of the

---

[471]Ibid. 160-162.

[472]George Eldon Ladd, *A Theology of the New Testament,* rev. ed. (Grand Rapids: Eerdmans, 1993), 509.

use of this and other anthropological terms used by Paul in "conflict settings," Robert Jewett finds that he first brings the term *flesh* into full dialectic with *spirit* in Galatians 4:21-31 and describes that dialectic in this way: "He correlates flesh with the old aeon, the law, slavery, the present Jerusalem and the agitating Judaizers, while opposing flesh with spirit, which in turn was correlated with the new aeon, the promise given to Abraham, freedom, and the church."[473] Thus Walter Russell concludes that "Any understanding of the σάρξ/πνεῦμα conflict in Galatians must recognize at a foundational level that this terminology grew out of the polemics of the Judaizing controversy."[474]

This interpretation enables us to see Paul's contrast between the old aeon (the present age) and the new aeon (the age to come) inaugurated by the death and resurrection of Christ. In Romans and Galatians it becomes most obvious in the context of the overriding issue of the criterion for inclusion in the family of Abraham. The Judaizers, which Paul confronts so sharply in the Galatian situation, were arguing that to be a true son of Abraham the Gentile believer must embody the marks of identity that included particularly circumcision but also kosher food and Sabbath observance. The basis of their argument was an appeal to Genesis 17:11—"You shall circumcise the *flesh* of your foreskins and it shall be a sign of the covenant between me and you." Paul's argument was that Abraham was "justified" by faith long before the sign of circumcision and 430 years before the law was promulgated. Hence the appropriate identifying mark of the children of Abraham was faith, not a mark of the "flesh." Thus Paul stands their argument from "flesh" on its head making "flesh" a negative concept.

The central issues of Galatians were two-fold as described by John Barclay: "The issues at stake in the Galatian crisis were the *identity* of these Galatian Christians and their *appropriate patterns of behaviour*: should they regularize and confirm their place among God's people by getting circumcised and becoming proselytes? And should they adopt the ritual and ethical norms of the Jewish people?"[475]

---

[473]Robert Jewett, Paul's *Anthropological Terms: A Study of Their Use in Conflict Settings* (Leiden: E.J. Brill, 1971), 113.

[474]Russell, "The Apostle Paul's Redemptive-Historical Argumentation in Galatians 5:13-26," *Westminster Theological Journal* 57 (1995), 335.

This analysis highlights the contrast between the old aeon and the new. The old aeon is characterized by law, which is the norm of behavior under the old covenant. This is why "flesh" and "law," or Torah, are so closely identified in Paul's apologetic. The new aeon is characterized by the gift of the Holy Spirit made available through the death and resurrection of the Messiah Jesus. The question in both Romans 7-8 and Galatians 5:13-26 is which is the most effective as affecting behavior. Paul's argument in Romans 7 demonstrates the failure of Torah to accomplish this (see below) and in Romans 8 the effectiveness of the Spirit. The same argument is present in Galatians dramatically portrayed in the contrast between the "works of the flesh" and the "fruit of the Spirit."

Old man/new man. This dichotomy (found in Romans 6:6; Ephesians 4:17-25; and Colossians 3:9) has served as the most extensive imagery of the early holiness apologists as an argument for the necessity of a second work of grace. This is done by interpreting the "old man" as a more or less ontological entity, or a "nature" that continues to exist alongside the "new man" until "crucified" and thereby put to death.[476] The "inward struggle" with "carnality" in the "merely regenerated" person is thereby described and the groundwork laid for the second grace that "eradicates" the source of the internal conflict.

A.M. Hills graphic description is typical:

This is the vile fountain from which the stream of sin flows. This is the traitor in the citadel of the soul, which responds to every outside solicitation to evil and longs to deliver us into the hands of our enemies. This is the internal cancer that eats away at the spiritual life, to consume it utterly. "For from within," said Jesus, "out of the heart of men, evil thoughts proceed, fornications, thefts, murders, adulteries, covetings, wickedness, deceit, lasciviousness, an evil eye, railing, pride, foolishness: all these proceed from within and defile

---

[475]J. M. G. Barclay, *Obeying the Truth: A Study of Paul's Ethics in Galatians* (Edinburgh: T. and T. Clark, 1988), 73.

[476]Two early examples of extensive arguments for this interpretation were A.M. Hills, *The Establishing Grace*, and Beverly Carradine, *The Old Man*, both found on the NNC "holiness classics" website.

the man." This is the "bent to backsliding" in the hearts of unsanctified believers, of which God justly complains. This is "the root of bitterness" by which so many Christian hearts are despoiled of their loveliness. This is what expresses itself in the easily besetting sin, in the fierce uprising of ungovernable temper, and in the smoldering embers of hate. Oh, this is that "carnal the sin [?] that is enmity against God," and will not bow to God and tries to keep us from doing it, and is the relentless foe of all deep spirituality in every life.[477]

A more recent attempt to make the same point was presented by Ross Price in a series of eleven articles in *The Nazarene Preacher* from February, 1970 to December 1979. This apologetic was rebutted in a significant article by J. Kenneth Grider in the same periodical in February 1972. Grider argued more soundly that "old man" did not refer to "original sin" as Price had contended but rather referred to the pre-regenerate life.[478] He does argue that "flesh" does refer to "original sin." In a rather curious turn of the argument Grider further attempted to import entire sanctification as a second work of grace into his otherwise rather sound exegesis. But the contention of numerous contemporary New Testament scholars is that this idiom, like the other dichotomies, refers to the two aeons that inform Paul's theology.

It is important to recognize that these references are corporate rather than individualistic in nature. The reference in Romans 6:6 makes this explicit since the "putting off" of the "old man" results in the destruction of the "body of sin." The early holiness exegetes saw this as simply a repetition of a reference to "original sin" resident within the individual but as N.T. Wright points out in his commentary on Romans, "since the abolition of 'the body of sin' is the result of the crucifixion of 'the old self' they cannot be identical," and argues that "it is probably better to take 'body' in the wider sense of 'solidarity'."[479] In one of his writings, Oswald Chambers interprets the "body of sin"

---

[477]*The Establishing Grace*, NNU website. Later published as *Holiness in the Book of Romans*.

[478]Greathouse concurs with Grider's interpretation but quickly comes close to affirming the position proposed here: "The expressions **our old self** and **the body of sin** refer to our corporate existence in Adam—*our old humanity*—that comes to an end as we participate in Christ—the new humanity." *Romans 1-8*, 182.

[479]*Romans*, 540.

in the same way drawing a parallel with the idiom of the church as the body of Christ:

> Every time a man or woman by identification with Jesus enters into the experimental [experiential] knowledge that his "old man" is crucified with Christ, the ultimate defeat and destruction of the body of sin becomes clearer. . . . Paul's argument is that the purpose of "the old man" being crucified is that the body of sin might be destroyed, i.e. that the connection with the body of sin might be severed. . . . There are two mystical bodies—there is the mystical body of Christ and the mystical body of sin.[480]

The two references to this idiom in Ephesians and Colossians seem to have a different context. While the Romans passage is found in the context of the Jew and Gentile (probably converted God-fearers who were originally semi-converts to the Jewish faith) question focusing on the law and the question of the identity of the true children of Abraham, and the behavioral implications vis-à-vis the Torah, these two references seem most appropriate to Gentiles converted from paganism. For them, the old aeon was characterized by idolatry and immoral practices foreign to Jewish ethics. Hence the appeal to put the "old *anthropos*" away is an appeal to abandon the characteristics of the old aeon as embodied in paganism. It is in these two epistles that the most explicit references to the eschatological dualism of the two ages is found (cf. Eph. 1:21).

This finally brings us to take notice of the much controverted seventh chapter of Romans. With the shift in the make-up of the early church referred to above, the Pauline emphasis on the Jew and Gentile question also shifted from a corporate concept to an individualistic interpretation focused on essentially Gentile issues. Thus the question became one of whether Paul was describing a Christian or a non-Christian experience and was it an autobiographical reference. The Eastern fathers tended to refer the struggle to his Jewish, pre-converted state but under the influence of St. Augustine's later view, the Western

---

[480]*My Utmost for His Highest*, ?.

interpreters tended to interpret it as the experience of his Christian experience.

Some of the early holiness apologists followed the Western tradition using Romans 7 to describe the experience of the "merely" regenerated but not yet entirely sanctified believer. Whether or not this had an actual counterpart in the experience of their contemporaries it served as a powerful argument for the importance of a "second blessing" to remove that which was the source of this "divided mind."

Since applying this interpretation to Paul's pre-Christian experience is totally contradictory to his own testimony in Philippians 3:4-6, those who still interpret it in individualistic categories ascribe the situation to Christian experience. But when placed within the narrative structure of Paul's argument, a different picture emerges that transcends a personal application. The central question of the chapter concerns Torah (not law in the abstract or a principle like Kant's categorical imperative), is it a good thing or a bad thing. Paul's answer is that it is a good thing (7:12) but it could not do what it was intended to do, namely give life. Instead it brought death, not because it was bad but because of sin, a power that was introduced into the world by Adam's sin. As N.T. Wright described it: "The problem lay elsewhere [than with the Torah]: in the 'flesh'—not the physicality of human nature, which was God-given and will be reaffirmed in the resurrection (8:11), but in the present rebellious and corruptible state of humankind, within which sin had made its dwelling (7:18, 20, 23, 25)"[481] Here is a powerful argument for what later theologians came to call original sin. Paul's argument as chapter 7 merges into chapter 8 is that now, instead of the law, we have Christ and the Spirit. Together they do what the law could not do (8:1-4).

N.T. Wright's exegesis of this section of Romans places it in the context of the Old Testament expectation of a new exodus that will produce what the old exodus never really produced, freedom from sin. Thus the narrative structure reflects the larger narrative of the history of Israel beginning with the exodus itself where the slaves passed through the waters to freedom. This is the imagery of Romans 6:1ff. The believer has passed through the waters of baptism, like the Red Sea, and entered into a new era of freedom. But Romans 7:7-12 takes them to Sinai where, as soon as the law was given Israel recapitulated

---

[481]*Romans*, 577.

the sin of Adam by the Golden Calf apostasy. This, it is suggested, is the significance of 7:9 referring to the coming of the Mosaic Law at Sinai.[482] The rabbis came to refer to this event as the fall of Israel and it resonates through Israel ever since.

This raises the question of why Paul used the "I" to refer to this situation. The simplest answer would be to recognize the corporate nature of the biblical mind and see Paul doing here what he did in chapters 9-11, and what Moses did in Exodus 32:11-14 and 33:12-16 and Daniel in 9:1-19. He was identifying with his people and avoiding referring to the repeated failures as "they."

This analysis, brief as it may be, highlights the fact of the corporate nature of "original sin," and militates against a "two-nature" anthropology that explains the struggle in Romans 7 as "not a battle between my better and worse self." In a word, as is the case with all anthropological references in scripture, it is a reference to the whole person.

But W. M. Greathouse offers a significant modification of the entire picture that fits comfortably in the personal dimension of this narrative. He suggests that the problem in the chapter is not a two-nature battle but rather "a discrepancy between my purpose and my performance." Neither is it "the inevitability of failure when my noble aspirations encounter law's impossible demands (despite the tradition of Lutheran-Reformed Protestant interpretation)." Rather what is being described is "a discrepancy between my purpose and my performance. . . . between my good intentions and my poor achievement." In other words, "my will presents no problem, my problem is my failure to achieve what is right."[483]

What this proposal both implies and presupposes is the distinction between what the Old Testament refers to as "high-handed sin," and "inadvertent sin," and corresponds to John Wesley's distinction between sin properly so-called and sin improperly-so

---

[482]This interpretation is also followed by D. J. Moo, "Israel and Paul in Romans 7:7-12," *New Testament Studies* 32 (1986), 122-135. Also A. Katherine Grieb, *The Story of Romans* (Louisville: Westminster John Knox Press, 2002), 71-76.

[483]*Romans 1-8*, 216.

called. In practical terms it distinguishes the sin that is willfully and knowingly committed from sin that Wesley would refer to as the falling short of the perfect law of love that is not the result of intention.

N.T. Wright's exegesis of Romans 8:1-4 explicitly supports this interpretation. The failure to see this in a superficial reading is partly in the translation. The (pre-2011) NIV botches the translation by once again rendering *sarx* as "sinful nature," and the NRSV leaves it unclear, but the RSV (and NRSV also) footnote makes the matter abundantly clear: "There is therefore now no condemnation for those who are in Christ Jesus ("the age to come"). For the law of the Spirit of life in Christ Jesus has set me free from the law of sin and death ("the present age"). For God has done what the law, weakened by the flesh, could not do: sending his own Son in the likeness of sinful flesh and *as a sin offering* [footnote], he condemned sin in the flesh."

As in 2 Corinthians 5:21 the term usually translated as "sin" is the "regular phrase that, in the LXX [Greek translation of the OT] translates the Hebrew terms for the specific sacrifice known as the sin offering." John Wesley translates it this way. The sin offering is designed for dealing with sin that has been committed ignorantly or unwillingly, "either one did something without realizing it was sinful; or knowing it was sinful, one did it despite intending not to."

Wright's concluding summary puts it all together: "The sin offering thus answers exactly, not indeed to any and every sin [that is not what this phrase was designed to do] but to the problem so carefully analyzed in chap. 7. The 'I' of 7:15, as we saw, does not 'know,' and does not 'will,' the actions committed. The sin in question is precisely, in Jewish terms, sins of ignorance, unwilling sin."[484]

---

[484]*Romans*, 578-579. This admittedly raises a question of tension between this interpretation and the correlation with the history of Israel's apostasy, which he also supports.

BIBLIOGRAPHY

Allport, Gordon W. *Becoming.* New Haven: Yale University Press, 1955.

Anderson, Ray S. *On Being Human.* Grand Rapids: Eerdmans, 1982.

Atkinson, Baines. *The Beauty of Holiness.* N. Y.: Philosophical Library, 1953.

Aulén, Gustav. *Christus Victor,* trans. A.G. Hebert. N. Y.: Macmillan Co., 1951.

_____. *The Faith of the Christian Church,* trans. Eric H. Wahlstrom & G. Everett Arden. Philadelphia: The Muhlenberg Press, 1948.

Barclay, J. M. G. *Obeying the Truth: A Study of Paul's Ethics in Galatians.* Edinburgh: T. and T. Clark, 1988.

Barclay, William. *The Promise of the Spirit.* Philadelphia: The Westminster Press, 1960.

Barker, J.H.J. *This is the Will of God.* Salem, OH: Schmul, 1975.

Bassett Paul M. and William M. Greathouse, *Exploring Christian Holiness, The Historical Development.* K.C.: Beacon Hill Press of Kansas City, 1985.

Bassett, Paul M. et. al. "A White Paper on Article X," www.didache.nts.edu; (summer, 2010)

_____. "Culture and Concupiscence: the Changing Definition of Sanctity in the Wesleyan Holiness Movement, 1870-1920." *Wesleyan Theological Journal* 28 (1993).

Blackman, E.C. "Sanctification," *Interpreters Dictionary of the Bible*, ed. George Buttrick, 4 vols. (N. Y.: Abingdon Press, 1964).

Bauckham, Richard. "The Holiness of Jesus and His Disciples in the Gospel of John," *Holiness and Ecclesiology in the New Testament* ed. Kent E. Brower and Andy Johnson (Grand Rapids: Wm. B. Eerdmans Pub. Co., 2007.

Berkouwer, G. C. *Man: The Image of God.* Grand Rapids: Wm. B. Eerdmans Pub. Co., 1962.

Bonhoeffer, Dietrich. *Creation and Fall.* London: SCM, 1959.

Booth, Roger P. *Jesus and the Laws of Purity: Tradition, History and Legal History in Mark 7.* SNT Sup 13; Sheffield: JSOT, 1986).

Brand, Chad Owen, ed., *Perspectives on Spirit Baptism, Five Views.* Nashville: Broadman and Holman Pub., 2004.

Bright, John. *The Authority of the Old Testament.* Nashville: Abingdon Press, 1967.

Brockett, Henry E. *Scriptural Freedom from Sin.* K.C: Beacon Hill Press, first printing 1941.

Brower, Kent E. "1Thessalonians," *Asbury Bible Commentary* ed. Eugene E. Carpenter & Wayne McCown. Grand Rapids: Zondervan Publishing Company, 1992.

Bruce, F.F. *Commentary on the Book of Acts.* Grand Rapids: Wm. B. Eerdmans Pub. Co., 1973.

Cairns, David. *The Image of God in Man.* N. Y.: Philosophical Library, 1953.

Calvin, John. *Institutes of the Christian Religion*, 2 vols. Trans. Henry Beveridge. Grand Rapids: Wm. B. Eerdmans Pub. Co., 1970.

Carter, Charles W. *The Person and Ministry of the Holy Spirit*. Grand Rapids: Baker Book House, 1974.

Cerfaux, L. *The Church in the Theology of Paul*. N. Y.: Herder & Herder, 1959.

Chadwick, Samuel. *The Call to Christian Perfection*. K.C.: Beacon Hill Press, 1943.

Chambers, Oswald. *The Psychology of Redemption*. London: Marshall, Morgan & Scott, 1955.

Chapman, J.B. *The Terminology of Holiness*. K.C.: Beacon Hill Press, 1947.

Clines, David J. A. "The Image of God in Man," *Tyndale Bulletin* 19 (1968)

Cook, Thomas. *New Testament Holiness*. London: The Epworth Press, 1950.

Corlett, D. Shelby. *The Meaning of Holiness*. K.C.: Beacon Hill Press, 1944.

Cox, Leo G. "The Imperfections of the Perfect," *Further Insights into Holiness*. K.C.: Beacon Hill Press, 1963, 179-196.

Dayton, Donald W. "Asa Mahan and the Development of American Holiness Theology," *Wesleyan Theological Journal*, 9, 1974, 60–69.

_____. "Pneumatological Issues in the Holiness Movement," *The Spirit and the New Age*, ed. Alex R.G. Deasley and R. Larry Shelton. Anderson, IN: Warner Press, 1986.

212

Deasley, Alex R. G. "Entire Sanctification and the Baptism with the Holy Spirit: Perspectives on the Biblical View of the Relationship," *Wesleyan Theological Journal*, vol. 14, no. 1 Spring 1979.

_____. "The Spirit in the Pauline Epistles," *The Spirit and the New Age* ed. Alex R.G. Deasley and R. Larry Shelton. Anderson, IN: Warner Press, 1986.

Dieter, Melvin. *History of the 19th Century Holiness Movement.* K.C.: Beacon Hill Press of Kansas City, 1998.

Dodd, C. H. *The Epistle of Paul to the Romans.* Fontana Books, n.d.

Douglas, Mary. *Purity and Danger.* London: Routledge, 1992.

_____."The Forbidden Animals in Leviticus," *Journal for the Study of the Old Testament* 59 (1993), 3-23.

_____. "Atonement in Leviticus," *Jewish Studies Quarterly*, vol. 1 (1991-94), 109-130.

Dunlap, E. Dale. "Tuesday Meetings, Camp Meetings, and Cabinet Meetings: A Perspective on the Holiness Movement in the Methodist Church in the United States in the Nineteenth Century," *Methodist History/A.M.E. Zion*, 13, no. 3, Apr. 1975.

Dunn, James D.G. *The Theology of Paul the Apostle.* Grand Rapids: Wm. B. Eerdmans, 1998.

Dunning, H. Ray. *Becoming Christlike Disciples* (Bloomington, IN: Westbow Press, 2010.

_____. "Ethics in a Wesleyan Context," *Wesleyan Theological Journal*, vol. 5, No. 1, Spring, 1970.

_____. *Grace, Faith and Holiness.* K.C.: Beacon Hill Press of Kansas City, 1988.

213

_____, *Our Standard of Conduct.* K.C.: Beacon Hill Press, n.d.

_____. *Partakers of the Divine Nature.* Salem, Ohio: Schmul Pub. Co., 2006.

_____. *Superlative Christ.* K.C.: Beacon Hill Press, 2001.

_____. "Christian Perfection: Toward a New Paradigm," *Wesleyan Theological Journal* vol. 33, no. 1, spring, 1998.

_____."Nazarene Ethics as seen in Historical, Theological and Sociological Context," Ph.D. Dissertation, Vanderbilt University, 1969.

Earle, Ralph. *Sanctification in the New Testament.* K.C.: Beacon Hill Press of Kansas City, 1988.

Eby, Patrick Alan. "The One Thing Needful: The Development of Charles Wesley's Theology of the Restoration of the Image of God," Ph.D. diss. Drew University, 2010.

Ehrensperger, Kathy. "'Called to be saints'—the Identity-shaping Dimension of Paul's Priestly Discourse in Romans," in *Reading Paul in Context: Explorations in Identity Formation* ed. Kathy Ehrensperger and J. Brian Tucker. N.T.: T & T Clark International, 2010.

Failing, George E. "Developments in Holiness Theology After Wesley," *Insights into Holiness,* comp. by Kenneth Geiger. K.C.: Beacon Hill Press, 1963.

Fee, Gordon D. *God's Empowering Presence.* Peabody, Mass: Hendrickson, 1994.

Flew, R. Newton, *The Idea of Perfection in Christian Theology: an historical study of the Christian ideal for the present life.* N.Y.: Humanities Press, 1968.

Ford, Jack. *What the Holiness People Believe, A Mid-Century Review of Holiness Teaching.* Palm Grove, Birkenhead, Cheshire: Emmanuel Bible College and Missions, n.d.

Foster, R.S. *Christian Purity* Holiness Data Ministry, NNU website, 1997.

Fraser, M. Robert. "Tensions in Perfection: A Study in Theological Transmission," Ph.D. diss, Vanderbilt University, (1988).

Gäster, B. *The Temple and Community in Qumran and the NT.* Cambridge: UniversityPress, 1965.

Gilkey, Langdon. *Maker of Heaven and Earth.* N.Y.: Doubleday, 1959.

Gordon, T. David "The Problem at Galatia," *Interpretation* 41 (1987), 32-43.

Gorman, Michael J. *Cruciformity, Paul's Narrative Spirituality of the Cross.* Grand Rapids: Wm. B. Eerdmans, 2001.

Greathouse, W. M. "A Pauline Theology of Sanctification," *Biblical Resources for Holiness Preaching,* 2 vols. Ed. H. Ray Dunning and Neil B. Wiseman. K.C.: Beacon Hill Press of Kansas City, 1990.

_____. *Wholeness in Christ.* K.C.: Beacon Hill Press of Kansas City, 1998.

_____. "Sanctification and the Christus Victor Motif," *Wesleyan Theological Journal,* vol. 38, No. 2, Fall, 2003.

_____. *Romans 1-8* in *New Beacon Bible Commentary.* K.C.: Beacon Hill Press of Kansas City, 2008.

_____. "The Dynamic of Sanctification: Biblical Terminology," a paper presented at the 1969 Nazarene Theology Conference.

Gregory, James F. "The Holiness of God," *Further Insights into Holiness*. K.C.: Beacon Hill Press, 1963.

Grider, J. Kenneth. *Entire Sanctification*. K.C.: Beacon Hill Press of Kansas City, 1980.

_____. "Carnality and Humanity." *Wesleyan Theological Journal*, Vol. 11, Spring, 1976, 81-91.

_____, "Entire Sanctification: Instantaneous—Yes; Gradual—No," *The Preacher's Magazine*, March-April, 1971.

Grieb, A. Katherine. *The Story of Romans*. Louisville: Westminster John Knox Press, 2002.

Haggard, Cornelius P. "Temptation and the Sanctified Life," *Further Insights into Holiness*. K.C.: Beacon Hill Press, 1963, 197-212.

Hall, Douglas John. *Imaging God* (Grand Rapids: Wm. B. Eerdmans Pub. Co., 1985.

Hamilton, Victor P. "Recent Studies in Leviticus and Their Contribution to a Further Understanding of Wesleyan Theology," *A Spectrum of Thought* ed. Michael Peterson. Wilmore, KY: Asbury Pub. Co., 1982.

Harrington Daniel J. & James F. Keenan. *Jesus and Virtue Ethics*. N.Y.: Rowman and Littlefield, 2002.

Hays, Richard B. *The Moral Vision of the New Testament*. N.Y.: Harper Collins, 1996.

Hayes, Christine E. *Gentile Impurities and Jewish Identities*. Oxford: University Press, 2002.

Heath, Elaine A. "Becoming a Bible Christian: Toward a New Reading of Phoebe Palmer's Sanctification Theology in Light of Roman Catholic Mystical Traditions," Ph.D. diss. Duquesne University, 2002.

Heitzenrater, Richard. *The Elusive Mr. Wesley*, 2 vols. Nashville: Abingdon Press, 1984.

Heron, Alasdair I.C. *The Holy Spirit*. Philadelphia: Westminster Press, 1983.

Horst, F. "Face to Face. The Biblical Doctrine of the Image of God," *Interpretation* 4 (1950), 259-170.

Houston, Walter. *Purity and Monotheism*. Sheffield: Sheffield Academic Press, 1993.

Howard, Richard E. *Newness of Life*. K.C.: Beacon Hill Press of Kansas City, 1975.

Hunter, A. M. *The Gospel According to Paul*. Philadelphia: Westminster Press, 1966.

Jennings, Ortho. "Areas of Growth After Sanctification," *Further Insights into Holiness*. K.C.: Beacon Hill Press, 1963, 141-162.

Jenson, P. P. *Graded Holiness: A Key to the Priestly Conception of the World*. Sheffield: Journal for the Study of the Old Testament, 1992.

Jewett, Robert. *Paul's Anthropological Terms: A Study of Their Use in Conflict Settings*. Leiden: E.J. Brill, 1971.

Jones, W.T. *A History of Western Philosophy*, Vol. 1, *The Classical Mind*. N.Y.: Harcourt, Brace & World, 1969.

Kinlaw, Dennis. "Old Testament Roots of the Wesleyan Message," *Further Insights Into Holiness*. K.C.: Beacon Hill Press, 1963.

Kiuchi, N. *The Purification Offering in the Priestly Literature*. Sheffield: Sheffield Academic Press, 1987).

Klawans, Jonathan, *Sin and Purity in Ancient Judaism*. Oxford: Oxford University Press, 2000).

_____. "Notions of Gentile Impurity in Ancient Judaism," *AJS Review* 20/2 (1995), 285-312

Knight, Henry H. III. *The Presence of God in the Christian Life: John Wesley and the Means of Grace*. Metuchen, N.Y.: Scarecrow Press, 1992.

Knight, John A. "John Fletcher's Influence on the Development of Wesleyan Theology in America," *Wesleyan Theological Journal*, 13. 1978, 13–33

Kugler, Robert A., "Holiness, Purity, the Body and Society," *Journal for the Study of the Old Testament* 76 (1997), 3-27.

Ladd, George Eldon. *A Theology of the New Testament*, Revised Ed. Grand Rapids, Eerdmans Pub. Co., 1974.

Lee, Hoo-Jung, "The Doctrine of New Creation in the Theology of John Wesley," Ph.D. dissertation, Emory University, 1991.

Lennox, Stephen. "Biblical Interpretation, American Holiness Movement, 1875-1925," *Wesleyan Theological Journal*, vol. 33, no. 1, Spring 1998.

Lim, Kor Yong. "Paul's Use of Temple Imagery in the Corinthian Correspondence: The Creation of Christian Identity" in *Reading Paul in Context: Identity Formation*. London: T & T Clark, 2010.

218

Lindsey, Jr., Leroy E."Radical Remedy: The Eradication of Sin and Related Terminology in Wesleyan-Holiness Thought, 1875-1925," Ph.D. diss, Drew University, 1996.

Lindström, Harald. *Wesley and Sanctification.* Wilmore, KY: Francis Asbury Pub. Co., reprint, 1980.

Lowrey, Asbury. *Possibilities of Grace.* Chicago: The Christian Witness Co., 1884.

Lowrey, Kevin T. "A Fork in the Wesleyan Road: Phoebe Palmer and the Appropriation of Christian Perfection," *Wesleyan Theological Journal*, vol. 36, no. 2 (2001).

Lyons, George. "The Spirit in the Gospels," *The Spirit and the New Age* ed. Alex R.G. Deasley and R. Larry Shelton. Anderson, IND: Warner Press, Inc., 1986.

Lyon, Robert W. "Baptism and Spirit-Baptism in the New Testament," *Wesleyan Theological Journal*, vol. 14, no. 1 Spring 1979.

MacIntyre, Alasdair. *After Virtue.* Notre Dame, IN: University Press, 1981.

Maddox, Randy, ed. *Aldersgate Reconsidered.* Nashville: Kingswood Press, 1990.

_____. *Responsible Grace.* Nashville: Kingswood Books, 1994.

_____. "Reconnecting the Means to the End: A Wesleyan Prescription for the Holiness Movement," *Wesleyan Theological Journal*, vol. 33, No. 2, Fall, 1998.

_____. "The Use of the Aorist Tense in Holiness Exegesis," *Wesleyan Theological Journal*, vol. 16, No. 2, Fall 1981.

Marsden, George M. *Fundamentalism and American Culture.* N.Y.: Oxford University Press, 1980.

Martins, Elmer. *Gods' Design.* Grand Rapids: Baker Book House, 1981.

Meyer, Paul W. "The Holy Spirit in the Pauline Letters," *Interpretation* 33 (1979).

McCown, Wayne. "God's Will . . . For You; Sanctification in the Thessalonian Epistles," *Wesleyan Theological Journal,* vol. 12, Spring 1977, 26-33.

McCumber, W.E. *Holiness in the Prayers of St. Paul.* K.C.: Beacon Hill Press of Kansas City, 1955.

McGonigle, Herbert. "Pneumatological Nomenclature in Early Methodism," *Wesleyan Theological Journal,* 8, 1973, 61–72.

McKelvey, R. T. *The New Temple.* London: Oxford University Press, 1969.

McLaughlin, George Asbury. *A Clean Heart.* Holiness Data Ministry, 1995, from NNU website.

Metz, Donald. *Studies in Biblical Holiness.* K.C.: Beacon Hill Press of Kansas City, 1971.

Meyers, Ben M. *The Aims of Jesus.* San Jose, CA: Pickwick Pub., 2002.

Milgrom, Jacob, "Rationale for Cultic Law: The Case of Impurity," *Semeia* 45 (1989).

_____. "Sin-Offering or Purification-Offering?" *Vetus testamentum,* 21 no 2 Apr. 1971, p 237-239.

_____."Sacrifices and offerings, OT," *Interpreters Dictionary of the Bible,* supplementary volume, Keith R. Crim, et. al. eds. Nashville: Abingdon Press, 1976.

Miller, Chris A., "Did Peter's Vision in Acts 10 Pertain to Men or the Menu," *Bibliotheca Sacra* 159 (July –September 2002), 302-317.

Moore, Don Marselle. "Development in Wesley's Thought on Sanctification and Perfection," *Wesleyan Theological Journal.* Vol. 4 (1969).

Moo, D.J. "Israel and Paul in Romans 7:7-12," *New Testament Studies* 32 (1986).

Nausner, Helmut."The Meaning of Wesley's General Rules; An Interpretation," trans. Steven O'Malley, *The Asbury Theological Journal*, vol. 44, No. 2 (1989).

Neusner, Jacob, *The Idea of Purity in Ancient Judaism.* Leiden: Brill, 1973).

Newport, Kenneth G.C. *The Sources and Sitz im Leben of Matthew 23.* JSNT Sup. 117; Sheffield: Sheffield Academic Press, 1995.

Newton, Michael, *The Concept of Purity in Qumran and in the Letters of Paul.* Cambridge, Cambridge University Press, 1985.

Neyrey, Jerome H., "The Idea of Purity in Mark's Gospel," *Semeia* 35 (1986):91-128.

Noble, T. A. "Doctrine of Original Sin in the Evangelical Reformers," *European Explorations in Christian Holiness*, Summer, 2001.

Olsen, Mark. "John Wesley's Doctrine of Sin Revisited," *Wesleyan Theological Journal*, Volume 47, No. 2, Fall 2012.

Outler, Albert C. *Theology in the Wesleyan Spirit.* Nashville: Tidings, 1975.

_____, Ed. *The Works of John Wesley, The Sermons*. 4 vols. (Nashville: Abingdon Press, 1984-85.

Pak, Myung Soo. "Concepts of Holiness in American Evangelicalism: 1835-1915," Ph.D. dissertation, Boston University, (1992).

Peters, John L. *Christian Perfection and American Methodism*. Nashville: Abingdon Press, 1956.

Peck, Jesse T. *The Central Idea of Christianity*. K.C.: Beacon Hill Press, 1951.

Powell, Samuel M. *Holiness, Why it Matters Today*. San Diego, CA: Point Loma Press, 2010.

Purkiser, W. T. *Exploring Christian Holiness: The Biblical Foundation* (K.C.: Beacon Hill Press of Kansas City, 1983.

_____. *Interpreting Christian Holiness*. K.C.: Beacon Hill Press of Kansas City, 1971.

Quanstrom, Mark *A Century of Holiness Theology*. K.C.: Beacon Hill Press of Kansas City, 2004.

Reasoner, Victor. "The American Holiness Movement's Paradigm Shift Concerning Holiness," *Wesleyan Theological Journal*, vol. 31, No. 2, Fall, (1996).

Regev, Eyal. "Moral Impurity and the Temple in Early Christianity in Light of Ancient Greek Practice and Qumranic Ideology," *Harvard Theological Review*, 97.4 (2004).

Rhodes, Arnold B. *The Mighty Acts of God*. Richmond, VA: CLC Press, 1964.

222

Ridderbos, Herman. *Paul: An Outline of His Theology*, trans. John Richard de Witt. Grand Rapids: Eerdmans Pub. Co., 1966.

_____. "The Redemptive-Historical Character of Paul's Preaching," in *When the Time Had Fully Come, Studies in New Testament Theology*. Grand Rapids: Eerdmans, 1957.

Robinson, H. Wheeler. *The Christian Doctrine of Man*. Edinburgh: T. & T. Clark, 1972.

Robinson, John A. T. *The Body*. Philadelphia: Westminster Press, 1952.

Rosner, Brian S., "Temple and Holiness in 1 Corinthians 5:1," *Tyndale Bulletin* 42.1 (1991), 137-145.

Runyon, Theodore. *The New Creation*. Nashville: Abingdon Press, 1998.

Russell, III, Walter Bo. "Insights from PostModernism's Emphasis on Interpretive Communities in the Interpretation of Romans 7," *Journal of the Evangelical Theological Society*, (December 1994).

_____. "Does the Christian have 'Flesh' in Gal. 5:13-26?" *Journal of the Evangelical Theological Society* 36/2 (June 1993).

_____. "The Apostle Paul's Redemptive-Historical Argumentation in Galatians 5:13-26," *Westminster Theological Journal* 57 (1995.

Saldarini, Anthony J. *Matthew's Christian-Jewish Community*. Chicago: University Press, 1994.

Sanchez, Jr., Juan Ramon. "The old man versus the new man in the doctrine of sanctification: A critique of the two-nature theory," M.Th. thesis, Southern Baptist Theological Seminary, 2002.

Sanders, E. P. *Paul and Palestinian Judaism*. Philadelphia: Fortress, 1977.

_____. *Paul, the Law and the Jewish People*. Philadelphia: Fortress, 1983.

Sandifer, Brian K. "A Critical Analysis of the Two Nature View of Regenerate Man: Toward an Understanding of the Cause of Sin in the Life of the Believer." Ph.D. diss, Southeastern Baptist Theological Seminary, 2010.

Sangster, W.E. *The Path to Perfection*. N.Y.: Abingdon Press, 1943.

Scott, Jr.,J. Julius "The Cornelius Incident in the Light of its Jewish Setting," *Journal of the Evangelical Theological Society* 34 (December, 1991): 475-484.

Smith, Timothy L. *Called Unto Holiness*. K. C.: Beacon Hill Press of Kansas City, 1962.

Snaith, Norman. *Distinctive Ideas of the Old Testament*. London: Epworth Press, 1955.

Spaulding, Henry. "A Reconstruction of the Wesleyan Understanding of Christian Perfection," *Wesleyan Theological Journal*, vol. 33, No. 2, Fall, 1998.

Spohn, William C. "The Return of Virtue," *Theological Studies* 53 (1992), 60-75.

Spross, Daniel B. "Sanctification in the Thessalonian Epistles in a Canonical Context," Ph. D. diss., Southern Baptist Theological Seminary, 1987.

Stacey, W. David. *The Pauline View of Man*. London: MacMillan, 1956.

224

Staples, Rob L. "John Wesley's Doctrine of Christian Perfection: A Reinterpretation," Ph.D. diss. Pacific School of Religion, 1963.

Steele, Daniel. *Antinomianism Revived*, digital reproduction, NNU website.

_____. *Milestone Papers*, Digital Edition, 07/14/95, Holiness Data Ministry, NNU website.

Stendahl, Krister. "The Apostle Paul and the Introspective Conscience of the West," *Harvard Theological Review* 56 (1963) 199-215.

Stewart, James S. *A Man in Christ*. N.Y.: Harper and Row, Pub., n.d.

Strickland, William J. and H. Ray Dunning, *J.O. McClurkan: His Life, His Theology, and Selections from His Writings.* Nashville: Trevecca Press, 1998.

Stumpf, Samuel E. *Philosophy: History and Problems*. N.Y.: McGraw-Hill Publishing Co., 1989.

Sugden, E. H., Editor.*Wesley's Standard Sermons*, 2 vols. London: Epworth Press, 1964.

Swanson, Dwight D. "Offerings for Sin in Leviticus, and John Wesley's Definition," *European Explorations in Holiness*, vol. 1.

Tannehill, Robert C. *Dying and Rising with Christ*. Berlin: Verlag Alfred Töpelmann, 1967.

Taylor, Richard S. *A Right Conception of Sin.* K.C.: Nazarene Publishing House, 1939.

_____. *Exploring Christian Holiness: The Theological Formulation*. K.C.: Beacon Hill Press of Kansas City, 1985.

_____. "Why the Holiness Movement Died," *God's Revivalist*, vol. 111, No. 2, March, 1999, 7-27.

_____. "Holiness and the Meaning of Maturity." *The Preacher's Magazine*, September/October/November, 1994.

Telford, John, ed.,*The Letters of John Wesley,* 8 vols. (London: Epworth Press, 1931), 1:152.

Temple, William. *Nature, Man and God.* London: Macmillan & Co., 1935.

Thomas, Gordon. "The Need," in *Re-minting Holiness,* a project of the faculty of Nazarene Theological College, Manchester, England.

_____. "Re-Minting Christian Holiness: Our Global Opportunity," European Explorations in Christian Holiness on World Wide Web.

_____. "Old Testament Proof-texts for Original Sin," *European Explorations in Christian Holiness (2).*

Tillich, Paul. *Systematic Theology,* 3 vol. in 1. Chicago: University Press, 1967.

Tracy, Wesley D. et. al., *The Upward Call.* K.C.: Beacon Hill Press of Kansas City, 1994.

Truesdale, Albert. "Christian Holiness and the Problem of Systemic Evil," *Wesleyan Theological Journal,* Vol. 19, no. 1, Spring 1984.

_____. "Reification of the Experience of Entire Sanctification in the American Holiness Movement." *Wesleyan Theological Journal,* vol. 31, No. 2, Fall, 1996.

Turner, George Allen. *The More Excellent Way,* republished as *The Vision that Transforms.* K.C.: Beacon Hill Press of Kansas City, 1964.

Wall, Robert W. "The Acts of the Apostles," *The New Interpreter's Bible Commentary.* Nashville: Abingdon Press, 2010.

Webster, John. *Holiness.* Grand Rapids: Wm. B. Eerdmans, 2003.

Wells, Jo Bailey. *God's Holy People: A Theme in Biblical Theology.* EBSCO Publishing: e-book collection.

Wenham, Gordon J., *The Book of Leviticus.* Grand Rapids: William B. Eerdmans Pub. Co., 1979.

_____. "The Perplexing Pentateuch, *Vox Evangelica* 17 (1987).

_____. "The Theology of Unclean Food," *Evangelical Quarterly* 53.1 (January/March 1981).

Wesley, John. *The Works of John Wesley.* 14 vols. K.C. Nazarene Publishing House, reproduction of the 1872 edition.

_____.*Explanatory Notes upon the New Testament.* London: The Epworth Press, 1954.

Whiteley, D. E. H. *The Theology of St. Paul.* Oxford: Basil Blackwell, 1964.

Whittle, Sarah. "Purity in Paul," in *Purity in Bible & Theology,* eds. Andrew Brower Latz and Arseny Ermakov. Eugene, OR: Wipf and Stock, 2014.

Wiley, H. Orton. *Christian Theology* 3 vols. K.C. Beacon Hill Press, 1947.

Winchester, Oliver M. and Ross Price, *Crisis experiences in the Greek New Testament: an investigation of the evidences for the definite, miraculous experiences of regeneration and sanctification as found in the Greek New Testament, especially in the figures emphasized and in the use of the aorist tense.* Kansas City: Beacon Hill Press, 1953.

Witherington, III, Ben. *The Indelible Image*, 2 vols. Downers Grove, Ill.: IVP Academic, 2009-2010.

Wood, J. A. *Purity and Maturity*, abridged by John Paul, K.C.: Beacon Hill Press, 1944.

_____. *Perfect Love*, abridged by John Paul. K.C.: Beacon Hill Press, n.d.

Wood, Laurence W. "Exegetical-Theological Reflections on the Baptism with the Holy Spirit," *Wesleyan Theological Journal*, 14 (Fall 1979).

Wright, Christopher J. H. *An Eye for an Eye*. Downers Grove, ILL: Intervarsity Press, 1983.

Wright, N. T. *After you Believe*. N.Y.: Harper Collins, 2010.

_____. *Jesus and the Victory of God*. Minneapolis: Fortress Press, 1996.

_____. *The Letter to the Romans* in *The New Interpreter's Bible Commentary*, vol. 10 (Nashville: Abingdon Press, 2002.

_____. *The New Testament and the People of God*. Minneapolis: Fortress Press, 1992.

_____. "Jesus and the World's True Light," Intervarsity Press Conference, January 1999.

_____. *Simply Christian*. N.Y.: HarperCollins, 2006.

228

_____. "Mind, Spirit, Soul and Body: All for One and One for All, Reflections on Paul's Anthropology," Lecture given to the Society of Christian Philosophers, March 18, 2011.

_____. "Redemption from the New Perspective? Towards a Multi-Layered Pauline Theology of the Cross" published in *Redemption*, ed. S.T. Davis, et. al. Oxford: University Press, 2006, 69-100.

Wynkoop. Mildred B. *Foundations of Wesleyan-Arminian Theology*. K.C.: Beacon Hill Press of Kansas City, 1967.

_____. *A Theology of Love*. K.C.: Beacon Hill Press, 1972.

_____. "John Wesley—Mentor or Guru?" *Wesleyan Theological Journal*, vol. 10, Spring, 1975, 5-15.

Person Index

4

Subject Index

Scripture References

Genesis
1:1   90
1:1—24a   90
1:26   78
2:25   92
3:5   84
3:10   85
3:22   84
5:2   77
9:6   77
11:1-9   127
12:1-3   119
15   138
17:11   200

Exodus
14:30   133
19:3-6   48
19:5   49
20   89
32:11-14   205
32:12-16   205

Leviticus
1-7   138
1-15   62
11:44-45   43
10:10   66
16-17   62
19:2   43
19:18   52
20:26   43
21:5-6   52

Numbers
9:13, 20   62
11:24-30   118
13:23   178
19   62
25:1-9   178

Deuteronomy
4:4   178
4:5-8   179
6:3   45
6:4-5   88
6:4   71
6:5   102
6:4-5   178
7:6
10:20   179
14:2, 21   49
26:19   44
28:9   44

Judges
13:25; 14:6   118

Psalms
24:3, 4   59
51:2, 7, 10   59
86:11   71
103:14   89

Isaiah
40-55   125
53   151

Made in the USA
Monee, IL
25 March 2022